THE GREAT BOOK OF
SAN FRANCISCO BAY AREA
SPORTS LISTS

THE GREAT BOOK OF SAN FRANCISCO BAY AREA SPORTS LISTS

BY DAMON BRUCE

RUNNING PRESS
PHILADELPHIA · LONDON

Printed in the United States

This book may not be reproduced in whole or in part, in any form or by
any means, electronic or mechanical, including photocopying, recording, or
by any information storage and retrieval system now known or hereafter
invented, without written permission from the publisher.

9 8 7 6 5 4 3 2 1
Digit on the right indicates the number of this printing

Library of Congress Control Number: 2008926968
ISBN 978-0-7624-3521-0

Cover and Interior Designed by Matthew Goodman
Cover and Interior photographs by Pat Johnson
Edited by Greg Jones

Running Press Book Publishers
2300 Chestnut Street
Philadelphia, PA 19103-4371

Visit us on the web!
www.runningpress.com

Contents

Dedication

To the fans sitting in the upper deck and the bleachers—if I weren't in the press box, I'd be right there with ya.

Acknowledgements

Thanks to my mother and father who never once told me, "Get a real job," and to my friends and family, who've stood by me through thick and thin. To everyone who contributed a list or conversation or suggestion that made the book, and to everyone whose facts and blurbs were left out. Thanks to Greg Jones at Running Press and Lisa Jones at Verbal Construction for their support. To my press-box compatriots: . . . Joe Salvatore, Ryan Leong, Jeremy Kahn (Go Blue,) George Devine (Junior and Senior,) Bruce Macgowan, Dean Johnson, Auggie the 49ers fan, Ken Dito, Joe Starkey, Greg Papa, Mycahael Urban, Bruce Grimes, Hal Ramey, Louis Alberto Torres, Carlos Nunez and several others . . . without you guys, this wouldn't have even been an interesting e-mail, much less a book. Extra special thanks to Tony "Malibu" Hayes, who's the closest thing this book has to a co-author. Thanks so much to my Sportsphone 680 audience, and to the "real fans, who listen late." Last but certainly not least, a very special thanks to my beautiful fiancée, Sara (along with her family, who raised her in the Church of 49ers Football), for her endless love and support.

Introduction

When I was approached to write this book, I decided to take on the task and treat it like a chance to earn a graduate degree in Bay Area sports. It has been my pleasure to cover these teams since I was hired as a host on KNBR 680 in October, 2005. But I have always admitted that many of my listeners know more about their teams' histories than I do. I didn't grow up in San Francisco, so I wanted to educate myself about this city's glorious sports history. What can I say? I don't have a serious job, but I do take it seriously. Now that I'm finished with this book, I realize my education has merely begun. This truly is an amazing place, with a stunning sports past. That my fingerprints are even a small smudge on the picture. . . well, I consider it an honor. I truly hope you enjoy this book as much as I enjoyed the process of putting it together.

—Damon Bruce

Ten Reasons Why Joe Is God

This book on Bay Area sports opens and closes with Joe.

10. All I've said is Joe and you know exactly who I'm talking about. One of the most common names on Planet Earth means just one man in San Francisco—and for that matter, in the NFL. Montana is more Joe than any other Joe in the history of sports, and that's saying something.

9. 99 wins for the San Francisco 49ers. Thanks, Joe. Forty losses, too, but who's counting?

8. 244 TD and 123 INT.

7. 476 yards in a game. Destroyed the Falcons on October 14, 1990, in Atlanta for a team record—and a 100-percent embarrassing 476 passing yards.

6. Six touchdown passes on the same afternoon in Atlanta, for the career and team records.

5. Joe hung 55 on the Broncos in Super Bowl XXIV. The Niners offense ran 77 plays that Sunday afternoon, gaining 461 yards.

4. 4,600 attempts, on the dot. Plus, 2,929 completions. Both are team records.

3. Thirty-five 300-yard games. That's a Niners record—as are six of his 300-yard passing efforts coming in consecutive games.

2. 22 consecutive completions over the stretch of two games. In 1987, versus Cleveland and Green Bay.

1. 35,124 passing yards that changed the position of quarterback forever. One could argue that no quarterback in the history of the position has been more studied than Montana. As coaches adopted Bill Walsh's West Coast Offense, Montana has likely flickered in more film rooms than anyone who's ever played.

No team in the Bay Area can claim longer residence than the 49ers. From their days at Kezar Stadium to Candlestick Park, no single franchise has been able to bring more glory to San Francisco than the Niners. Boasting five Super Bowl championships, a coach who forever changed football and a list of legends who have become household names, the fingerprints of this franchise can be seen in every NFL team. Every man on this list, except one, has a bust resting in Canton, Ohio, and an ugly yellow jacket to go with it.

10. Roger Craig (1983-90). I'll start with Roger only because he's the lone man on this list without a H.O.F. ring. What bullshit. He's a big reason why a few of these guys are in Canton. The first running back in NFL history to gain 1,000 yards both rushing and receiving in a season, Craig helped San Francisco win three Super Bowls (XIX, XXIII, XXIV) and is still the only RB to lead the NFL in receptions in a single season. After eight seasons with the 49ers, he played one year for the Raiders and two more for Minnesota before retiring. He qualified for the playoffs in every single season of his eleven-year NFL career.

9. Leo Nomellini (1950-63). The first draft pick the 49ers ever selected, "The Lion" played in every game for fourteen consecutive seasons and was named to ten Pro Bowls. A two-way player, the Italian import was one of the bricklayers on which the long road to success would be built.

8. Dave Wilcox (1964-74). A seven-time Pro Bowl linebacker, "The Intimidator" was the Dick Butkus of the West Coast. He changed the other team's offensive game plan with his aggressive nature, athleticism and ability to get around, under or through blocks. Wilcox was one of the NFL's first hybrid linebackers who could play the run and pass, and took pride in doing both equally well.

7. Jimmy Johnson (1961-76). So talented, at first the 49ers didn't know if they should play him at corner or on offense after drafting him out of UCLA. After a year or two of juggling, they made the right choice. Johnson was one of the NFL's first premier shutdown cornerbacks. A five-time Pro Bowler, Jimmy is regarded as one of the best man-to-man defenders in NFL history, and finished with 47 interceptions.

6. Bob St. Clair (1953-63). When the legend outgrows the truth, print the legend. Bob St. Clair was your grandfather's definition of tough and the stories about his losing teeth on punt blocks, and eating raw meat before games, are now somewhere between truth and legend. Fact is, St. Clair was a bad-ass offensive lineman in his day and was named to five Pro Bowls and three all-NFL teams. Born, raised and educated in San Francisco, St. Clair still gets around and serves as a living link to the past. He's one of the few players in sports history to ever play his high school, college and pro careers all in the same stadium.

5. Steve Young (1987-99). One of the greatest athletes to ever play quarterback, Young guided the Niners to the Super Bowl XXIX title and was named MVP of the game, finally getting that monkey off his back. Along with primate extermination, Young also managed to win two league MVP titles while becoming the most accurate passer in NFL history. His legs made him one of the most dangerous scramblers ever, and with all due respect to Mr. Montana, it's often argued that no 49ers offense was ever more dangerous than the one Young guided in 1994. Don't believe me? Ask the AFC Champion San Diego Chargers of the same season what they think.

4. The Million Dollar Back Field: Quarterback, Y.A. Tittle, fullback John Henry Johnson, and halfbacks Hugh McElhenny and Joe Perry. All right, so I'm cheating a bit, but you can't have one without the other three. The Fearsome Foursome consisted of one of the game's first superstar QBs, a bone-crunching blocker and short yardage specialist, and two thrilling runners, one known as "The King," and the other, "The Jet." Now that would be cool in 2008, much less 1958.

3. Ronnie Lott (1981-90). The defensive leader of four Super Bowl teams and ten-time Pro Bowler, Lott moved from cornerback to safety as his body grew along with his reputation for being one of the game's most vicious tacklers. His NFL-record nine post-season interceptions equal the number of fingers he's got left after cutting his pinky off in 1985 to keep playing. San Francisco won eight division titles in Lott's ten seasons with the team. His stellar play was honored with three amazing accomplishments: Lott was named to the all-Eighties and all-Nineties teams, and the NFL's seventy-fifth anniversary team.

2. Jerry Rice (1985-2000). Considered slow coming out of Mississippi Valley State, all Rice did, after struggling at times during his rookie season, was become the greatest pound-for-pound player in NFL history, regardless of position. Rice is, hands down, the single best wide receiver to ever play football. He is the leader in every single career receptions category, and was the textbook definition of dedicated. Rice's legendary off-season workout program allowed him to enjoy a twenty-year-long NFL career, with thirteen Pro Bowl appearances. Along with three championship rings and an MVP performance in Super Bowl XXIII, Rice joins Ronnie Lott on two all-decade teams, as well as being named the No. 1 wide out on the seventy-fifth anniversary team.

1. Joe Montana (1979-92). Elway? Brady? Maybe Favre? All in the conversation with Joe for best QB ever, right? Well, those are fighting words in one of America's most peaceful cities. In San Francisco, Joe Montana is the Alpha and the Omega. The forward pass did not matter until it came from the right hand of "Joe Cool." When you revolutionize the passing game, win two MVPs, start one of football's most iconic plays with an off balance lob to a TE in the back of the end zone to beat the arch rival, then go to four Super Bowls and win all of them, they tend to remember you. Of course, none of this happens without the true mastermind of the franchise, Head Coach Bill Walsh, who would become the most important figure in the history of football on the West Coast. But when it comes to strapping on the helmet, no 49er was ever greater—or more revered—than Joe Montana.

In 1958, owner Horace Stoneham picked up his New York Giants and moved to the majestic city of San Francisco, forever changing the landscape of Major League Baseball. Since that season, these are the best of the best.

10. Kevin Mitchell (1987-91). A two-time All-Star in just five seasons, Boogie Bear won the 1989 MVP, powering the Giants to the NL Pennant with 47 homeruns, 125 RBI and a .635 slugging percentage. However, a bare-handed, running catch to rob Ozzie Smith of a deep double down the line at old Busch Stadium became his signature play that year. "This Week In Baseball" can't roll closing credits without it. His time in San Francisco was short, but sweeter than most of his stops. Pegged for having an attitude, and sometimes living up to it, Mitchell is the only MVP to be traded to five different teams before his thirty-second birthday, and he's the only MVP to play for a grand total of eight teams in his career.

9. Gaylord Perry (1962-71; H.O.F. 1991). One of four pitchers in team history to win 100 or more games, Perry is one of the most beloved and notorious icons in baseball. A gifted pitcher and the first to ever win the Cy Young in both the National and American Leagues, Perry is also known for doctoring the ball. He's one of only seven pitchers in history to win 300 games with 3,500 strikeouts. Of his 134 victories in San Francisco, 125 were complete games, and 21 of those were shutouts. The legend of his "tinkering with lubricants" far outweighs the truth, but his place in the game's history as lovable scamp is one he relishes. Perry is the first Giants player to make historians and Hall of Fame voters consider how much cheating would be tolerated when weighing the greatness of a player; he would not be the last.

8. Matt Williams (1987-96). The third overall pick of the 1986 amateur draft, Williams turned into a sturdy right-handed bat and a Gold Glove third baseman. A four-time All-Star in S.F., Williams was on pace for 61 homers when play was suspended due to the strike of 1994. He has had to settle for a NL best and career-high 40. In 1990, "Matty" shattered the team record for RBI by a third baseman with 122— along with having one of his four, thirty-or-more home run seasons.

7. Jeff Kent (1997–02). He's the only player on the list who's still playing, and the only player Giants fans are equal parts happy to see on the list, and pissed off to see he made the list. No other player in team history has gone from so loved to so hated. The feisty second baseman was the only man with the guts—or numbers—to push back when Barry Bonds pushed him. Recall the infamous near dugout brawl between the two. Kent won NL MVP in 2000, thanks in large part to pushing Bonds across home plate. Kent finished with 125 RBI, 33 home runs and a .334 average. For anyone, that's a monster year, but for a second baseman, that's sick. In a six-year stretch, Kent averaged nearly thirty homers while driving in more than 100 runs. Someday, he'll go to the Hall of Fame—and he'll go in wearing a Giants cap, to the delight and chagrin of many a fan.

6. Will Clark (1986-93). As if God built a player for Giants fans to fall in love with, Clark embodied the raw talent and hard work ethic that made you feel OK about having to pay money to watch men play a child's game. "The Thrill" also possessed one of the sweetest swings in Giants history. With a home run off HOF pitcher Nolan Ryan in his first career at-bat, Clark became a career .303 hitter, and the walking definition of clutch. Somewhere, a guy is drinking at a bar and talking about a certain Clark performance in the 1989 NLCS when he hit .650, which remains one of the greatest postseason performances of all-time.

5. Orlando Cepeda (1956-1958; H.O.F, 1999). Not only did the city of San Francisco get the Giants in 1958, it got Rookie of the Year Orlando Cepeda. "The Baby Bull" started at first in the inaugural game on city soil. It was only the beginning of pioneering career. Cepeda was one of baseball's premier Latino superstars, and became the first Puerto Rican to win home run and RBI titles, and to start in the All-Star Game, which he did six times for the Giants. Cepeda and Roberto Clemente are the only two players from Puerto Rico in the Hall of Fame. PS. Try the Cha-Cha Bowl, some of the best ballpark food in the game next time you're at AT&T Park.

4. Juan Marichal (1960-1973; H.O.F. 1983). His 238 wins are the most by any pitcher in club history since relocating to the Golden Gate. A twenty-game winner on six different occasions, Marichal's sky-high leg kick—once the cover story of Time Magazine—was a warning sign to any hitter who dared dig-in too deep. With 2,303 strike outs against only 709 career walks, when a Marichal fastball buzzed you or worse, it was almost always intentional. Control and brute force from the mound, Marichal was a unique mixture of grace and destruction. He's without question the best pitcher the club has seen since moving West.

3. Willie McCovey (1959-1973; 1977-'80; H.O.F 1986). It didn't take very long for the original "Big Mac" to show Giants fans they had something special in a young first baseman, who'd also become known as "Stretch" for his long, lanky frame. In his debut, McCovey went four-for-four off H.O.F. pitcher Robin Roberts, and would go on to win Rookie of the Year. His 19 seasons in a San Francisco uniform are the most by any player in team history. A first-ballot Hall of Famer, member of the 500 HR club and MVP in 1969, McCovey still holds the record for NL career grand slams at 18, and is the only player on this list to have a body of water named after him. McCovey Cove, beyond the right field wall at AT&T Park, is one of the more charming aspects of any ballpark, anywhere.

2. Willie Mays (1958–1972; H.O.F. 1979). No player in the history of baseball captured the imagination of fans everywhere, or remains as revered, as the "Say Hey Kid." The living legend remains somewhere between a memory and a dream. His stunning career numbers can't measure his legacy because Mays still lives in people's hearts, not box scores. It's not the humble opinion of Giants fans that he was the greatest center fielder ever—it's fact. Immortalized with a bronze statue outside of 24 Willie Mays Plaza (address of AT&T Park) the two-time MVP was named the starting center fielder of the all-century team. As a player, Mays is still adored by fans everywhere. Ted Williams once famously said, "The All-Star Game was made for Willie Mays." And why not? He appeared in 24. His pre-game tribute before the 2007 All-Star Game in San Francisco left me in chills. Hundreds of readers think this list is garbage because he is not ranked number one.

1. Barry Bonds (1993–07; H.O.F ???). For all the right and wrong reasons, the most significant player in franchise history didn't wear number 24 on the back of his uniform—he wore 25. Bonds' staggering career numbers may be as suspect as they are mesmerizing, but his sheer impact on the Giants franchise and economy of San Francisco will never be fully measured or appreciated. Neither AT&T Park nor the surrounding neighborhood outside the privately financed stadium would exist without the left fielder who generated the greatest home run circus ever. Bonds' ascendancy to the top of the records books left an impact on pitchers' ERAs, the legacy of MLB and the FBI. He casts the longest shadow in team history, and thanks to a little help from BALCO, Barry Lamar Bonds is the greatest home run hitter—and Giants player—of all time.

With both franchises dating back to New York, the roots of this rivalry are deep. The California coastline may have put more miles between the two teams, but it did nothing to cool the intense dislike between the two fan bases. Winning alone isn't enough. You have to leave the opponent battered and broken. It's amazing how much each fan base relishes the chance to make the other miserable. And each has caused the other a great deal of misery. Here are ten of the best chapters between the two rivals since relocating to California. Yes, the bitter comes with the sweet.

10. The Twi-night Doubleheader from Hell, July 26, 1988. It's known as the ugliest, rowdiest night in the history of Candlestick Park. Over 100 fans were detained or arrested after an evening of drinking during the Giants doubleheader sweep of the Dodgers. Total game time was seven hours and ten minutes. Fans climbed the foul pole, scuffled over home run balls behind the left field fence and erupted in pockets of brawls all night long. At one point, the media even locked the doors of the press box, fearing fans would come streaming through in a hazy, drunken conga line. Giants president Al Rosen apologized to NL president Bart Giamatti and to the Dodgers for the crowd's behavior. He called the night "frightening," famously saying, "This was the worst I've seen since I've been born. And I've been in World War II."

9. Trevor Wilson's War. Just a game behind the Atlanta Braves, the Dodgers needed a strong showing on the final weekend at Candlestick to head to the 1991 post-season. The Giants, meanwhile, were far from contention. But as is often the case between the two, the team that needs the win the most, usually doesn't get it. San Francisco won two of three with Trevor Wilson tossing a complete game shutout on the day the Dodgers were eliminated.

8. Steve "F-ing" Finley in 2004. Up 3-0 in the ninth inning, the Giants bullpen couldn't hold off the Dodgers lineup. After loading the bases, Steve Finley rang a grand slam home run off Wayne Franklin, which sealed the division for L.A. Had the Giants held on to win that evening, San Francisco would have forced a one-game playoff with the Dodgers for the NL West crown.

7. Seventy-three Home Runs and Nothing to Show For It. Barry Bonds shattered the single-season home run mark with a pair of home runs off Chan Ho Park in the final series of the season, but all those 73 long balls brought Bonds was an MVP award and a one-way ticket back to Beverly Hills. The Dodgers took two of the final three games, allowing the Diamondbacks to clinch the division on the same day Bonds became the single-season home run king. Again, a Dodgers fan's pleasure became a Giants fan's pain. Giants fans would have to settle for an individual record instead of team success—a reoccurring theme over the next several seasons.

6. Holding off the Dodgers in 1971. L.A. had come back from six and a half games behind to get within one game of the West-leading Giants, with one game to play. The Dodgers lived up to their end of the bargain with a win over the Astros. But the Giants beat the Padres on the last day of the season to hold off the Dodgers' strong charge, and win the division.

5. 103 Wins and We're Going Home? On the final day of the 1993 season, Dodgers catcher Mike Piazza clubbed two home runs to back a complete game performance by Kevin Gross. San Francisco was clobbered 12-1, and L.A. had spoiled October once again for Giants fans. The Braves won the division by one game. The result was so dramatic that the Wild Card was installed by the following season.

4. Two-Game-Sweep-and-a-Twirl. In a two-game series in late September 1997, the Giants swept the Dodgers, sending both franchises in opposite directions for the next decade. In the Giants first win, Barry Bonds infamously spun around, coming out of the batter's box after a prolific home run. The second win was cemented by a twelfth-inning homer off the bat of Brian Johnson, which pulled San Francisco even with L.A. atop the NL West. The Giants would win the division and enjoy more playoff appearances over the next seven seasons than any time since the decade of the 1930s. The Dodgers, meanwhile, would blow out the front office, rebuild the team and basically send the whole plan back to the drawing board.

3. Juan Marichal vs. Johnny Roseboro, August 22, 1965. In one ugly instant, the Giants and Dodgers had a moment as heated as the rivalry itself. After brushing back two Dodgers hitters with pitches, Juan Marichal came to bat, and faced Sandy Koufax. However, it was Dodgers catcher, John Roseboro who tried to intimidate Marichal, and returned the ball to Koufax by throwing it as close to Marichal's head as possible. Juan took exception and cracked Roseboro in the head with his bat, opening a gash that required fourteen stitches, and sparked a brawl that some insist is still going on. Juan was suspended for eight games and missed two starts—the same number of games the Giants finished behind the Dodgers in the standings.

2. Joe Morgan Sends Dem Bums Packing! With the Giants and Dodgers tied for second place behind the Braves, there would be a three-game showdown at Candlestick to sort it out and end the 1982 season. It didn't go the way Giants fans wanted. The Dodgers won the first two games by a combined score of 19-4, killing postseason hopes for S.F. But in the final game of the season, Joe Morgan cracked an eighth-inning, three-run home run that kept the Dodgers from winning the pennant, too. Since the Giants haven't won a World Series, preventing the Dodgers from a chance at another is as good as it gets around here.

1. The 1962 Season. The season came down to the wire with the Giants and Dodgers tied after the final day of the regular season. For the last time in Major League History, a three-game series to decide the pennant was needed. The Giants took two of three, with the final blow coming with four runs in the ninth inning to beat the Dodgers in L.A. When the team plane landed at San Francisco International Airport, there were 75,000 fans waiting to greet the NL Champs. Many Giants players, unable to find their own rides home due to the throngs of people, hitchhiked home with strangers who were thrilled to chauffeur their hometown heroes who had just put San Francisco in its first World Series.

Dodgers Killers: Top Ten Home Runs

The Giants franchise has always coveted the long ball. Here's the list of the Giants who "touched 'em-all" the most against the Dodgers.

10. Will Clark—8 seasons—15 HR. He could hurt you with his average or his power. Clark used every chance he had vs. the Dodgers to endear himself to Giants fans, who still give him standing ovations in the bathroom.

9. Jeff Kent (6 seasons) Darrell Evans (8 seasons) Jeffrey Leonard (8 seasons)—16 HR. Even though they all wore different uniforms during their careers, fans in San Francisco can't forget what they meant to the team. Neither can Tommy Lasorda.

8. Jim Davenport—13 seasons—17 HR. He got to the see the rivalry from the batter's box, and from the dugout as the team's manager. He was more successful as a hitter when it came to beating L.A.

7. Jim Ray Hart—9 seasons—19 HR. The original "Ray by the Bay."

6. Bobby Bonds—7 seasons—20 HR. It runs in the family. Bobby joins his son and his son's godfather on the list of Dodgers Killers.

5. Orlando Cepeda—9 seasons—24 HR. Try the Tri-Tip sandwich. It's the only good taste Cepeda left in the mouths of Dodgers fans.

4. Matt Williams—10 seasons—27 HR. Have I mentioned how much they hated Matty in SoCal?

3. Willie McCovey—19 seasons—41 HR. Stretched Dodgers pitchers beyond the outfield wall on several occasions. Along with Willie Mays, he shares the team record with 261 games vs. L.A.

2. Barry Bonds—15 seasons—53 HR. Another amazing Bonds stat: his home run total vs. the Dodgers came in 595 at-bats. It took Willie Mays 953 ABs to reach his total, and he hit just three more home runs.

1. Willie Mays—14 seasons—56 HR. Say Hey, Willie's beating L.A.! See, it runs in the family.

If the game's about scoring runs, then driving them in must be important. Here are the Giants who took the time to shine with runners in scoring position.

10. Jeffrey Leonard (8 seasons) Jim Davenport (13 seasons)—58 RBI. Same RBI total vs. L.A., different personalities.

9. Chris Speier—10 seasons—60 RBI. Yes, that Chris Speier.

8. Felipe Alou—6 seasons—61 RBI. Not only did his brothers taste the rivalry, his son would as well.

7. Jim Ray Hart—9 seasons—64 RBI. He's the only Giants player besides Willie Mays to appear top ten against the Dodgers on the RBI, HR and AVG lists. Now that's a Dodgers Killer.

6. Bobby Bonds—7 seasons—69 RBI. The only man on the list the Dodgers never walked intentionally. His son would make up for it with 71 of his own free passes.

5. Will Clark (8 seasons) Matt Williams (10 seasons)—71 RBI. It's fitting these two finished with the same total. As teammates, they're responsible for tons of Dodgers damage from the late Eighties to the mid-Nineties.

4. Orlando Cepeda—9 seasons—107 RBI. With 156 hits in 145 games, Orlando was always ready for the Dodgers.

3. Barry Bonds—15 seasons—121 RBI. A .465 on-base percentage made Bonds a true table setter as well. His 136 runs against L.A. is the second most in franchise history, behind Willie Mays, of course.

2. Willie McCovey—19 seasons—151 RBI. He also came around to score 111 runs vs. the Dodgers, making up for his .249 lifetime average against them.

1. Willie Mays—14 seasons—155 RBI. At the top of yet another All-Time Giants list. I'm sensing a pattern here.

Dodgers Killers: Top 25 Batting Averages

Giants who laid the most pine on Dodgers pitching.

25. Joel Youngblood—6 seasons—.262 avg. Finished his career with San Francisco. The .265 career hitter nearly lived up to his average when L.A. was in town.

24. Darren Lewis—5 seasons—.264 avg. Dusty Baker named his son after Lewis. Maybe it's because of how good he made Daddy look vs. L.A.

23. Omar Vizquel—4 seasons—.269 avg. And just think of all the hits he took away from L.A.

22. Dan Gladden—4 seasons—.269 avg. The Twins color commentator let his bat do the talking when he tasted the West Coast rivalry.

21. Dave Rader—5 seasons—.269 avg. The Giants' first pick of the 1967 draft, this defensive catcher saved his best swings for the Dodgers.

20. Ron Hunt—3 seasons—.270 avg. After just one season in L.A., Ron always relished the chance to show up his former teammates.

19. Jack Clark—9 seasons—.273 avg. Seeing him put on a Padres uniform later in his career was hard enough. Giants fans are thankful that one of their beloved sluggers never wore Dodgers blue.

18. Barry Bonds—15 seasons—.274 avg. Surprising to see Bonds this low on the list. Elsewhere, he more than makes up for his 18th place showing.

17. Marquis Grissom—3 seasons—.277 avg. After two seasons in L.A., this journeyman finished strong against the Dodgers in his final three professional seasons.

16. Jeffrey Leonard—8 seasons—.279 avg. Saved some of his best hacks for when it mattered the most.

15. Matt Williams—10 seasons—.281 avg. Hard-nosed, hardheaded, hard on L.A. pitching.

14. Candy Maldonado—4 seasons—.283 avg. Hated in San Francisco when he played in L.A., he made up for his time with the Dodgers by taking it to them when he moved north.

13. Ray Durham—8 seasons—.284 avg. Ray-by-the-Bay usually saves his best for the Dodgers and his contract years.

12. Orlando Cepeda—9 seasons—.286 avg. The Dodgers never enjoyed running with "The Baby Bull."

11. Rich Aurilia—10 seasons—.286 avg. One of the classiest guys in baseball, and one of the most beloved by fans, Richey knows how much the rivalry means, and plays like it.

10. Daryl Spencer—2 seasons—.288 avg. An original N.Y. Giants player, he came to the West Coast to play for San Francisco, and the Dodgers before his career ended.

9. Felipe Alou—6 seasons—.288 avg. His long and storied history with the team begins with him being a thorn in L.A.'s side.

8. Edgardo Alfonzo—3 seasons—.290 avg. Not even coming in eighth on this list changes the way Giants fans feel about this underachiever.

7. Bill Madlock—3 seasons—.293 avg. The Mad Dog was another Giant who would cross rivalry lines and play for the Dodgers as well.

6. Willie Mays—14 seasons—.302 avg. Over the span of 261 career games vs. L.A. in a San Francisco uniform, Willy racked up 288 hits, 56 doubles and 12 triples, scored 187 runs and walked 158 times.

5. Larry Herndon—6 seasons—.305 avg. The only time you'll see Larry Herndon ranked above Mays.

4. Jim Ray Hart—9 seasons—.314 avg. Now everyone knows why Jimmy Ray was a fan favorite: It's all the "Hart-ache" he caused in L.A.

3. Will Clark—8 seasons—.315 avg. He thrilled fans and killed Dodgers.

2. Randy Winn—4 seasons—.320 avg. Professional hitter who many Giants fans will be surprised to see coming in #2 in the rivalry's history.

1. Brett Butler—3 seasons—.322 avg. Showed what a solid hitter he was in just 52 games. First he beat 'em; then he joined 'em.

It's not enough to score a bunch of runs. Giants fans feel true ecstasy only when the L.A. lineup is shut down. Here are the pitchers who visited the win column the most against the Dodgers.

25. Vida Blue—6 seasons—5 wins. The Hall of Famer shares the same fate as Ron Bryant. Both posted 5-12 records. That's just a .294 winning percentage, which ties them for dead last on this list. Hard to believe the Dodgers were probably happier to see him than he was to see them.

24. Ron Bryant—6 seasons—5 wins. With a good-enough win total to make this list, Bryant didn't exactly dominate the Dodgers. In fact, it was the other way around. His career record of 5-12 becomes even less impressive with his 4.93 ERA, which is highest on this list.

23. Livan Hernandez—4 seasons—5 wins. Yes, he did beat the Dodgers, but not in a dominating manner. His 4.84 career ERA vs. L.A. is the second worst of the all the pitchers here.

22. Fred Breining—4 seasons—5 wins. In 69.2 innings pitched vs. L.A., Breining allowed only 17 Earned Runs and posted a 2.20 ERA. Both rank him number one in those categories on this list.

21. Scott Garrelts—9 seasons—6 wins. A career Giants pitcher, Garrelts went 14-5 in 1989, helping the Giants reach the World Series. More important, he left some baffled Dodgers hitters along the way.

20. Billy O'Dell—5 seasons—6 wins. Won a career-high 19 games in 1962, before taking the Game One loss in the World Series. Oh well. At least he could "Beat L.A."

19. Stu Miller—5 seasons—6 wins. His career dates back to the Polo Grounds, when he made his major league debut the season before the team moved. Miller would become a 100-game winner who also led the NL in saves in 1961. He's the only pitcher on this list to close multiple games against L.A. without a blown save. Miller was eight for eight.

18. Bill Laskey—5 seasons—6 wins. His thirteenth win in 1982 made him the team leader his rookie season. Laskey is now teaching the rivalry to fans at Giants fantasy camps in Scottsdale. Hell of a guy.

17. Mark Davis—5 seasons—6 wins. Two of his wins came via the shutout. Not bad, blanking the Dodgers a third of the time you beat them.

16. Ray Sadecki—4 seasons—6 wins. Held the Dodgers to just a .208 team average in his 16 appearances against them. It's the second best opponent batting average on the list, behind Jason Schmidt's dominant .189.

15. Greg Minton—11 seasons—7 wins. Minton really kept the L.A. bats from showing any thump. He allowed just four home runs to the Dodgers—the least of anyone else on the list.

14. Mark Gardner—6 seasons—7 wins. His 7-2 lifetime record vs. the Dodgers gives him a .778 winning percentage, tops in franchise history vs. Los Angeles.

13. John Burkett—5 seasons—7 wins. Went 22-7 in 1993 for San Francisco before becoming a strikeout artist in two sports. Burkett is a part-time professional bowler with a dozen perfect games under his belt.

12. Randy Moffitt—10 seasons—8 wins. Moved the bullpen later in his career and leads this list of players with 11 saves vs. the Dodgers as well.

11. Jim Barr—10 seasons—8 wins. Served the Giants well as a ten-game winner in five consecutive seasons. However, his thirteen career losses against the Dodgers are the most by any Giants pitcher since the 1971 season.

10. John Montefusco—7 seasons—8 wins. You could count on "The Count" to raise his game vs. L.A. His no-hitter against the Braves—the season after Halicki threw his—remains the last no-hitter in Giants history.

9. Ed Halicki—7 seasons—8 wins. Hard on Dodgers hitters, he was even tougher on August 4, 1975, when he no-hit the Mets.

8. Kelly Downs—7 seasons—9 wins. Never won more than thirteen games in any one season, Downs had a knack for mowing down the Dodgers.

7. Kirk Rueter—8 seasons—10 wins. He may have looked like Woody from *Toy Story*, but when the Dodgers were in his sights, he pitched like Buzz Lightyear.

6. Jack Sanford—7 seasons—10 wins. He finished second to Don Drysdale for the 1962 Cy Young Award with a stellar 1.93 postseason ERA.

5. Mike Krukow—6 seasons—10 wins. That's some serious "ownage" over L.A. Now "grab some pine, meat."

4. Jason Schmidt—6 seasons—10 wins. 141 strikeouts rank Schmitty tops among the group of hurlers tied for fourth place, and third all-time in the rivalry. Good news for Giants fans, the pitcher they got to enjoy is not the same guy who left San Francisco for big free-agent money with the Dodgers. Injuries have mostly kept Schmidt out of the rotation, and therefore out of the rivalry from the Dodgers' point of view.

3. Gaylord Perry—10 seasons—12 wins. No team complained more about Perry's pitching antics than L.A. Now we know why. His 143 strikeouts rank him second behind Marichal.

2. Mike McCormick—9 seasons—15 wins. An original Giants player, he wasted no time making sure the rivalry made it to the West Coast. He blanked L.A. on five different occasions.

1. Juan Marichal—14 seasons—37 wins. The franchise career leader in virtually every major pitching category, it's only fitting that Juan is tops here, too. His 305 strikeouts in the rivalry are also number one, nearly doubling the second closest total. He pitched 64 times against the Dodgers and finished all but one of his starts.

The Giants and Dodgers have been feuding and will continue to draw battle lines as long as we're playing baseball. But it's not all baseball that fuels the fire between the two. Here are ten more reasons, beyond the field, that will keep these two clubs from ever liking the other.

10. Dodgers Dogs vs. Gilroy Garlic Fries. There's a battle on the field and a battle in the concession line. Boasting some of the best ballpark food anywhere, both fans stand behind their signature ballpark dishes as the best tasting in the game.

9. "Beat L.A." Predating the Celtics and Lakers rivalry, one of the best chants in all sports started in the bleachers, not courtside seats.

8. Back to "Giants Suck." For years, Barry Bonds had become the target of Dodgers fans; they weren't rooting against the Giants as much as they were rooting for him to fail. Now Bonds is gone. "Barry Sucks" has been replaced with "Giants Suck." Good to see balance restored to the force.

7. Orange vs. Blue. What good is a classic rivalry with terrible uniforms? In a funny way, great rivals' uniforms usually complement each other. In this case, it's no different. Both the Giants and Dodgers have great uniforms, and seeing both of them on the same field just looks like baseball to me.

6. Jackie Robinson hated the Giants. In December of 1956, Robinson was traded from the Dodgers to the Giants, but he refused to report to his new club, choosing to retire instead. The man who broke baseball's color barrier couldn't see himself in Giants colors; it was the sort of integration Jackie wanted no part of.

5. Classic Battlegrounds. Just look at the iconic diamonds these two have called their own: The Polo Grounds, Ebbets Field, Seals Stadium, LA Coliseum, Candlestick Park, Dodgers Stadium, AT&T Park.

4. Broadcaster Heaven. Baseball and the radio go together like no other sport and broadcast. An everyday friend for six months of the year, a team's broadcaster becomes part of the family. Thanks to some of the greatest voices to ever settle behind the microphone, Giants fans have enjoyed top notch play-by-play from the likes of Jon Miller, Lon Simmons and Russ Hodges. I heard the Dodgers guy isn't bad either.

3. Shot Heard Round the World. OK, it didn't happen in San Francisco, but it did happen, and it happened to the Dodgers. It has been 57 years since it happened, and it's still the greatest call in the history of baseball, so it deserves to be mentioned. Can someone please remind me: Who won the pennant in 1951? Oh, "The Giants win the pennant! The Giants win the pennant! The Giants win the pennant! The Giants win the pennant!" Thank you, Mr. Hodges.

2. The New York Roots. If the Giants and Dodgers were both expansion teams operating on opposite sides of the same street, the rivalry couldn't get any better. That's because it's not about location—it's about history, and these two have been at each other's throats since the Big Apple wasn't that big. Say what you will about East Coast bias, New York City matters, especially when it comes to baseball history.

1. Forever Linked at the Hip. Both from N.Y., both moved to California in the same year, both had visionary owners; both realized that their success was relative to the other's failures. Say what they will about the other, they need one another. You can't have a hero without a villain. You can't have the Hatfields without the McCoys. And you can't have the Giants without the Dodgers. Baseball just wouldn't be the same.

NOTE: Bruce Jenkins has been with the *San Francisco Chronicle* since 1973, started writing for them in earnest in 1977, and got his column in 1989. He is mandatory reading for all Bay Area fans, and in my opinion, one of the finest writers in any medium. Here are his ten favorite Bay Area sports events he's ever covered, in no particular order.

Kansas City Chiefs at Oakland Raiders, 1970. It wasn't so much the game, which I was covering as a stringer for United Press International while still a student at Cal, but the scene. My assignment was to get quotes from the Kansas City locker room, and I was a pretty impressionable kid then, but to this day, I've never seen such a collection of physical specimens. Ernie Ladd, a professional wrestler in the off-season, was built much like a redwood tree. Bobby Bell was insanely chiseled and had virtually no waist (and by the way, I will always claim he's the best pure football player in history. Forget Jerry Rice and look it up; Bobby Bell played every skill position dating back to high school, including quarterback, and played all of them well, eventually becoming one of the NFL's greatest outside linebackers of all time). Jim Tyrer, E.J. Holub, Willie Lanier—it was just one distinctive stud after another. I may be slightly off on the year, but I remember Fred Biletnikoff beating Jim Marsalis in the end zone for a huge Raider touchdown in that game. Those Oakland teams weren't too shabby, either. In fact, no current NFL rivalry can touch that one in terms of pure talent.

Will Clark singles to center, 1989. It was one of those stone-perfect weather days at Candlestick, the kind only found in autumn, and it was Game 5 of the NLCS. It's rare that you get a perfect convergence of sporting elements, but this was one of them. The Cubs had Mitch Williams on the mound, and for all the misfortune that befell the "Wild Thing" later, he was an almost untouchable closer that year, a flame-throwing lefty who made the All-Star team and truly put the fear of God in opposing hitters. At the plate was Clark, who in those early years with the Giants showed all the qualities of a future Hall of Famer. He was the best hitter alive, and he knew it, and he talked it, and he backed it up. With the score tied 1-1 in the bottom of the eighth, Williams threw his fabled fastball, Clark lined a two-run single, and Candlestick was bedlam. That game's final out sent the Giants into the World Series.

Oakland A's at Kansas City Royals, Game 1 of the strike-forced "mini-series," 1981 playoffs. This was Billy Martin at the peak of his powers. I covered the A's for the *Chronicle* that year, with the endurance-crazed pitching rotation and the superb outfield of Rickey Henderson, Dwayne Murphy and Tony Armas. They went into Kansas City to play George Brett's Royals, Mike Norris scheduled to pitch Game 1, and nobody gave the A's much of a chance (just one year prior, Brett hit that epic homer into the upper deck of Yankee Stadium off Goose Gossage). I was among a group of writers who happened to run into Martin at the A's hotel that afternoon—it was the Adams Mark, right across the freeway from the ballpark—and Billy was feeling so good, he invited us into the bar. The man decided to have a cocktail or two on the day of the game. The A's won that night, and swept the series—Billy Ball at its finest. You'll never hear me say a bad word about Martin in any context. I've got a soft spot for the mad geniuses in life, no matter what their flaws. In 10 years, that's the best season I had as a baseball beat writer.

Bob Brenly writes a book, 1986. This was a September day game at Candlestick against the Atlanta Braves. Getting a breather from the catcher's position, Brenly got the start at third base, and he made four errors in the top of the fourth, tying a major-league record and virtually handing Atlanta a 4-0 lead. Slowly, methodically, Brenly got the Giants back in the game. He hit a solo homer in the fifth inning. He cracked a two-run single in the seventh to tie the game, 6-6. And in the bottom of the ninth, he homered off Paul Assenmacher for an incredible walk-off win. I'll never forget the wonderful quotes from Mike Krukow, the king of perspective, afterward. "That wasn't a game," he said. "That was a novel." Brenly was a prince, too. When I asked him about those four errors, he said, "Believe me, I could have made many more."

Kenny Lofton wins the pennant, 2002. It wasn't long before Game 6 of the World Series cast a pall that still hovers over the Giants' organization. That was a game so horrific, so unspeakably wrong; it rendered meaningless everything else that happened that year. So we're still talking about Robb Nen's arm falling off, and Scott for-cryin'-out-loud Spiezio, and Dusty Baker handing the ball to Russ Ortiz. Just a week earlier, though, there was—for me—an equally unforgettable scene around Pac Bell Park. Lofton's single to right-center had sent the Giants to the World Series, and the South-of-Market atmosphere that night was absolutely priceless. I ducked into a stately old tavern with a bunch of sportswriter friends and soaked it up until the wee hours. Dusty had managed his way through the minefield of the Atlanta Braves, and then the St. Louis Cardinals, and this was his crowning touch. If only the story ended there.

Warriors wrap up the Dallas series, 2007. When my sports editor asked if I'd mind writing columns on that series, I didn't give it much thought. It didn't seem like a particularly choice assignment, probably a quick playoff exit for the Warriors, but I figured what the hell, let's see how Dallas looks this time of year. It turned into the most stunning upset in NBA playoff history and the greatest sustained madness at the Coliseum Arena I'd ever seen—including the 1975 title run (a weird one, admittedly, with the Finals games played at the Cow Palace). The atmosphere inside the arena was truly electric, and a big reason behind the Warriors' success. People got hooked around the country and surely hated to see the Warriors' run end in Utah.

Cal baseball goes to San Quentin, 1968. A strange entry, I know, but this was definitely the strangest event I ever covered. I don't know how the thing even got arranged, but Cal was invited inside the prison gates to play hardball against the inmates, and I went along as the sports editor of the *Daily Cal*. We had to wear specific clothing, got shaken down big-time at the gate, the whole thing. We were walked through aisles of prison cells, wondering what lurked inside, and once out on the field, I found myself alongside a number of inmates in the bleachers. I'll never forget this one shirtless African-American guy whose head came to a point, like the old Coneheads routine on *Saturday Night Live*. He never spoke a word, exuding danger by his mere presence. My friend Tony Murray had a no-hitter going for about five innings in that game, something we feared was a bad idea, but no problem: The coach took him out, put in a reliever named Biff, and next thing you knew, the San Quentin boys were in business. At one point late in the game, a country-and-western band full of inmates set themselves up in the outfield. And I mean, shallow right-center—totally in play. Nobody dared argue. Amazing day.

Eckersley strikes out Boggs. This was Game 1 of the 1988 ALCS at Fenway Park. God, I loved covering Fenway games back then, before the construction of the worthless "400 Club" forced a pitiful renovation of the press box (make no mistake, though; it's still the best atmosphere in the game). The A's had a 2-1 lead in the ninth inning, Eckersley on in relief of Dave Stewart, two runners on, and here came Wade Boggs. Eck had saved 45 games that year. Boggs, in winning his fourth straight batting title, hit .366. "So classic, it was a cliché," wrote the *New York Times* of that matchup. Boggs never struck out in those days. Eckersley certainly didn't figure to retire him that way, and Eck was hardly a popular figure in Boston back then. He'd been with the Red Sox in his hard-partying days, a pretty boy with the world on a string, and that didn't go over too well with the aging, crusty, red-faced Irishmen frequenting the press box. I can still hear one of them muttering in mid-at-bat, "Throw the damn ball, ya queerie." Yeah, you heard it right. Well, Eck took a gamble, threw a high fastball, and Boggs swung and missed—plainly shocking both men. Game over. A classic, indeed.

Cal-UCLA at Harmon Gym, 1969. This was a significant college basketball game on so many fronts. John Wooden brought his fabled Bruins to Berkeley that March with just a single loss, led by the great Lew Alcindor. They were the very definition of basketball perfection: talented, unified, proud and brilliantly coached. The Cal team was a symbol of the rebellion swirling around Berkeley at that time. Like so many students battling tear gas and the National Guard, they had some incandescent moments and very little discipline. The coach Jim Padgett was a tremendous recruiter who couldn't coach a lick. But he had Jackie Ridgle, Charlie Johnson and Bob Presley leading a team that could leap out of the building and throw a big-time scare into anyone. This was a night of excruciating tension, the Bears taking Alcindor into overtime before finally taking a heartbreaking loss. Difficult as it was to absorb, everyone felt privileged to have been there. As the years went on, Alcindor became Kareem Abdul-Jabbar and scored more points than anyone in NBA history. The troubled Bob Presley became a vagrant, somehow found his way up to the great Northwest, and jumped off a bridge to his death. The only plausible explanation was suicide.

The Super Bowl at Stanford. I've never covered much pro football for the *Chronicle*. I can't stand the six days between games, all the pompous blowhards, everybody (including writers) strutting around like they're Vince Lombardi, knowing far more than you or anyone else. I like a game where you can trust your eyes, not one where you can't possibly scrutinize 22 guys at once and where a coaching staff can talk you out (or at least try) of any critical stance. But this was a treat: the 1984 49ers playing Miami for the NFL championship at the old Stanford Stadium. I was part of a massive *Chronicle* task force, my only assignment being a locker-room story from the Dolphins' angle (the press box was so overcrowded, I was actually sitting in the stands). If you recall, Miami stormed into town on the heels of a frighteningly efficient destruction of the Pittsburgh Steelers in the AFC title game, featuring Dan Marino at his very finest. I don't think anyone would have been shocked if Marino had humbled the 49ers with five touchdown passes and a convincing win. Instead, they turned him into a grocery-store clerk. He did nothing, nor did any of the Dolphins. The only question was which unit impressed you more, the 49ers' offense or defense. A thorough, comprehensive, historic win.

When you think about the great franchises in Major League history, chances are you left the A's off your list. Truth is, the franchise's eleven World Series wins ranks third all-time. Four of those championships were won since the team moved to Oakland in 1968. In 1972, the A's won their first of three straight titles, then, in 1989, swept the Giants. Still, they'll always be "the other team." A's fans and ownership have to deal with that reality each season. However, there are zero image problems with this list: the ten greatest players to wear the Green and Gold.

10. Jose Canseco (1985-92). Thanks to steroids, a big kid from Cuba got bigger and slugged his way into baseball infamy right from the start by winning the Rookie of the Year award in 1986. Two seasons later, Canseco added an AL MVP. A season after missing half the season with a wrist injury, he rejoined the A's in time to help win the Bay Bride World Series. The first player to join the 40/40 Club with homers and steals, Canseco was an amazing player in his prime. However, we now know the source of his strength, and his place in history is somewhere in between cartoon-like sideshow and whistleblower of the Steroids Era.

9. Bert Campaneris. "Campy" came with the A's from Kansas City and would become one of the enduring fixtures on the back-to-back-to-back title teams of 1972-74. A small, speedy player, the Cuban-born shortstop and six-time all-star Dagoberto Campaneris is still the franchise's all-time leader in games played (1,795) hits (1,882) and at-bats (7,180).

8. Rollie Fingers (1968-76; H.O.F 1992). Owner of the single most identifiable mustache is sports history—and one of baseball's hardest sinking fastballs—Rollie redefined a pitcher's role out of the modern day bullpen, and was once the owner of the all-time saves record. A member of three World Series teams, and a World Series MVP in 1974, Fingers is one of just eight players in history to have his number (34) retired by two teams. He won an AL MVP and Cy Young in Milwaukee in 1981.

7. Dennis Eckersley (1987-95; H.O.F. 2004). In nine seasons with the A's, "Eck" established himself as one of baseball's most intimidating closers. Born in Oakland, Eckersley averaged 44 saves over a five-season stretch that saw him win an MVP and the Cy Young in 1992. During that time, the A's won four division crowns, three American League Pennants and a World Series.

6. Jim "Catfish" Hunter (1965-74; H.O.F. 1987). With a made-up nickname fresh from the desk of owner Charlie Finley, Catfish would win twenty games in five consecutive seasons for the A's in the early Seventies. With a perfect game thrown against the Twins in 1968, Hunter established himself as an elite pitcher who would go on to be named Cy Young winner in 1974, his final season in Oakland. A member of three consecutive title teams, and two more with the Yankees, Hunter fell down the stairs at his home in 1999 after suffering a long batter with Lou Gehrig's Disease, and died. I was there in Oakland the day he was honored. It was a beautiful moment that paid respect to one of baseball's best.

5. Vida Blue (1969-77). One of the most electric pitchers to pass through the Bay Area—he'd play two stints with the Giants as well—Vida overpowered hitters during his time with the A's and won three championships. Blue one-hit the Royals in his Major League debut, and ten days later, no-hit the Twins. He would shine the brightest however in 1971, when he was named the AL MVP and Cy Young winner. He partied as hard as he pitched, and has had a couple of semi-serious league issues because of it. But Vida remains a lovable reminder of some of the Bay Area's baseball glory days.

4. Mark McGwire (1986-97). Before he became "Big Mac" in St. Louis, McGwire was Jose Canseco's "bash brother" and assaulted AL pitchers wearing Green and Gold. Beginning with a 49 home run campaign during his first full season in the Bigs, McGwire became a nine-time All Star with the A's. His body grew along with his legend, but the steroids wind didn't blow until after he was with the Cardinals due to injuries that helped wear out his welcome at the Coliseum. Pure or not, he's Oakland's all-time home run leader to this day with 363 round-trippers, and a member of two World Series teams, winning it all in 1989.

3. Dave Stewart (1986-92; 1995). From Oakland's St. Elizabeth High School, "Smoke" would stare you down then strike you out without remorse. He posted four straight twenty-win seasons, and helped the A's win the Series with an MVP performance in 1989. His big-game reputation would serve him well on five different teams, as Stewart compiled a career 10-6 postseason record, with a 2.84 ERA, including a 7-1 mark versus Roger Clemens.

2. Reggie Jackson (1968-75, 1987; H.O.F. 1983). Of the biggest personality on the three title teams it was once said, "There wasn't enough mustard in the world to cover Reggie Jackson." His opinion of himself couldn't have been higher than in 1973, when Jackson won the lone MVP of his career, hitting .293 with 32 homers and 117 RBI. Mr. October's reputation may have been cemented with the high-profile Yankees, but the legend was born in the Oakland Coliseum. He would play in a grand total of 21 Major League seasons, and reach the playoffs eleven times, winning six pennants and five World Series.

1. Rickey Henderson (1979-84; 1989-93; 1994-95; 1998). As you can see, the A's could never get over Rickey Henderson. The finest leadoff hitter in baseball history, Rickey swiped a major league record (and worldwide record) 1,406 bases. He is also the game's all-time leader in runs scored, with 2,295. His only MVP season came in 1990, during the second of four appearances he made in an A's uniform. His love of the game had him playing long beyond is prime. His desire to stay in baseball had him slapping base hits around independent leagues long after his Major League career ended. Rickey's Oakland roots run deep. He moved here as a very young child, and graduated from Oakland Technical High School, where he was also an All-American running back. If he's not a first ballot Hall of Famer, Cooperstown should be shut down.

The Oakland A's have won four World titles. Still, they're a "might have been" franchise. Throughout Oakland's history, no matter what goes right, there seems to be another force—usually cheapness on ownership's part—causing something to go wrong. Would you break up a team that had won three straight World Series because you were frugal? My hat is off to A's fans who've put up with all-star caliber players and future Hall of Famers leaving for richer destinations. More have left the A's than any other team in baseball. Before the talent leaves, there's usually a little magic in the air, making the departure that much more painful. Here are ten memories that should warm the hearts of even bitter A's fans.

10. First Game. Major league baseball came to the East Bay on April 17, 1968 as the Baltimore Orioles defeated the newly minted Oakland Athletics 4-1, on a two-hitter by Dave McNally. Rick Monday collected the A's first hit, a booming home run to lead off the sixth in front of 50,164.

9. Catfish Hunter's Perfect Game. Only 22 days after playing their inaugural game in Oakland, A's fans had their first major memory. On May 8, 1968, Catfish Hunter twirled a 4-0 perfect game over the visiting Minnesota Twins. But we also have our first look at a major problem that haunts the A's to this day: after drawing more than 50,000 to opening day, only 6,298 attended Catfish's masterpiece.

8. Vida Blue, 1971. In his first full big league campaign, Vida lapped the majors with a 24-8 ledger and 1.82 ERA. Vida threw eight shutouts and completed 24 of his starts. At the end of the season, after leading the A's to their first Western Division title, Blue was honored with both the AL MVP and Cy Young Awards. No pitcher before or since brought the buzz to the Coliseum like Vida in his day. Every home performance during his first year was electric.

7. Reggie Jackson 1971 All-Star Home Run. It may have been an individual moment, but it belongs to A's fans—and pinstripes are nowhere to be seen. Oakland introduced the nation to the next great slugger at the 1971 All Star Game in Detroit, when Reggie Jackson crushed a titanic home run off Dock Ellis that caromed off the right field light standard.

6. 1972 World Series title. Reggie, Catfish, Rollie, Campy and Captain Sal won the AL West, beat the Tigers in the playoffs, and then threw a monkey wrench into the "Big Red Machine," rubbing out the favored Reds in seven games in the World Series. Gene Tenace earned Fall Classic MVP honors, belting four long balls to go with a .348 average.

5. 1973 World Series title. "Mustache Gang" version 2.0. Oakland earned its third straight division title, and then downed the Orioles in the ALCS before running up against the gritty Mets in the World Series. New York took the A's to seven games, but couldn't stop the power of facial hair. Oakland won its second straight championship in seven games. Reggie Jackson earned MVP honors, batting .310 with three doubles, a triple and a home run. I believe George Steinbrenner watched that game.

4. 1974 World Series title. A new skipper; players upset about the cheapness of ownership; clubhouse problems—none of it mattered. Alvin Dark replaced Dick Williams without skipping a beat, managing the A's to their third consecutive crown. Bert Campaneris hit .353, but Rollie Fingers ('stach power) took home the MVP, going 1-0 with two saves and a 1.93 ERA. Even Giants fans enjoyed this one. Oakland took out the Dodgers in five games.

3. Rickey Henderson breaks single season all-time stolen base record. In his fourth big league season Henderson went bananas on the base paths, swiping 130 bags to break Lou Brock's single-season record of 118. Rickey had 84 pilfers by the All-Star break. No other player has stolen as many as 84 bases in a full season since. The man redefined how the game was played. Rickey Henderson's greatness really can't be overstated—unless of course you hand him the microphone, which happened in 1991. After breaking Brock's all time stolen-base record, Rickey declared, "Now, I'm the Greatest." Nice, Rickey.

2. 1989 World Series title. Sandwiched between disappointing Fall Classic results in 1988 and 1990, the powerhouse A's and their "Bash Brothers" wiped out San Francisco for the 1989 world championship in four games. Of course, the most memorable part of the series had nothing to do with baseball. The series was delayed for nine days because of the deadly Loma Prieta Earthquake. Tony LaRussa went with his aces Dave Stewart and Mike Moore as a two-man rotation.

1. Twenty-Game Winning Streak, 2002. Why is this number one? Because other American League teams have their world titles, and have had great performances in great games, but never twenty in a row. From mid-August to early September in 2002, Oakland players and fans went 24 days without experiencing the agony of defeat, setting an AL record. Crowds grew by the game, culminating in a regular season Coliseum attendance record of 55,528 for the dramatic 20th consecutive win. After blowing an 11-0 lead, Scott Hatteberg hit a walk-off home run to give the A's a 12-11 victory over the Royals. Miguel Tejada put a stamp on his MVP season campaign with game-ending hits in wins 18 and 19. He was in another uniform by the next season, of course. Oakland finished 2002 with a 103-59 record, winning the AL west before losing to the Twins in the division playoff series. It marked the third straight season the A's had been sent home in the 5th game of the ALDS. But it was, without a doubt, the best ride anyone ever took, only to come up short in the post-season.

A visionary owner at his best—and an outside-the-box thinker at the very least—Charlie Finley may have been short of cash, but never short on ways to tinker with the game. Here's a list that can only be described as, "The Good, The Bad and The Furry."

10. Orange Balls and the Two-Strike K. Finley proposed that big leaguers play with orange colored baseballs so they would show up better on TV. He also proposed a three-ball walk and two-strike strikeout to quicken the pace of action. To get Finley off their backs, MLB allowed the A's to experiment with both in spring training exhibitions; obviously, the ideas never took.

9. Designated Runner. Finley loved action. What better way to create action than to have players whose sole responsibility was to wreak havoc on the base paths? Herb Washington, a former track star who had no baseball experience, swiped 31 bases in 1974-75, without one official at-bat or defensive inning in the field.

8. Ball Girls. Bless his heart. It was Charlie's fantastic idea to put comely young lasses in short shorts on each base line to scoop up foul balls.

7. Colorful Uniforms. When he first bought the Kansas City A's, Finley switched the team colors from navy and gray to Green and Gold. He wanted the team to look flashier in the days of psychedelics.

6. Joe DiMaggio. More than 15 years after DiMaggio was last in uniform, Finley got Joe D. out of his Marilyn Monroe stupor and into matching white cap and spikes during the A's first season in Oakland in 1968. What Joe did with baseball operations is anybody's guess, but it was great to see him back on the field.

5. MC Hammer. Long before you couldn't touch him and his parachute pants, Hammer (a.k.a. Stanley Burrell) was a gofer for Charlie Finley, running errands, serving as a bat boy or clubhouse attendant, and even describing the action over the phone to Finley back in his Chicago headquarters. Players gave the pop-star-to-be his nickname because he resembled Hammerin' Hank Aaron.

4. Harvey. Before Finley came along, no one ever gave two hoots about the exchange of baseballs between batboy and home plate umpire. But for the A's owner this was a wasted motion. For the first two seasons in Oakland he installed a mechanical rabbit nicknamed "Harvey" that would pop up behind home plate at the Coliseum with a fresh supply of baseballs.

3. Charley O. Presently, most clubs employ people dressed in furry costumes to be dorky mascots. They just leave a bad impression. Finley's mascot "Charley O." was a real live mule that, all too often, left something else on the field.

2. Mustaches. The "Grand Old Game" had become decidedly square by the Sixties. While hippies were running around the Bay Area with long hair and flowing beards, the local nines looked like Joe Friday wannabes. So in 1972, Finley offered $300 to any Athletic who would wear lip fur. Nearly everyone took him up on the offer.

1. Cheapskate. Despite all his good, bad and sometimes funny ideas, Finley is best known in Oakland for his idea to pay players as little as possible. His penny-pinching ways were notorious from his earliest days as A's owner. The reason he moved the club to Oakland was the nearly free Coliseum rent. But his stingy business practices caught up to Finley in the Seventies when his star players immediately left town when free agency allowed them to. Who knows how many World Series titles the Seventies' A's would have won if that club had been kept intact.

Ten All-Star games, two World Series rings, MVP, Comeback Player of the Year, 13 major league contracts with a total of 9 different teams—there could never be enough numbers to explain how good Rickey Henderson was at baseball.

10. Twenty-five straight seasons. Rickey is the only position player since 1900 to have a career that spanned a quarter century. His durability secured his next two records as well. The rest of this list depended on his quick feet, bat and sharp baseball mind.

9. Twenty-five consecutive seasons with at least one stolen base.

8. Twenty-five consecutive seasons with at least one HR.

7. Caught stealing 335 times. Players who are perceived as fast these days may not be allowed this many attempts in their careers, much less have their managers watch them get gunned down 335 times.

6. Eight stolen bases in a single postseason series. Rickey could run in October, too.

5. Unintentional walks: 2,129. Bonds holds the total walks records, but with tons of intentional walks. Henderson took his "base on balls" the old fashioned way; he earned them.

4. Eighty-one games with a leadoff HR. By today's standards, someone with that much power wouldn't be allowed to hit in the leadoff spot.

3. Career runs scored: 2,295. If Bonds had played in 2008, Rickey's record would have been in jeopardy. Barry was just 68 runs away from Henderson.

2. Stolen bases in a single season: 130. As untouchable a modern record as there can be. Managers these days are too busy waiting for their long ball to put runners—and, in this case, history—in motion.

1. Career stolen bases: 1,406. On May 1, 1991, Henderson stole his 939th base to pass Lou Brock as the all-time stolen base king. Forget what he said. What he did will never be done again. His career total is 468 more than Brock, who is still securely in second place.

Greatest A's Hitters by Average

Of all the guys who grabbed lumber and swung it for the Green and Gold, these are the best by career average. Number one on this list was good when he was in town, but I never would have guessed he'd lead all Oakland hitters.

10. Jose Canseco—.264. Say what you want about Canseco and steroids, the guy could hit the ball like no one else for a couple of his nine seasons in Oakland.

9. Reggie Jackson—.264. The same average as Jose, but there's no doubting Reggie was only fueled by an even more toxic performance enhancer: his own ego.

8. Mark Ellis—.266. In six unheralded seasons in Oakland, Ellis has established himself as the one of the game's most dependable middle infielders.

7. Eric Chavez—.269. Thanks to a never-ending stream of injuries, Chavey's eleven seasons have been viewed through strained eyes at times. But he's always been a professional hitter, not to be confused with "clutch."

6. Miguel Tejada—.270. A's fans still can't get over the fact that the team couldn't find the cash to re-sign this former MVP sparkplug who never missed a game. He's one of the good ones that got away after seven seasons.

5. Joe Rudi—.273. When Joe showed up with the club from Kansas City, he brought a solid bat with him for ten seasons' worth of work.

4. Terry Steinbach—.275. He had lots of hits and three American League pennants in eleven seasons with the A's.

3. Carney Lansford—.288. The South Bay native thrived in the East Bay even though he saved his best for the Back Bay of Boston.

2. Rickey Henderson—.288. When it came to getting aboard, no one did it like Rickey. The most complete player in franchise history.

1. Jason Giambi—.308. Twenty points higher than Rickey and Carney, Giambi lived up to the motto on his famous t-shirt: "Party like a rock star; fuck like a porn star; hit like an All Star." His power may have been not completely genuine, but he sure was.

Greatest Homerun Hitters in Oakland A's History

From the swing-away Seventies to the Bash Brothers of the Eighties, the A's can boast as hard-hitting a lineup as any other franchise in baseball history.

10. Terry Steinbach—132 HR. Smacked a pinch-hit HR in his first major league plate appearance as a September call-up in '86.

9. Dwayne Murphy—153 HR. A little pop was waiting for hitters behind Rickey Henderson in the lineup's #2 hole. Murphy, from nearby Merced, spent ten seasons producing in Oakland and took plenty of hits away with six gold gloves.

8. Miguel Tejada—156 HR. Not completely sure of his age, but this is a number I have full confidence in.

7. Rickey Henderson—167 HR. His career record of 81 leadoff homeruns will stand for decades, as will about ten other "Rickey Records."

6. Jason Giambi—187 HR. Turned his East Bay power into Broadway riches when he inked his mega-deal with the Yankees.

5. Sal Bando—192 HR. Captain Sal slugged his way to respectability and 5th place on the list.

4. Eric Chavez—229 HR. Nearly as many trips to the Disabled List.

3. Jose Canseco—254 HR. Third on the all-time Oakland list, and first to appear on a reality TV show. Oh, how the mighty have fallen.

2. Reggie Jackson—268 HR. Forget the Bronx; the legend of REG-GIE begins in Oakland.

1. Mark McGwire—363 HR. He may never make it to Cooperstown, or outside again for that matter, but Mark McGwire will always be a fond memory for most A's fans.

Greatest Strike-Out Artists in Oakland A's History

Here are the top A's gunslingers who sent hitters back to the dugout talking to themselves.

10. Dennis Eckersley, 658 Ks. And nearly every one of them punctuated with a fist pump.

9. Mark Mulder, 668 Ks. He's the first of three young arms on this list who are still active but no longer pitching in Oakland. The real lesson of moneyball is that it takes money to keep players who are good at throwing a ball.

8. Blue Moon Odem, 675 Ks. They just don't out give nicknames like that anymore.

7. Bob Welch, 677 Ks. He rang in the decade of the Nineties with a Cy Young award with 27 wins. No pitcher in either league has won that many games in a single season since. As a matter of fact, no pitcher has even won 25 games since Welsh had his monster season in 1990.

6. Rollie Fingers, 784 Ks. All those strikeouts, and I still think the moustache is the best thing about the guy.

5. Tim Hudson, 899 Ks. Left for richer dollars in Atlanta, and has pitched well for the Braves when not injured.

4. Barry Zito, 1096 Ks. Let for richer dollars in San Francisco, and has been the Giants' problem ever since. He's nothing like the former Cy Young winner and three-time all-star he was in Oakland.

3. Catfish Hunter, 1139 Ks. Threw a perfect game, in a near perfect career that landed him in the Hall of Fame and made the man a household name.

2. Dave Stewart, 1152 Ks. Don't let his second place finish on this list fool you. Stewart led the A's in intimidation when he was on the mound.

1. Vida Blue, 1315 Ks. When Vida pitched, it wasn't a game; it was an event. Fans would pack the Coliseum to watch Vida pitch every four days, and rarely went home unhappy. His 1971 season was good enough to win Blue both Cy Young and AL MVP.

Ten Best Closers in Oakland A's History

The way teams use their bullpen began in Oakland. From the early days of Rollie, to the modern musings of Tony LaRussa, the A's have always been ahead of the curve concerning their bullpen. When LaRussa convinced one of his best pitchers to end games instead of start them, the value and glamour of the closer role became what it is today. Here are the best nails in the coffin in Oakland A's history.

10. Paul Lindblad—34 saves. Known more as a middle reliever, Lindblad, an original A's player, once went 385 consecutive games without an error. He pitched two shutout innings, the ninth and tenth in Game three of the 1973 World Series, and was credited with the win.

9. Bill Caudill—37 saves. In just two seasons with the A's, he managed to find himself on this list. He also managed to find his way out of baseball after breaking his hand in a parking lot fistfight.

8. Keith Foulke—44 saves. Started with the Giants but made a name with the A's after a few seasons with the White Sox. But like all good A's pitchers, he went on to have his greatest success elsewhere, and was on the Red Sox World Series team in 2004. After a brief retirement, Foulke found himself back in the A's bullpen in 2008.

7. Billy Koch—44 saves. Yes, he's tied with Foulke, but he needed just one season to match his save total and 88 percentage, which is best in team history.

6. Jay Howell—61 saves. A two-time All Star with the A's, he was ironically on the Dodgers team that beat Oakland in the 1988 World Series, but there must have been some Green and Gold left in his veins. Howell was kind enough to serve up a home-run ball to Mark McGwire in the ninth inning of Game 3 for the A's only win of the series.

5. Jason Isringhausen—75 saves. Before leaving for bigger free-agent dollars in St. Louis, Izzy was a poster child for Billy Beane's strategy of showcasing a player in the closer role, then enjoying the compensatory pick after he leaves.

4. Huston Street—94 saves. In just four seasons, Street has established himself as one of the best closers in team history. He must be seen as a valuable commodity by the A's front office because normally, players this good are on another team by now.

3. Billy Taylor—100 saves. Drafted in 1980, it took Taylor 14 years of grueling minor league baseball before he got his big league break. He made the most of it. Taylor became a dependable closer over the better part of five seasons. Not bad for a guy who made his major league debut at the age of 32.

2. Rollie Fingers—136 saves. It's only fitting that the last two players on this list are arguably the two most important closers of all time. Fingers was the guy the A's turned to in late innings. More often than not, he would work more than one frame for his saves.

1. Dennis Eckersley—320 saves. More of a one-inning specialist than the durable Fingers, Eckersley is the prototype of the modern major league closer. A good measuring stick between the two great closers is to look at their innings pitched. Both were with the A's for nine seasons. Eck pitched in 637 innings, while Fingers pitched 1016 innings and faced nearly twice the number of hitters. Both were perfect for their time. Both were uniquely gifted and trusting of a manager's unique vision and both are in the Hall of Fame.

Winningest Pitchers in Oakland A's History

"Just Win, Baby!" may be the slogan of the other team that calls the Coliseum home, but these ten pitchers wasted no time adopting that mantra for their own personal gain.

10. Blue Moon Odem—71 wins. Luckily the victories came more frequently than the celestial event he was named after.

9. Rick Langford—73 wins. Pitched 22 consecutive complete games in 1980, which is still the American League record.

8. Ken Holtzman—77 wins. Career ERA of 2.92 in four seasons in Oakland, that's the lowest of all the ERAs on this list.

7. Mark Mulder—81 wins. After a rocky rookie season, Mulder turned into a dependable pitcher who helped the eternally cash-strapped team reach four straight postseasons from 2000-2003.

6. Tim Hudson—92 wins. After his 11-2 rookie season, he never looked back until he looked to Atlanta for a bigger paycheck. He joined Mulder and Zito as the Ace of the A's "Big Three Pitchers."

5. Bob Welch—96 wins. Turned his on-field experience into solid advice for the World Champion Diamondbacks in 2001 when he served as the team's pitching coach.

4. Barry Zito—102 wins. The third of the Big Three, Zito in his prime featured one of the greatest curveballs the AL had ever seen. Now with the Giants, it's unlikely Zito will reach the 200-win mark before his durable career is over.

3. Dave Stewart—119 wins. I'd show Dave that he's 3rd on the team's all-time wins list, but he'd just stare me down.

2. Vida Blue—124 wins. 28 shutouts, 105 complete games, 1,945.2 innings over nine seasons. All are team records.

1. Catfish Hunter—131 wins. Not only is Jim "Catfish" Hunter #1 in Oakland's win column, he held hitters to just a .227 average, which is also tops among starters in Oakland A's history.

NOTE: One of my favorite people in the world to talk baseball with, Marty Lurie turned a distinguished legal career into his real passion: covering the Grand Old Game. The host of A's pre-game, and regular Bay Area media contributor, Marty's stories about the game and the people he has met are endless. Alas, his list is not, so here are just ten of the most colorful Oakland Athletics he's ever covered.

10. Miguel Tejada. "Miggy Magic" was a phrase used to describe the wonderful things this young man (at least we thought he was young) did on the diamond. A's fans got to watch Tejada grow from a raw infielder into a league MVP. Miguel became an outstanding fielding shortstop after many hours of working with the best fielding coach in the majors, Ron Washington. After a slow start Miggy led the club to the playoffs and won the hearts of the fans forever. He could field his position expertly, hit with power, and ignite the fans when he came to the plate. He did all he could for the franchise and whenever his name is mentioned it is done with fondness. Not signing Miggy is the biggest mistake of the Schott era. The A's chose to sign Eric Chavez and let Tejada walk in his free agent season. ·

9. Dave Henderson. No one captured the spirit of the three-time pennant winning teams of 1988-90 than Hendu. He was a team leader motivating Rickey Henderson when the moody left fielder wasn't sure he wanted to play that day. Hendu would tell Rickey that some other player was catching up to Rickey in some statistical category. Rickey would say "Really?" and then put his name in the lineup for that day. When Dave Stewart threw his no-hitter in Toronto, Hendu ranged from his centerfield position to catch the final out in left centerfield, calling off Rickey because he wanted to be on television every time that no-hitter would be shown in the future. Hendu hit homeruns in the post season, entertained his "Hendu's Bad Boys" fans in centerfield talking to them every game, and along with Dave Stewart and Carney Lansford, was a leader of the ball club; he ran the outfield, Carney the infield, and Stew the pitchers. Hendu's smile never left during his tenure with the A's from 1988 through 1993.

8. Mike Norris. This talented righty's best pitch was the screwball . . . perfect for this young native of San Francisco who struggled with substance issues during his tenure in Oakland. When players remember the top-pitched games in A's history, Norris' 14-inning complete game against Baltimore always comes to mind. Hall of Famer Bob Gibson took Norris aside in 1979 and called him a disgrace when Norris didn't pitch inside often enough. It worked and Norris's career took off as the screwball artist won 22 games in 1980. Norris had the best stuff of any of the starters in the early '80s. In heartwarming fashion, he returned to Oakland in 1990 after working out numerous personal issues, winning his only decision for the club. Mike Norris still is an inspiration to those trying to overcome challenges in life.

7. Billy North. The centerfielder fought with Reggie Jackson, never backing down when confronted by the superstar right fielder. North teamed with Campy Campaneris, giving the A's a dynamic base-stealing duo at the top of the lineup. He won the respect of his teammates when he charged the mound after routinely swinging and missing at a Doug Bird pitch, losing his bat in the process. Seems Bird hit North with a pitch while the two were in the minor leagues, sending North to the hospital. North vowed he would get Bird if the two ever met again. They did when North faced the Kansas City Royal righty for the first time in the majors. North's teammates followed his lead and ran to the field to join North's fight, not knowing why. North became a Swingin' A on that day and no one messed with him thereafter. North had an edge that showed when he played baseball. However, North is also remembered for breaking the wrong way on a fly ball with two out in the ninth inning, costing Ken Holtzman his third career no-hitter.

6. Billy Martin. A Bay Area native, Martin's hiring by Charlie Finley to manage the 1980 ball club brought respectability back to the franchise. Fans came out to see Billy Ball, a freewheeling, base-stealing, take-no-prisoners style of play. In 1981, Martin presided over a pitching staff that threw more complete games than any other team in baseball history, other than some squad that played in 1880. Martin might have ruined the careers of Rick Langford, Matt Keough, Mike Norris and Brian McCatty but it sure was fun to see the A's pitch that year. Billy drank, swore and fought his way out of a job by 1984, being replaced by the studious Steve Boros. Pitching coach Art Fowler had the best line when he would go out to the mound to talk with a struggling pitcher. Art would say in his South Carolinian drawl, "You better start throwing strikes because you're starting to piss Billy off." Fowler's words usually did the trick.

5. Vida Blue. His fastball was called "The Blue Blazer," and to this day, Vida is still the most dynamic pitcher ever to play for the A's in Oakland. Blue threw a no-hitter during a late season call-up in 1970. In 1971, Blue won the league's MVP and Cy Young awards going 24-8 with a 1.82 ERA and 301 strikeouts. In 1972, Finley made a mint having Blue pitch on Monday nights at the Coliseum on half-price night, filling up the joint with 50,000 wildly excited fans. Finley wanted Vida to change his name to "True Blue," but Vida told Charlie to get lost. When Charlie refused to pay Vida what he was worth for his 1972 contract, he held out, threatening to sell plumbing supplies instead of pitching baseballs for the A's. When Vida was traded to the Giants for half the Giants farm system, the spirit of the 1970s Swingin' A's left, too. Vida was something to see. His save in game five of the ALCS in 1972 sent the A's to the series and the first of three straight world titles.

4. Jason Giambi. When the A's won the AL West in 2000 Giambi carried the club on his back in September. His homeruns and big hits against the Yankees will never be forgotten. Giambi was a terrific hitter who epitomized the A's patient yet powerful approach at the plate. Unbelievably, A's owner Steve Schott, a noted spendthrift, offered Giambi $95 million to stay in Oakland as free agency loomed for the slugger. But he turned the club down and bolted for New York. Giambi told the world via David Letterman's show that there was "no there there" in Oakland. Still Giambi is cheered more than he's booed when he returns to the Coliseum in pinstripes.

3. Jose Canseco. Mister 40-40 was a huge hit with the fans, winning the AL Rookie of the Year award in 1987. If you were coming out to the game you showed up early just to see Jose take batting practice. Jose had fast cars, glamorous wives and famous girlfriends (Madonna). Jose was a good outfielder before becoming bored by standing around in right field while waiting his turn to hit. Jose had a line that irked his teammates and manager Tony LaRussa when he whined that the season was too long if the A's had to play in October.

2. Rickey Henderson. Rickey is the next A's Hall of Famer, a sure first-ballot selection in 2009. Rickey said it all when he broke Lou Brock's all-time stolen base record as he held the pilfered bag aloft, proclaiming to the world that he was now the greatest base stealer in baseball history. Rickey toyed with his American League opponents as a precocious little leaguer would toy with other 12-year-olds. Rickey was that good. Rickey took over the game once he entered the batter's box. In 1981, Rickey single-handedly took the Royals apart in the ALDS. When Rickey returned from N.Y. in June 1989, the ball club came alive and won the pennant.

1. Reggie Jackson. Mr. October was the first legitimate superstar in Oakland, bursting onto the scene with 47 homeruns in the A's second season in 1969. Reggie met with the media when other players shied away, and routinely fought with owner Charlie Finley. If there was a fight in the clubhouse, Reggie could nearly always be found in the middle of the fracas. When Reggie came to bat you didn't get up to buy a hot dog; watching Reggie play on the diamond was all the hot dog one needed. Reggie was AL MVP in 1973. When he left the club in a trade with the Orioles in 1976, the team lost its swagger.

With two football teams and two baseball teams dividing fans—and sometimes, households—the Warriors are a welcome rallying point for the Bay Area. The Warriors truly are the Bay Area team, having played regular season home games in San Francisco, Oakland and San Jose during their existence. I've always thought it was appropriate they don't claim a city, settling for "Golden State" instead of setting up rooting boundaries. Known more for the lean times over the last 30 years than winning titles, Golden State has enough all-time depth to run with any team in NBA history, make no mistake.

10. Jerry Lucas (1969-71). It was only two seasons, but the former Buckeye who was crowed NCAA champ in San Francisco city limits, made the most of it, averaging 17 points and 15 rebounds. With too many big men, the Warriors traded the power forward to the Knicks. Yup, these are yourrrrrrrrrr Golden State Warriors!

9. Purvis Short (1978-87). For nine of his 12 NBA seasons, Short played big for the Warriors, justifying their using the fifth pick of the 1978 NBA draft on the small forward out of Jackson State. He would average better than 17 points per game. On November 17, 1984, he dropped a career-high 59 points on the Nets.

8. Mitch Richmond (1988-91). Drafted with the fifth overall pick, Richmond won Rookie of the Year, averaging 20 points per game. Three years later the Warriors pulled a typical Warriors move and traded Richmond—and his 22 points per game— to Sacramento. His slashing style turned him into a six-time all-star, and a mere memory for fans who still reminisce about the days of Run TMC.

7. Tim Hardaway (1989-96). Out of Texas El Paso, Hardaway UTEP two-stepped his way into the hearts of Warriors fans right from the start. He was a double-double machine at the point, and guided the Warriors to some of their most memorable regular season successes. But in typical Warrior fashion, right as he entered the prime of his career, the team traded him to Miami, where he immediately became first-team all-NBA.

6. Tom Meschery (1962-67). The son of Russian immigrants, Tomislav Nikolayevich Mescheryakov was born in Manchuria, China. Tom-for-short was imported to the Bay Area along with the Philadelphia Warriors in 1962. Funny thing was it wasn't his first time in San Francisco. When his family fled to America, Meschery landed here. He went to Lowell High School before playing his college ball at St. Mary's in the East Bay. Alongside Wilt, he established himself as a solid low post player who eventually would see his number retired by three franchises.

5. Wilt Chamberlain (1962-64; H.O.F. 1978). I wonder how many women Wilt went through in his two years with the Warriors. Considering it was San Francisco, and the early Sixties, I'm guessing the bedroom statistics were as impressive as his on-court numbers. Chamberlain averaged 44 points per game with 24 rebounds in the team's first season on the West Coast. Someone worth keeping around, unless you're struggling as a newly relocated franchise, which the Warriors were. And so it was.

Wilt was traded for players and cash, and San Francisco saw the first officially terrible decision by its new NBA team. We'd get used to it. One of the greatest forces ever unleashed on humankind, Wilt is also the only player in NBA history to battle Conan the Destroyer.

4. Chris Mullin (1985-97; 2000-01). Now the Warriors General Manger, Mully was a sharp-shooting small forward with one of the sweetest strokes in NBA history. The three-time Big East Player of the Year, and John R. Wooden Award Winner out of St. Johns, flourished when Don Nelson started calling his name during timeouts. He's the only player in Warriors history to average 25 points per game over five seasons who didn't sleep with 20,000 women. An original Dream Teamer, Mullin won Olympic gold twice and came back to Oakland for a sentimental, on-court goodbye to end his career in 2001. He remains one of the favorite players in team history.

3. Al Attles (1962-71). He came so close, and then he took us so far. An African American coaching pioneer, Attles was a career Warrior dating back to the team's Philly days. The durable forward—whose battles down low became more of a roll down low—used the time to make mental notes on how he thought the game should be played. During his playing days, the Warriors lost in the NBA finals twice. But as a coach, he was prepared to win it all in 1975-76. It remains the Warriors only NBA Championship.

2. Nate Thurmond. (1963-74; H.O.F. 1985). "Nate the Great" was one of the few centers whom the NBA's legendary centers feared. He grew up backing-up Wilt, but came into his own after Chamberlain was traded. In back-to-back seasons, Nate averaged 20-20, but wasn't with the Warriors when they won their only title. Nevertheless, he is remembered as one of the best rebounding, shot-blocking big men of all-time.

1. Rick Barry (1965-67; 1972-78). He averaged a whopping 35 points in his second NBA season and developed into one of the most complete, all-court players in the history of basketball. With his underhanded free throw shooting style, four prime seasons in the ABA with the Oakland Oaks (he's their number one, too) Rick did things his own way, including sitting out a season, and never asked what you thought. He irritated defenders and often, his own teammates, like Mike Dunleavy, who once said, "You could send him to the U.N., and he'd start World War III." Didn't matter. Barry is and will forever be the only man on planet Earth to have led the NCAA, NBA and ABA in scoring. Inside, outside, however you want it, in whatever league you want it, Barry's brightest professional moment came when he helped the Warriors sweep the Washington Bullets to win the NBA finals. On a personal note, it was my pleasure to get to talk basketball with Rick on more than a few occasions. He was working at KNBR when I arrived. He was great to me, and if today's players listened to him, the game would be better. And if he were 24-years-old again, he'd tear the NBA apart.

Franchise-Defining Raiders Moments Before Al Davis Sold His Soul to Los Angeles

The Raiders we watch today are Raiders version 2.0, downloaded back to Oakland after Al Davis ripped the heart and soul out of Raider Nation with a move to Los Angeles. Breaking that trust is something many Silver and Black fans in Northern California will never forget. To others, it's water under the bridge. Truthfully, it was one of the biggest miscalculations in sports history. Testing the L.A. market left the Raiders as the NFL's definitive second-class citizen. As far as hardcore Oakland fans are concerned, there is no history between the years 1982–1994. Consequently, "The Team of the Decades" really hasn't had a decade that's mattered since the Seventies. As far as the East Bay is concerned, these ten things define the REAL Oakland Raiders.

10. The Ageless George Blanda, 1970. Longhairs in Berkeley may not have trusted anyone over 30, but Raiders fans couldn't get enough of 43-year-old Blanda in 1970. The lantern-jawed oldie but goodie was named AFC Player of the Year and NFL Man of the Year after leading the Silver and Black to an AFC West title with several late-game field goals and spot-on relief quarterbacking.

9. Monday Night Mayhem. The Raiders made *Monday Night Football* appointment viewing in the 1970s, going 12-1-1 under the lights during the disco decade. It was the high water mark of intimidation for the Silver and Black. On Dec. 11, 1972, the Jets' Joe Namath threw for 403 yards, but left the Coliseum with a broken jaw and a 24-16 loss.

8. Ghost to the Post, 1977. The Raiders trailed late in their 1977 playoff game at Baltimore when Dave Casper (the Friendly Ghost) was slated to run a post pattern. He opted for a shorter curl, hauled in a feathery pass from Kenny Stabler, and sprinted 42 yards to set up a game-tying field goal. The Raiders would win 37-31 when the Ghost made a ten-yard TD grab in the second overtime period.

7. The Holy Roller, 1978. Trailing 20-14 with just about a minute on the game clock, Ken Stabler fumbled on purpose rather than take a sack. Pete Banaszak tried to scoop it up but only managed to push the ball forward. Dave Casper attempted to pick up the elusive pigskin, but kicked it over the goal line before falling on it for a most unlikely touchdown. The PAT gave Oakland a miraculous 21-20 victory. The following season the rules were changed to allow only the fumbling player to advance the ball.

6. Snake Comeback, 1979. Stabler was a two-minute-drill master, leading Oakland to many last minute comebacks with the Raiders. In his final campaign with Oakland in 1979, Stabler did it one more time, overcoming a 35-14 second-half deficit at New Orleans to lead the Raiders' dramatic comeback win. The coup de grace was a 66-yard touchdown pass to Cliff Branch late in the fourth quarter.

5. Sea of Hands, 1974. Miami held a 19-14 lead late in the action, but the Snake and Co. slithered to another win. Cliff Branch caught a 72-yard pass to make it 21-19. Miami came back quickly, scoring on a 78-yard drive that took all of four plays. But the Dolphins had scored too quickly. There was still 2:08 on the clock, and Kenny had all his timeouts. With 35 seconds left, a triple-teamed Clarence Davis, out-leaping several outstretched arms, somehow snatched a pass for the winning score in a 28-26 win.

4. Super Bowl XI, 1976 season. After going 13-1 during the regular season and two, thrilling playoff wins—including a fourth-quarter nail-biter comeback over the Patriots in round one—the Raiders redeemed their Super Bowl II loss with a 32-14 blowout of the Vikings at the Rose Bowl. Clarence Davis rushed for 137 yards. Dave Casper caught a TD, Pete Banaszak rushed for a pair and Willie Davis returned a Fran Tarkenton interception 75 yards for another score.

3. *Heidi* Game, 1968. With the Raiders trailing 32-29 to the visiting Jets, NBC cut away from its game broadcast with about five minutes on the clock to show the scheduled feature film *Heidi*. As the east coast watched children in lederhosen, the Raiders stormed back to score two touchdowns on a 43-yard pass play from Daryle Lamonica to Charlie Smith. Then, immortal special teamer Preston Ridlehuber fell on a kickoff fumble in the end zone. NBC's switchboard went berserk. Since that night, no game has been cut away from in the name of "regularly scheduled programming," all thanks to *Heidi* and the Raiders' comeback win.

2. Immaculate Reception, 1972. "We was robbed" is a birthright mantra of all Raiders fans. But could anything sting worse than being on the wrong end of one of sports' all-time highlights? On December 23, 1972, the first round of the AFC playoffs would turn to mayhem in the waning seconds. The pass from Pittsburgh's Terry Bradshaw reached receiver Frenchy Fuqua at the same time as a forearm shiver by Jack Tatum. The ball caromed in the air and into the arms of Franco Harris who rumbled 60 yards for a winning score, 13-7 Steelers. A case for illegal touching indeed, but the game was played at Three Rivers Stadium, and home cooking prevailed. Tatum swears he never touched the ball, and a coy Fuqua has always said he knows what happened, but will never tell, adding fuel to what is, according to NFL films, the greatest play in NFL history, which altered the course of history for both franchises.

1. 1980 Playoffs and Super Bowl XV. After making the playoffs as a wild card entry, the Raiders went on to work playoff magic, snatching a win out of the Browns hands when Mike Davis intercepted a Brian Sipe pass in the end zone, whipping the heavily favored Chargers. They were underdogs again in Super Bowl XV. But it quickly became apparent the Eagles were no match for the Silver and Black. Led by three Rod Martin interceptions and MVP Jim Plunkett's 261 passing yards and three TDs, Oakland rolled to a 27-10 win, made bittersweet with the move to L.A. in 1981.

Where's Howie Long? Where's Marcus Allen? Where's Bo Jackson? Sorry kids, but they're Los Angeles Raiders. This list is all Oakland—well, mostly Oakland.

10. Jack Tatum (1971–1979). Although the Raiders have two HOF cornerbacks in Mike Haynes and Willie Brown, no member of the Silver and Black secondary was ever as feared as "The Assassin." His hard-hitting reputation was sadly cemented when he paralyzed Patriots WR Darryl Stingley in a pre-season game. In nine seasons with the Raiders, the former Buckeye and eventual Super Bowl Champ led the NFL in bone-crushing hits, and was named All Pro five times.

9. Fred Biletnikoff (1965–1978; HOF 1988). Second-most catches in franchise history, and named MVP of Super Bowl XI. A four-time Pro Bowler and Raiders lifer, Biletnikoff returned as a WR coach for several seasons until his retirement in 2006.

8. George Blanda (1967–1975; HOF 1981). The only player in the history of the NFL to have a 26-year career, Blanda threw and kicked his way into the annals of Raiders history. Holder of the single-season scoring record, Blanda played in seven title games with the Raiders.

7. Kenny Stabler (1968–1984). Oh, how Al Davis loves the vertical passing game, and because of that, he loved Kenny Stabler. His touch on the deep ball was thing of beauty; good enough to have him lead the NFL in TD passes twice. A party man, a ladies' man, an MVP, Stabler embodied all that the Raiders represented— which of course, used to mean a championship, which he won in Super Bowl XI. Eventually, knee injuries slowed "The Snake" to a crawl, and out of Oakland.

6. Tim Brown (1988–2003). Sure, Tim was drafted when the team was in L.A., but I can't hold that against him. After all, the Heisman Trophy winner from Notre Dame is "Mr. Raider." Holds the team record for all-purpose yardage, and owns every significant team receiving record, as well as several NFL records. As the team's image degenerated into something unsavory, it was Brown's dignity and passion for the game that made him great.

5. Gene Upshaw (1967–1981; HOF 1988). regarded as one of the greatest guards in football history, Upshaw made an even greater impact off the field as the head of the NFLPA until he passed away in 2008. A six-time Pro Bowler, with an AFL All-Star Game appearance, Upshaw helped pave the way to two world championships, and unspeakable player riches when his blocking days were through.

4. Art Shell (1968–1982; HOF 1989). Prototype offensive tackle, regarded as one of the greatest, if not the greatest, to ever play the position. An eight-time Pro Bowler, Shell moved mountains and provided stellar pass protection for an often deep-dropping quarterback. He had two stints as team coach. One was semi-successful, but is unspoken here because it was in L.A. The other go-around lasted one horrific 2-14 season, and should also remain unspoken.

3. Jim Otto (1960-1974; HOF 1980). Named to a dozen Pro Bowls, and the only all-league center the AFL ever selected, Otto defined Raiders toughness. His #00 seemed to perfectly fit his intimidating style of play. He was the centerpiece, no pun intended, of one of the greatest offensive lines football has ever seen.

2. Ted Hendricks (1975-1983; HOF 1990). A member of the NFL's 75th Anniversary Team, "The Stork" dominated running backs and anyone brave enough to go over the middle during his nine-year tenure with the franchise. Even though he departed to L.A. with the rest of the team, Ted has to qualify for this classic list because of the way he upheld Al Davis's beloved Raiders image. A three-time Super Bowl Champion, he also played for the Colts, winning Super Bowl V, and may be the greatest defensive player in the history of the University of Miami.

1. Jim Plunkett (1978-1986). Sure, one of his two Super Bowl rings came in the city of Angles, but Plunkett is all Bay Area, and to this day, #1 in the hearts of Raiders faithful. A Heisman Trophy winner at Stanford, Plunkett's massive hands guided the Raiders to one of the greatest turnarounds in NFL history in 1980, when he filled in for an injured Dan Pastorini. Plunkett won 9 of 11 games, and went on to be named MVP of Super Bowl XV.

Five Reasons Why the Raiders Are Fooling Themselves These Days

I don't have anything against the Raiders. I really don't. But in all my years covering sports, I've never seen a team buy into its own bumper-sticker bullshit more than the Oakland Raiders. Here's proof.

5. Silver and Blacked Out. Since moving back to Oakland in 1995, the Raiders quickly found out that slapping their fans in the face with a 13-year relocation to L.A. makes it hard to sell tickets. Routinely blacked out on local TV, the Raiders have been ranked 30th or worse in attendance every season since 2002.

4. The Media Guide. There are hundreds if not thousands of high schools with big football programs that put more effort and pride into their media guides. Honestly, there is nothing in professional sports more pathetic than the 2008 Oakland Raiders Media guide. Completely colorless. There's hardly an indent, paragraph, bullet point, graphic or photo to be seen in 296 underwhelming pages. Where's the pride, Al? Comparing it to the 49ers media guide, you'd think the Raiders were an expansion team that got the project finished in the middle of the night at Kinkos in Alameda.

3. Championship Rings. As written in the media guide: "The Raiders' World Championship rings are renowned as the most memorable pieces of championship team jewelry ever produced." Come on. Has anyone ever even considered the Raiders' Super Bowl rings? No special memories here. Come and sip from the Al Davis Kool-Aid. Gimme a break.

2. Team of the Decades? The Raiders claim to be the "Team of the Decades." Let's examine that. One of the great AFL franchises, the Raiders won a title before the NFL/AFL merger. For argument's sake, I'll give Oakland the decade of the Sixties. The Seventies were good to the Raiders, but better to the Steelers, who won four Super Bowls. As far as the decade of the Eighties goes, Niners lay claim to it without debate. Hop into the Nineties: Raiders begin the decade with a 51-3 drubbing by the Bills in the AFC title game, and it was all downhill from there. Since 1990, the Raiders have notched just seven winning seasons in 18 years, with one Super Bowl appearance—where they were crushed by the Buccaneers, 48-21. Team of the decades? OK, Mr. Davis, if you say so.

1. Commitment to Excrement—or, The Randy Moss Era. Forget the fact that the Raiders are 19-62 since 2003. The most telling indicator that the "Commitment to Excellence" is pure bullshit: Randy Moss. In two seasons, "Captain Randy" jogged his routes, took plays off and became the prime example of a guy who didn't care about anything other than his paycheck. To make matters worse, he shattered NFL receiving records as soon as he left. All Oakland had to show for it was a fourth-round draft pick. The fact Moss was able to get away with his act, and never even stripped of his captaincy, was proof the Raiders had lost control from the top down.

Despite speaking in Raiders clichés to his own detriment, there is no doubt that Al Davis achieved his life's dream: Building one of the most feared professional franchises the game of football has ever known. Here are ten things I'm certain he's thinking about right now as he stomps the halls of Raiders headquarters in his Silver and Black jogging suit.

10. Wins. Coming into the 2008 season, the Raiders have tasted victory exactly 400 times. The Raiders all-time record is 400-313-11.

9. Rushing. With a 92-yard TD scamper against Cincinnati, and a famous 91-yard TD run in his legendary romp over the Seahawks on Monday Night Football, Bo Jackson owns the two longest rushing plays in franchise history, but that's soooo L.A. The longest running play in Oakland Raiders history was ripped off by Kenny King, who went 89 yards to paydirt against the Chargers in 1980. Notice none of these records belong to Marcus Allen.

8. Passing. The longest pass play in Raiders history is the longest pass play in NFL history, and it's a record that can't be broken, only tied. Jim Plunkett connected with speedster Cliff Branch for a 99 yard TD in Washington in 1983. Yes, I know that's Los Angeles Raider territory, but Al loves NFL records, so I'm sure he'd want you to know.

7. It's hard to beat a Raider on a regular basis. Only five NFL teams have winning records over Al Davis' franchise: Philadelphia (4-5), Ravens (1-3), Jaguars (1-3), Houston Texans (0-3), and the archrival Kansas City Chiefs (43-50).

6. Super Bowls. Sure the 49ers have more Super Bowls. But one thing San Francisco doesn't have is a winning record over the Raiders. The two have met just ten times since 1970, with Oakland holding a 6-4 edge. The near-annual pre-season match-up favors the Raiders as well: 19-17.

5. Coach of the Year. Five coaches were named Coach of the Year while walking the Raiders' sidelines: Al Davis (1963), John Rauch (1967), John Madden (1969), Tom Flores (1982), and Art Shell (1990).

4. Decades. The Raiders are the only team in NFL history to appear in four Super Bowls in four different decades: Sixties, Seventies, Eighties and 2000s.

3. Winning Percentage. Of all the original AFL teams—Chiefs, Broncos, Patriots, Chargers, Titans/Oilers, Bills and Jets—the Oakland Raiders have the highest winning percentage: .561. FYI, the Jets have the lowest at .450. Good luck, Brett Favre.

2. Broncos and Chargers. The two opponents the Raiders have put a whoopin' on the most since 1960 are the Denver Broncos and San Diego Chargers. Both have bent to the power of Raider Nation. Denver has lost 54 times, and the Chargers 56 times.

1. Monday Night Mayhem. Under the lights, the Raiders came alive and into your living room on Mondays and usually went to bed with a win. Oakland is 36-23-1 on ABC's once-legendary program, dying on the vine since its move to ESPN. The Raiders won their first four *MNF* games, tied one, lost one, then won 14 in a row. It's really been a tale of Two Mondays for the Raiders. They were 29-6-1 before 1991, and just 7-17 since.

A model for expansion, the Sharks joined the NHL in 1991, and didn't take long to establish a rabid fan base and hockey credibility. After two seasons serving as a Western Conference whipping post, the Sharks moved to their permanent home, "The Shark Tank" in San Jose, and skated to one of the biggest turnarounds in NHL history. They went on to stun the hockey world with an upset over the heavily favored Detroit Red Wings in the first round of the 1993–94 Stanley Cup playoffs. Although the Cup eludes San Jose, the franchise has made the playoffs in 11 of 16 seasons, not including the lockout year. Much of the success is due to the effort of these ten men, who made the color teal . . . tough.

10. Jonathan Cheechoo. The right winger has been lighting the lamp in San Jose since he burst into the NHL in 2002. Drafted in 1998, he's the first player from Canada's Moose Cree First Nation (Native Canadian Indian) to skate in the NHL. In 2005-06, Cheech won the Maurice "Rocket" Richard Trophy for the most goals in season, 56, which is one of three team records he holds. The others are for most power play goals in a season (24) and most hat tricks in a season (5).

9. Vincent Damphousse. After skating with the Maple Leafs, Oilers and Canadians, Damphousse found a home in Northern California with the Sharks, and retired as one of the team's most vocal supporters of hockey in the area. He played in all 82 games in four of his six seasons, and had his best year in teal as the team's frontline center with 61 points in 2002-03.

8. Jeff Friesen. With the Sharks from 1994-2001, Friesen was the Sharks' first pick of the 1994 NHL draft, eleventh overall. The left winger is third on the franchise's all-time scoring list. Traded to the Ducks near the end of the '01 season, Friessen went on to win a Stanley Cup with the New Jersey Devils. Still skating, Friesen was invited to Sharks training camp heading into the 2008-09 season.

7. Mike Ricci. From 1997 through 2004, Ricci was the heart and face of the San Jose Sharks. He holds the team record with 228 consecutive games played. Captain Ricci became one of the best defensive centremen in the NHL. Without front teeth, and with a great mullet, Ricci was a rock on the first-and-only Sharks team to reach the Western Conference Finals in 2004, his final season skating with the team. An all-time fan favorite, Ricci rejoined the team as an advisor in 2007.

6. Doug Wilson. After 14 distinguished seasons with the Chicago Blackhawks, Wilson came west with NHL expansion to become the first Captain in team history. However, it's not his two seasons as a player that had the biggest impact on the franchise. In 2003, Wilson returned to the Sharks as General Manager. The team has finished first or second in the Pacific Division in each of his four seasons calling the shots.

5. Arturs Irbe. The foundation of the '93-'94 team that stunned the Red Wings, Irbe defined the term "hot goaltender" that season, and is still beloved in San Jose because of it. During that remarkable season, Irbe played a NHL record 4,412 minutes in goal, and became known as "The Wall." Archie, as he was called, wore every save he made and never washed the scuff marks off his mask. The build-up of rubber resulted in yet another nickname, "The Michelin Man." Irbe was released after his play declined due to a freak dog-mauling accident, but he went on to recover and continues to play professionally to this day.

4. Evgeni Nabokov. A two-time All Star, Nabokov burst onto the scene in 2000-01, winning the Calder Memorial Trophy as the NHL's best rookie. Drafted by San Jose, the man in the pipes with the funny name has left goal scorers stone-faced time and time again. Nabby is the franchise leader in nearly every goaltending category, including games played (430), wins (208), shutouts (40) and even goals scored, with one.

3. Joe Thornton. After defining the Boston Bruins for nearly a decade, Thornton was acquired in the best trade in team history. Joe joined the Sharks midway through 2005-06, and scored a whopping 92 points in just 53 games. It was just a hint of what was to come. The next season, Thornton won the Ross Trophy after leading the NHL with 114 points—a team record—and easily won the Hart Trophy as the league's MVP. Playing in two All-Star games in as many full seasons, Thornton is also one of the friendliest, most generous men in all of sports. If the Sharks know what's good for them, he'll retire in teal.

2. Owen Nolan. A three-time All Star, six-time Captain, and owner of two restaurants in San Jose, Nolan was and still is a fixture in Sharks history. Picked up in a trade for Sandis Ozolinsh in early 1995, the Sharks enjoyed the best of Nolan's career, which became injury prone after he was traded to Toronto at the deadline in 2003. Nolan finished second in the NHL with 44 goals and added 40 assists in his best season, 1999-00. That year he scored eight goals in the postseason.

1. Patrick Marleau. Drafted second overall, ironically behind Joe Thornton in 1997 by San Jose, Captain Marleau has played his entire career with a Shark on his chest. In just over a decade, Marleau has become the all-time leader in games (795), points (539), assists (301), goals (238), game-winning goals (43) and shots (1,669). His breakout season was in 2005-06 when he set a new career high for points, with 86. Although his harshest critics have questioned his toughness, it's really an indictment of the high expectations now placed on the franchise.

Ten Greatest Moments in San Jose Sharks History
:: by Drew Remenda

NOTE: Drew Remenda *is* Sharks hockey. He has been with the team first as an assistant coach, then as wildly popular announcer on both radio and TV. Originally from Saskatoon, Saskatchewan, Drew's intermission reports are mandatory viewing for Bay Area hockey fans, and have turned him into the most recognizable figure in the team's history. No one has seen more Sharks hockey than Drew, and no one is more qualified to offer us the team's ten greatest moments on ice.

10. First Game, Sharks vs. Canucks, Oct. 4, 1991. The team came from behind to tie the game but lost late, 4-3. California-born Craig Coxe scored the first-ever franchise goal.

9. First Game in San Jose, Oct. 14, 1993. Sharks lost 2-1 to Calgary Flames. The start of a great record-setting NHL season.

8. All Star Game in San Jose. The Sharks own Tony Granato and Owen Nolan are the hometown heroes. Nolan scored a hat trick, including the infamous "called shot."

7. Owen Nolan traded to San Jose. Promising Young Defenseman Sandis Ozolinsh moved to Colorado for the Sharks future Captain and face of the franchise, power forward Owen Nolan.

6. Sharks trade away opportunity to draft Chris Pronger. In a draft day switch with Hartford, the Sharks traded down and Hartford got Chris Pronger. Sharks settled for a lesser known but are able to gain short term, grabbing Sergei Makarov who becomes the club's first 30-goal man.

5. Sharks beat the Presidents' Trophy-winning St. Louis Blues in seven games. For the first time in nine years, a team had beaten the Presidents' Trophy winner in the first round. Owen Nolan scored from centre ice to crush the hopes of the Blues.

4. Sharks win nine in a row to secure first-ever playoff berth. Jamie Baker scored twice to beat the L.A. Kings. The Sharks set an NHL record for the biggest turnaround in one season to get to the playoffs.

3. Sharks reach Western Conference Finals. For the first, and so far, only time the Sharks beat Colorado in six games to reach the Conference Finals. Led by Evgeni Nabokov, the Sharks beat the Avs 3-1 and headed to uncharted waters.

2. Joe Thornton is traded to San Jose. In one of the biggest trades in NHL History, the Boston Bruins superstar is traded to San Jose for fan favorite Marco Sturm, Defenseman Brad Stuart and utility Forward Wayne Primeau. The Sharks and Thornton take off and Joe goes on to win the NHL's MVP and Scoring Leader (Art Ross) trophies.

1. Jamie Baker scores the biggest goal in franchise history. Baker pounces on a Chris Osgood giveaway and scores in the third period to give the Sharks the lead. The team holds off a furious push at the end of the game and celebrates the franchise's first-ever playoff series win, defeating the top-seeded Red Wings.

Top Ten Eats or Treats at the Park or Stadium

If there's one thing everyone in San Francisco and the surrounding Bay Area can agree on it's the fact we like our food, and the teams know it. The concessions here are routinely ranked among the best in all of sports. Cancel the reservations—dinner is served right in your seat.

10. The Carvery, AT&T Park. Good sandwiches. Turkey, pastrami, roast beef. Don't forget the mustard.

9. Boysenberry Lemonade, AT&T Park. One of the tastiest sips offered anywhere. Cool yourself off with this Club Level drink, found behind home plate.

8. Ghirardelli Hot Fudge Sundae. Served at a couple of stadiums around the Bay, it's a reminder that sometimes in life you must throw down $8 at the altar of the Chocolate master.

7. Bloody Mary, Acme Chophouse. It has saved several lives, and combs the hair of the dog that bit you the previous night. Essential for those who enjoyed a late Friday night, and have tickets to Saturday afternoon's game.

6. Cinnamon Roasted Almonds. Another treat you can find at several venues. Call me old fashioned, but I like my nuts hot. Insert joke here.

5. Crazy Crab Sandwich/Crab Louis Salad, AT&T Park. Behind the scoreboard in center field you'll find these two delicacies. As delicious as they are expensive, I limit myself to one per season, but it's worth it.

4. BBQ at Warriors Games. Seats in the nosebleeds may not be tasty, but the BBQ sold in the upper deck at Oracle Arena is worth the climb. I've made more than a couple of trips upstairs to douse my belly with ribs and brisket.

3. Oakland Hot Link, Coliseum. There's nothing extraordinary about the hot links in Oakland, but for some reason they taste better here than anywhere else. It's an annual rite of passage for me as I take in my American League ball.

2. The Cha-Cha Bowl/Tri-Tip Sandwich, AT&T Park. Orlando Cepeda's tent behind the scoreboard usually has more than a couple of people in line waiting for one of the best meals served in any sporting venue. Go with a buddy, get one of each and split them.

1. Gilroy Garlic Fries, Everywhere. Look out, sourdough bread. The garlic fry is quickly becoming San Francisco's signature food item. With the world-class garlic grown down in Gilroy, it didn't take long to realize that the french fry and the vampire spice were made for each other. I've yet to meet one Bay Area sports fan who can resist the smell.

If you live here, you already know. If you coming to visit, you're going to find out: Our fair city comes with a dear, unfair price. This place is expensive. So to help the budget conscious, here are ten places to fill your stomach without emptying your pockets. By the way, I define "cheap eats" is as under $15. Welcome to the big city.

10. Moishe's Pippic. A good old-fashioned Chicago-style Jewish Deli in the heart of Hays Valley. Bring your wallet for this cash-only sandwich shop that would make your mamma proud. Oh, that's *lean* corned beef. Brisket on Fridays only and it goes fast. Consider yourself warned. By the way, "pippic" is Yiddish for bellybutton.

9. Molinari's. Get ready to battle gawking tourists and exercise a little patience in the heart of North Beach. When you've been in business for over a hundred years, there's no reason to move fast. Every sandwich is made with care in this delicatessen that looks like it could have been used as a location when they filmed *The Godfather*.

8. Thai House Express. Make it spicy, make it fast, make it cheap; it's a formula that should never be ignored, but often is. Not at Thai House Express, a rare "chain restaurant" that I actually recommend. Did you know that Thai food can cure a bad hangover? Just trust me.

7. Mario's Bohemian Cigar Shop. Under the shadow of Coit Tower in North Beach, Mario's has been a staple for locals and tourist alike for its panini and focaccia sandwiches, and its ambiance. Your grandfather would have loved this place, and you will too. Grab something to eat, and maybe an espresso, and watch the world go by.

6. Taqueria El Castillito (on Golden Gate). The Burrito Wars in San Francisco take no prisoners. Friendships have ended over the question: Where's the best burrito? Although the Mission—S.F.'s center for Mexican food—boasts dozens of good options, my favorite is downtown by Civic Center, right on the edge of the Tenderloin. There are four other burrito places under the same name, so make sure you're near City Hall.

5. Gourmet Carousel. This place serves some of my favorite Chinese food in the city. Forget that the place has wood paneling and is pretty much a dump. The food is good, and you can eat well without busting the bank. Soups are great. Portions are huge. Order the salt-and-pepper quail, one of my favorites.

4. Marina Subs. Finding a good sub sandwich shouldn't be difficult in a city that's known around the world for its food, but it is. For years, the same guy has been making the same subs at the same place. He takes his time, caring more about your lunch than you do. After all, great sandwiches take time, and he's got plenty of it. Go Italian, or turkey and avocado. You won't be disappointed.

3. Tu Lan. On the corner of Sixth Street and Market, you'll find the dregs of humanity, the scent of urine, someone screaming about nothing, and the best Vietnamese food in the United States. Julia Child even gave this unassuming establishment her blessing. Dealing with the scumbags in the neighborhood will be worth it the second you sink your teeth into an Imperial Roll and some BBQ pork.

2. The Pork Store. Right in the middle of Haight/Ashbury stands a diner single handedly making sure we don't all go vegetarian at the same time. I give you the best breakfast in San Francisco; I give you The Pork Store. Don't be afraid of the Piggy Special, or ordering a couple of Pork Chops with breakfast. It's a bacon-lover's dream come true. If you wanted a fruit plate, you should have gone somewhere else. It's impossible to measure how many hippies have been nourished back to health here after a night of partying. Don't forget: Free mimosas on New Year's Day.

1. Yum-Yum Fish. Before I moved to California, I hated sushi and the idea of sushi. Oh, how times change. Cravings come and go, and when the beast needs to be fed raw fish, I go directly to Yum-Yum. With only four tables, they don't necessarily even want you there. The ambiance and service both get zero out of four stars. If you want something to drink other than water, bring it yourself. However, the portions are gigantic and the fish is off-the-boat fresh. Yum-Yum is a fish mart more than a restaurant. Don't bring your date, just your appetite for the best and least expensive sushi in San Francisco.

Ten Best Spots for Food and Drink Near AT&T Park
:: by Greg Quinn

NOTE: Besides being one of my best friends, Greg Quinn has been in the restaurant business for over a decade here in San Francisco. A true foodie, I can't think of a better fan of baseball and dining to send you on a tasty tour around the ballpark downtown. As Greg says: "San Francisco is one of America's great dining cities. From taquerias and noodle shops to the finest in haute cuisine, San Francisco has something exceptional to offer every taste and every budget. These restaurants are not the city's most elegant or expensive, but they reflect the diversity of S.F.'s vibrant food scene. Enjoy!"

10. Los Compadres, on the corner of Spear and Folsom St., S.F. San Francisco has an abundance of great Mexican food. While most of the best taquerias are located in the Mission District, the best Mexican food near the ballpark is served from a truck, which serves some of S.F.'s finest burritos and tacos at rock bottom prices. Nothing on the menu is over $5 and everything they serve is fresh and flavorful.

9. Tu Lan, 8 6th St., S.F. While not exactly in the same neighborhood as the ballpark, Tu Lan is a short, cheap Muni Metro ride away. San Francisco has a significant Asian population, and Thai, Vietnamese, Chinese, Japanese and other Asian noodle houses serve some of the best value meals in the city. Julia Child made Tu Lan famous by braving the dodgy neighborhood and declaring it some of San Francisco's finest food. (Insider's tip: Dish #17 is legendary).

8. Coco 500, 500 Brannan, S.F. Another restaurant people wouldn't usually associate with sports, Coco 500 is a perfect place to check out the latest developments in San Francisco gastronomy. Owner Loretta Keller oversees a menu using the freshest local ingredients with straightforward preparations. Their hip, understated décor and outstanding wine and liquor programs define a restaurant that is truly "in its time." Coco 500 is one of the best places in S.F. to drop in at the bar and enjoy a wide array of small plates and well-made cocktails.

7. Bacar, 448 Brannan St., S.F. "Trendy" and "baseball" don't go together in too many cities, but we San Franciscans love our vino, and Bacar has one of the best wine lists in town. The industrial chic atmosphere hearkens back to the dotcom era of excess, and the downstairs wine lounge is a very comfortable place to sample Bacar's 60+ wines by the glass. (Note: Historically, Bacar's food has been excellent, however, as of this writing Bacar is going through a chef change that may redefine their cuisine).

6. Hog Island Oyster Co., The Ferry Building. "The better the view, the worse the food," is a restaurant truism that has few exceptions, but the Ferry Building is one of them. A true food lover's paradise, the Ferry Building houses a wide array of locally owned retail shops, restaurants and bars. Hog Island farms their oysters 50 miles north of S.F. in the coastal town of Marshall. Their exceptional oysters are served in many of San Francisco's finest restaurants and they have built a nationwide reputation. Their oyster bar is a great place to get a table overlooking the bay and enjoy a wide range of fresh seafood. (Insider's tip: Monday and Thursday happy hours are from 5-7 p.m. and feature $1 oysters and $3.50 beers).

5. Hard Knox Café, 2526 Third St., S.F. A little bit of a hike from the ballpark, but it's worth it for some of the best fried chicken in the city. Owned by a Vietnamese couple from . . . yes, you guessed it: Texas! Hard Knox Café serves a wide range of delicious soul food in a down-home atmosphere. The mac 'n' cheese is exceptional, but their cornbread muffins really steal the show.

4. 21st Amendment Brewery, 563 Second St., S.F. Come to the 21st Amendment for decent food and an amazing pint of fresh, house-made beer. While they do make some lighter styles (including, I kid you not, a watermelon beer,) these guys really excel at flavorful, high-octane stouts and ales.

3. Red's Java House, Pier 30, S.F. A true local gem, Red's serves basic food and beer at cheap prices. The staff's no-nonsense attitude is summed up by the handwritten sign stating, "No lettuce or tomatoes ever, just don't ask."

2. Acme Chophouse, 24 Willie Mays Plaza, S.F. Actually part of the ballpark (right next to the Willie Mays statue), Acme Chophouse doesn't have to be as good as it is. Headed by local celebrity chef and Iron Chef America winner Tracy des Jardins, the kitchen serves amazing steaks and seafood, and the wine list and service are spot-on. If you're not in the mood for fine dining, this is also a prime spot for sitting out on the patio and enjoying a drink before the game. (Insider's tip: You can avoid long lines and ballpark prices by grabbing a drink at their bar and entering the park through the Chophouse's designated entrance).

1. Zeke's, 300 Third St., S.F. They serve perfectly fine bar food, but the main draw is Zeke's worn-out sports bar vibe. This place was here long before the ballpark came to the neighborhood, and it's one of the few spots that still does great business in the off-season. A dive bar for true dive bar lovers—extra points for their Denny Crum shrine.

Bay Area Baseball All-Time Dream Team

The amount of baseball talent that has graced the cities of San Francisco and Oakland is just staggering. From everyday players to pitchers to managers, it's amazing to see how many greats once called the Bay their home. In the interest of "going green," here's my hybrid: I'll take the Giants and the A's and smash their two great histories together to give you the all-time Bay Area lineup—rotation, bullpen, bench and coaching staff. I'm going American League rules so I can use a designated hitter in this full 25-man roster.

Lineup: Your Bay Area Starting Nine

LF—Ricky Henderson. Countless records and astonishing speed made Ricky the greatest leadoff hitter of all time.

Second Base—Jeff Kent. A dangerous hitter and scrappy player, he's got more power than anyone who's ever played the position.

CF—Willie Mays. 660 homers and the best defensive outfielder in baseball history should do nicely in the three hole.

DH—Barry Bonds. Now hitting clean up, the most feared slugger in modern times, and greatest home run hitter of all time.

First Base—Willie McCovey. Durable, powerful, and if you walk Bonds, you're going to pay.

RF—Reggie Jackson. You know you got a monster on your hands when "REG-GIE, REG-GIE, REG-GIE" is hitting sixth.

Third Base—Sal Bando. A four-time All Star and captain of three world title teams, Sal's my steady leader at the hot corner. He had some pop finishing with 242 homers, but was just a .254 career hitter. That's OK. This lineup can carry the low average.

C—Terry Steinbach. Three pennants, a championship, three All-Star games and MVP in the mid-summer classic, and a .271 career hitter from the squat!

SS—Bert Campaneris. Campy can pick it, and Campy can run. Perfect guy to flip the lineup around, and play the pivot in the dirt. Just so you can appreciate how good this lineup is—in case you don't—these nine players add up to 3,658 career homeruns with 12,237 career RBIs.

Rotation

1. Juan Marichal. Announces the staff's presence with a high kick and intimidating stuff. He's my ace.

2. Catfish Hunter. Can't beat him or his nickname.

3. Dave Stewart. "Smoke" is a bad, bad man; if you stare back into his eyes, you're a goner. Not to mention, Dave is Oak-town!

4. Vida Blue. Colorful? Yes. Hittable? No.

5. Gaylord Perry. Is he doing something to that ball? The fact that hitters were thinking about it was half the genius of his tinkering.

Bullpen

If a starter falters, no big deal; look who's waiting to pick him up.

CL—Dennis Eckersley. A sidearm slinger who fist-pumped his way into Cooperstown, he's my man to slam the door. Even though there are some others in the pen known for their final-inning excellence, I'm going with "Eck" to punctuate games.

RHP—Rollie Fingers. He helped change the way pitching staff are managed, and could really fill the bill all by himself.

LHP—Gary Lavelle. A two-time All Star and a decade-long lefty lifer in the Giants bullpen. I had to have one southpaw.

RHP—Rod Beck. A "Shooter" to gun you down if your lineup gets a little frisky. Hard to believe the arm stopped dangling so soon. He was loved and is missed.

RHP—Rob Nen. The "Nenth Inning" hasn't been the same in San Francisco since "Smoke on the Water" was blasting at then-Pac Bell Park.

Bench

Want some thump off the pine?

Mark McGwire. A homerun in every 10.6 at-bats. It all started quickly with a rookie-record 49 long-balls.

Orlando Cepeda. Career high 46 homers and 142 RBI back in 1961. The "Baby Bull" was a run-producing machine.

Kevin Mitchell. More power and a little style off the bench. It's boogie time.

Miguel Tejada. I don't care how old he is, his MVP season in 2002 was full of amazing moments that helped the A's win an American League record 20 games in a row.

Benito Santiago.

Matt Williams. Hard nose and no nonsense—that's what I want out of a team-mate, and that's what defined his decade-long Giants career.

Manager/Coaching Staff

MGR—Tony LaRussa. One of the greatest minds and animal lovers the game has ever known. LaRussa is one of just two managers to win it all in both leagues. That makes him perfectly equipped to manage the egos that are sure to flare up on this team.

First Base Coach—Alvin Dark. The 1948 Rookie of the Year grew up to be quite a skipper in his own right. Dark is the only man to manage both the Giants and the A's into the World Series.

Third Base Coach—Bill Rigney. Born in Alameda, Rigney played and managed the New York Giants before moving with the team back to his home on the West coast. He had two managerial go-rounds with the Giants.

Hitting Coach—Dusty Baker. Three-time NL manager of the year, Dusty was the man in San Francisco, and a consummate player's coach. Someone needs to keep Bonds happy. We know Dusty can do that.

Bench Coach—Art Howe. A real gentlemen, Howe was at the helm of a run of A's success that defied logic and baseball economics. Over a four-year run, Howe's A's tams would make the playoffs three times, while winning 383 regular season games—without a payroll.

It only took about four decades for Candlestick Park to go from state-of-the-art to complete dump, but the memories will always be pristine. Opened in 1960 for the Giants, enclosed for the 49ers in early 1970s, it's a cockeyed masterpiece, the likes of which will never been seen again. Some would say that's a good thing. Terrible wind, cold weather and an overall unpleasant outdoor environment are all hallmarks of "a day at The Stick." The iconic stadium has been ground zero for other major events in pop-culture and Bay Area history. Here are my top five.

5. The Rolling Stones, 1981. In the concert tour that married rock and roll with corporate America, the Rolling Stones came to Candlestick for two days in October and left quite an impression. When a half-dozen crusty sports reporters all insist this was one of the biggest events in the stadium's history, it's hard to argue with them. Promoter and San Francisco legend Bill Graham cranked out one of the most profitable tours in music history, grossing more than $50 million, forever changing the way summer concert tours were marketed and sponsored. The two shows at the Stick were the crescendo of the West Coast leg of the tour, and kicked much ass.

4. Papal Mass, September 18, 1987. Just two days after courting Southern California Catholics at Dodgers Stadium, Pope John Paul II came to Northern California to make sure millions of Catholic Giants fans didn't convert to something else.

3. Bill Walsh's Funeral, August 10, 2007. In an outpouring of love for the man who changed the NFL forever, thousands turned out for a public memorial service for the man called "Coach." Just mention the word "coach" at a Niners game. No one will assume you're talking about Mike Nolan. There's only one "Coach" in 49ers history. Politicians, Hall of Famers and even Cowboys fans paid their respects to the greatest leader of men, and greatest innovator, in the history of San Francisco sports.

2. Final Beatles Concert, August 29, 1966. The Fab Four from Liverpool had grown tired of touring. Fans didn't even listen to their music; girls were too busy screaming non-stop from the first note to the last. The Beatles couldn't even hear themselves, their own instruments or vocals, which makes it hard to play music, even for the Beatles. Only 24,000 fans were allowed in Candlestick Park for the concert, but it made no difference—the screaming never stopped. But the music did. After nine years of touring the world—and nearly 1,400 shows—the Beatles played for 33 minutes, walked off the stage and never, ever returned. No one knew it at the time, but the Beatles had just played their last public concert.

1. Loma Prieta Earthquake, 1989. Never before had a major seismic event been broadcast around the world live, as it happened. That changed on October 17, 1989. Only minutes before the first pitch of Game Three of 1989 World Series, an earthquake measuring 7.1 on the Richter scale rocked the Bay Area. Al Michaels and Tim McCarver, there to broadcast the game for ABC, instantly turned their play-by-play booth into a newsroom, adding some journalistic integrity to the world of sports casting. Michaels, who had been a Giants broadcaster earlier in his career, was exceptional in his knowledge and delivery. With all due respect to "Do you believe in miracles?" his quake coverage was his finest hour. A section of Bay Bridge collapsed, thousands were left homeless, and 67 people lost their lives. No one at Candlestick was injured.

NOTE: A self-described "shameless" Giants and 49ers fan, Brian Murphy is one half of KNBR's "Murph & Mac" morning show, and has covered Bay Area sports, in one way or another, for the better part of two decades. He authored the official Giants 50th Anniversary book, and was good enough to share with us his top ten moments in the history of Candlestick Park.

10. The Beatles' Final Concert, August 29, 1966.
The Fab Four on this day was not Mays, McCovey, Marichal and Perry. Instead, John, Paul, George and Ringo, on the final stop of their tour after recording *Revolver* arrived at Candlestick on a cold and windy Monday night. They were ferried in an armored car to a stage behind second base and played a 33-minute set for a reported 25,000 fans—far from a sellout. The set included "Day Tripper" and "Yesterday" and ended with a cover of Little Richard's "Long Tall Sally." The lads from Liverpool then climbed back into the armored car and drove off.

9. The Preston Riley Game, Dec. 23, 1972.
How unfair is sports? This unfair: nearly 3 decades after the fact, we're listing this as the "Preston Riley" game when, in fact, there were many reasons why the 49ers blew a 28-13 fourth-quarter lead to the rival Dallas Cowboys in this NFC Divisional Playoff Game. The 49ers endured the indignity of consecutive NFC Championship losses to the Cowboys in 1970 and 1971, but they had the Cowboys down and out in the fourth quarter, the Niners holding a 28-13 lead. Party time at Candlestick? Alas, Cowboys coach Tom Landry sent QB Roger Staubach in for Craig Morton, and Staubach only turned in a legendary performance, going 12 for 20 with 174 yards and two TDs in the fourth quarter alone. Still, it was the Niners' game for the taking. After Staubach hit Billy Parks for a TD to make it 28-23 with 1:20 left, all San Francisco needed to do was field the ensuing onside kick. But that dastardly Candlestick artificial turf of '72 pushed the onside kick off of 49ers special teams man Preston Riley—and into the arms of Cowboy Mel Renfro. Riley's muff would be the lingering image of another 49ers heartbreak at the hands of hated Dallas.

8. Joe Morgan, Terry Forster and October 3, 1982.
October 3 is an important day in Giants-Dodgers lore, most notably because of 1951, when Russ Hodges famously exulted about the Giants winning the pennant. Thirty-one years later, the Giants fought for a pennant, but were eliminated on Oct. 2 by the Dodgers in a loss at Candlestick. The only thing that could make it right was pure bloodlust: revenge. So, with the Dodgers needing to win on the season's final day to keep pace with the Atlanta Braves in the NL West, the Giants were tied 2-2 in the bottom of the seventh. With two Giants on, manager Tommy Lasorda brought in lefty Terry Forster to face Joe Morgan. Morgan, a Bay Area product, knew the importance of a Giants-Dodgers moment: He smoked a three-run HR over the chain-link fence in right field for a 5-2 lead in an eventual 5-3 Giants win. Lasorda ran his hand over his face in agony. Giants fans got their season-ending gift: The Dodgers were going home.

7. The Catch II, January 3, 1999. As if NFL history was doomed to repeat it-self, the 49ers found themselves in the late 1990s again with a January nemesis. Where it was Dallas from 1970-72, and the Cowboys again from 1992-93, from 1996-1998 Brett Favre and the Green Bay Packers bounced the 49ers from January each year. Finally, on this day that featured rumors about coach Steve Mariucci's future should he lose, the Niners had a chance, down 27-23 and driving, late. It came down to one play: The 49ers at the Green Bay 25, under ten seconds left, Steve Young nearly tripping as he dropped back in the pocket, and then a perfect pass—Niners OL coach Bobb McKittrick would call it the best pass he'd ever seen—to Terrell Owens for the game-winning TD with three seconds left. Owens, who'd dropped four passes including a sure TD earlier in the game, was sandwiched between two defenders but clung to the ball in the end zone and bawled as he was mobbed by his teammates. It wasn't The Catch . . . but it was The Catch, II.

6. The Brian Johnson/Rod Beck Game, September 18, 1997. Pick your Giants-Dodgers game at Candlestick and you can pick many for various meanings: history, import, emotion or revenge. Whatever the standard, it would be tough to top the 12-inning opera that saw the Giants pull into a tie for the NL West lead with the ri-vals from the Southland. In an unforgettable day game after a night game won by the Giants to pull within one game in the West, the Giants stood to lose the game when the Dodgers loaded the bases with nobody out in the top of the tenth. But Rod Beck, the gutsy closer whose mullet blew gently in the Candlestick breeze, struck out Todd Zeile and then induced Eddie Murray into an epic 4-2-3 double play. Beck roared as he came off the mound; so did 52,188. They'd roar even louder two innings later when Brian Johnson, the catcher who coaxed Beck through the jam, hit a leadoff HR off Mark Guthrie for the game-winner. The euphoric greeting he got at home plate spoke to the Giants' mood.

5. 1994 NFC Championship, Steve Young Slays a Dragon, January 15, 1995. Entering this pivotal game in Niner history, there was a cruel subtext: some thought Steve Young wore jersey No. 8 because he was only half the player of his predecessor, Joe Montana, who famously wore number 16. Losses to Dallas in the 1992 and 1993 NFC Championship games—the former with Montana standing on the sidelines, unused, in his final game in a 49ers uniform—only heightened the frus-tration among the Faithful. Could Steve Young ever win the big one? On this day, he did. The Niners blitzed the Cowboys with a 21-0 start, including a Young TD pass to Ricky Watters; then Young hit Jerry Rice for a critical TD just before half and a 31-14 lead. When Dallas cut it to 31-21, Young rushed for a key TD in what eventually was a 38-28 win. Young reacted like a man freed from prison. He ran around the Candle-stick field after the game, arms raised, basking in the "Steve! Steve! Steve!" chants from a manic sellout crowd. Two weeks later, he'd do what Joe used to do: He won a Super Bowl.

4. Game 7, World Series, McCovey Lines Out, October 16, 1962. How does this sound: New York Yankees 1, San Francisco Giants 0, Game 7, Fall Classic, bottom of the ninth, runners at second and third, two outs. Other than that, there was nothing special about the moment that Willie McCovey stepped into the batter's box to face Ralph Terry with everything on the line. The Giants were shocked that Terry pitched to McCovey, given that McCovey had tripled off Terry earlier in the game, and homered off Terry in Game 2. The Giants were even further shocked when McCovey crushed a line drive . . . right into the glove of Yankees 2B Bobby Richardson. In an instant, after a scalded shot off the bat of one of the game's most fearsome hitters, the Giants lost Game 7. The franchise would never forget it.

3. The Giants Tell It Goodbye, September 30, 1999. When it opened in 1960, and when Vice President Richard Nixon called it "the finest ballpark in America," nobody knew how happy the Giants would be to say goodbye to cold, windy, miserable Candlestick in 1999. With the gleaming new park in China Basin ready to open in 2000, the Giants left Candlestick with a mixture of unrestrained glee and, oddly, a fair bit of sentimentalism for days gone by. A massive crowd of 61,389 crammed into the 'Stick to see the Giants lose to the Dodgers in the final game, but that didn't matter. They stayed to roar for old heroes who returned to say goodbye: Juan Marichal, Ed Halicki, Dave Dravecky, Bobby Bonds, Jack Clark, Stu Miller, Chris Speier, Johnnie LeMaster, Bill Rigney, Dave Righetti, Hank Sauer, Robby Thompson, Tito Fuentes, so many more . . . and, of course, Willie Mays throwing the last pitch to Barry Bonds, with all the alumni standing behind him on the mound. Home plate was helicoptered to Pacific Bell Park. The Giants would play at Candlestick no more.

2. Loma Prieta, October 17, 1989. The Giants' first home World Series game in 27 years—and first since Willie McCovey lined out to Bobby Richardson—came on a warm October day, the kind of balmy climate some liked to call "Earthquake Weather." The Giants weren't thinking earthquake; they were only thinking about winning a game after losing the first two at Oakland in the Bay Bridge Series. But at 5:04 p.m., everything changed. A 7.1 earthquake, centered near the Loma Prieta peak in Santa Cruz County, rocked the Bay Area. Candlestick stood, but a section of the Bay Bridge did not, and the Nimitz Freeway collapsed, killing more than 40 people. As the Marina District burned, Major League Baseball Commissioner Fay Vincent cancelled Game 3, and players left Candlestick, many in uniform, and drove for safety. The Series did not resume for 10 days. Upon resumption Oct. 27, the A's would sweep the Giants.

1. The Catch, January 10, 1982. Every Bay Area sports fan with a pulse knows where he or she was when Joe Montana rolled right on 3rd and 3 from the Dallas Cowboy six-yard line with 58 seconds left in the 1981 NFC Championship Game. Chased by Ed "Too Tall" Jones and Larry Bethea near the right sideline, Montana pump-faked once, and then threw a pass high to the right corner of the end zone. To this day, only Montana knows if he was throwing the ball away—or if he meant for Dwight Clark to sky high above Dallas CB Everson Walls and catch the most important pass in San Francisco 49ers history with only the tips of his fingers. The 49ers and coach Bill Walsh would swear it was a play they'd run in practice. Either way, "The Catch" set off a wave of pandemonium that nearly reduced Candlestick to rubble. After Ray Wersching's extra point, and after Jim Stuckey recovered Danny White's subsequent fumble, the 49ers had a 28-27 win that put the 49ers in their first Super Bowl, and would bring the first world championship in San Francisco sports history back to the Bay—all thanks to "The Catch."

10. Ron Fairley. "The wind at Candlestick tonight is blowing with great propensity."

9. Catcher Bob Brenly. "I was the comeback player of the year—in one day." After his walk-off home run to beat the Braves, in the same game he committed four errors while making a rare start at third base.

8. Juan Marichal. "In 1968, I won 26 games and completed 30 games, but I couldn't get one vote for the Cy Young, because Gibson had a 1.12 ERA. . . . So, you know how big the rivalry was back then."

7. Jeffrey Leonard. "I'm the kind of guy that if you ask me to dinner at your mother's house and she made a cake and it wasn't very good and said, 'How's the cake?' I'd say, 'It stinks.'"

6. Detroit's Rocky Colavito. "If I was traded to the Giants and had to play here all the time under these conditions, I'd quit baseball." After playing in the 1961 All-Star Game.

5. Al Rosen. "I'm tired of seeing major league ballplayers hit a ground ball to the second baseman and run forty-five feet. If they can't run ninety-feet, they can't run forty-five feet for me."

4. Roger Marris. "Candlestick was built on the water. It should have been built under it."

3. Bobby Murcer. "Patty Hearst could be hiding in Candlestick's upper deck and nobody would ever find her." During his eleven-HR season in 1975.

2. Leo Durocher. "If somebody came up and hit .450, stole 100 bases, and performed a miracle in the field every day, I'd still look you right in the eye and tell you that Willie Mays was better."

1. Roger Craig, the man responsible for Candlestick's ultimate battle cry. "Humm Baby!"

Sometimes the fists do the talking; this list is a fisticuffs lecture. Someone ring the bell . . . . Let's get ready to rumble. Do I owe Michael Buffer money for typing that?

10. Omar Vizquel v. Jose Mesa. In addition to being a salsa dancer in his free time, Vizquel wrote an autobiography. While most of *Omar! My Life on and Off the Field* offers typical baseball-bio prose, it also offers therapeutic release for Vizquel, who vents some particularly strong opinions about former Cleveland teammate Mesa. Vizquel wrote that the closer essentially choked away the Indians' chances in the seventh game of the 1997 World Series, blowing a lead and the series to Florida. After cracking open the tome and discovering the belittling words, Mesa told a Philly scribe that he wanted to "kill" his former dominoes partner, vowing to hit him with a pitch every time. Mesa was a man of his word, striking the smaller Vizquel several times over the next few seasons, tallying up thousands of dollars in fines along the way. In 2006, with Vizquel on the Giants team and Mesa on the Rockies, they met again. Mesa promptly drilled Vizquel with a pitch in his back. The next day the Rox and Giants exchanged retaliatory brush backs and more nasty sentiments. Mesa was suspended four games and fined for his actions.

9. Michael Tucker v. Jeff Weaver, 2004. After bench-clearing incidents with the Dodgers at the Polo Grounds, Seals Stadium and Candlestick Park, the fight series moved into the Giants' home in June of 2004. Leading off the fifth for the Giants, Michael Tucker dragged a bunt down the first base line. Dodgers pitcher Jeff Weaver took the feed-through from first baseman Robin Ventura and applied a tag to the hustling base runner. When Tucker didn't accept Weaver's glove-handed shiver, offering a sharp elbow in response, the flaxen haired Dodger opened his yap. Tucker mouthed the word "bitch" and the dugouts emptied. The next night, Dodgers closer Eric Gagne backed Tucker off the plate with some French Canadian chin music. Again, the benches emptied.

8. Billy North vs. Doug Bird, 1973. If revenge is a dish best served cold, then the Food Network could have promoted this throw down. Three years after Oakland's Doug Bird beaned North in a minor league tilt, the pair faced each other again at the Coliseum. On Bird's first pitch, North swung and let go of his bat, feigning a slipped grip. On his way to retrieve the bat, Billy veered, hung a quick right and applied a quicker left hook to Bird's beak, knocking him to the ground. The future AL stolen-base leader landed a few more punches in the jumbled pile of players on the mound. Bird was totally caught off guard, commenting afterwards he had forgotten about the earlier incident.

7. John Montefusco vs. Bill Madlock and Dave Bristol. The Giants bois-terous Montefusco, a noted braggart, created a lot of enemies during his Giants ca-reer. Opposing teams didn't care for him either. During spring training in 1978, Giants teammate Madlock, a noted baseball pugilist, overheard "the Count" telling a reporter some bad things about the Giants lineup. Maddog decided to make some news right on the spot and cold cocked the 1975 Rookie of the Year with a right cross. Two sea-sons later, Montefusco and skipper Bristol got into it in the Candlestick home club-house. The 55-year-old manager quickly ended the discussion, connecting with a five-fingered forget-me-not that left Montefusco with a black eye.

6. Giants vs. Cardinals, 1988. If you were a Giants fan, the hard-nosed Will Clark played the game the right way. But if your rooting affections were with any other ball club, you probably hated "The Thrill." When Clark steamrolled Giants killer Jose Oquendo at second base, the Redbirds had their sharpened beaks at the ready. As Clark wrestled with the diminutive infielder, shortstop Ozzie Smith snuck in from be-hind, slapping Will's helmet. But like a superhero, Candy Maldonado, the batter on the play, came to the rescue. Maldonado zoomed toward the one-sided fight and took a flying leap. Soon, Ozzie was feeling the brunt of Candy's less-than-sweet haymakers.

5. Jeff Kent vs. Barry Bonds, 2002. Media members and Giants teammates didn't know whom to root for in this slobber knocker. Both Bonds and Kent were equally disliked. Each was an unfriendly, pompous and spoiled superstar, and the two happened to hate each other. After Kent criticized David Bell for a base-running gaffe during a game at San Diego, Bonds saw his opening and lit into his fellow MVP Award winner. Kent turned cherry red and told BaBo to sit down. In an instant, Bonds jumped on Kent like a Chan Ho Park fastball, wrapping his fingers around his throat and squeezing. It took an exasperated Dusty Baker and catcher Benito Santiago to peel Barry's grip away. Later, the combatants said the dugout altercation was no big whoop; they had mixed it up plenty of other times behind closed doors.

4. A's vs. Angels, 1981. The A's began the season 11-0 and seemingly had a fight with the opposition in each of those contests. Imagine that? A team led by Billy Mar-tin getting into frequent scrapes. This one began when Oakland's catcher seized the Angels' "Disco" Dan Ford's bat after a home run and began checking it for tell tale signs of a cork injection. After he completed his home run trot, Ford returned the favor by seizing Heath's right arm, igniting a sizable mid-game meet and greet. As the teams exited the field after the game, Martin squared off with Angels pitching coach Tom Martin, a former Yankees teammate.

3. Mike Marshall vs. Giants and fans, 1987. The unibrowed Marshall ranks among the most disliked Dodgers of the Candlestick era, and the feeling was clearly mutual. Tensions were predictably high and the suds were a-flowin' when the Dodgers visited a packed 'Stick in early 1987. The night was a particularly raucous one with arrests and stadium ejects nearing 100. The game was tied 8-8 with two outs in the tenth when Roger Craig walked Pedro Guerrero to get to Marshall. He smoked a long home run off Scotty Garrelts, putting the Dodgers up 11-8. During his home run trot, Marshall pumped his fists as if he were at a Billy Idol concert. When he reached home, Marshall offered a personal rebel yell to Craig and the rest of the Giants dugout. Garrelts' next pitch sailed over the Dodgers batter's head and the rumble was on. At one point, Marshall tried to climb the wall and reach a fan who had thrown his beer at him.

2. Giants vs. Cubs, 1976. The difference between baseball fights and common street brawls is that the paddy wagon is rarely called to the ball field. That wasn't the case in this free-for-all that started when the Giants' Jim Barr hit Jose Cardenal, who in turn heaved his batting helmet towards the mound. When the scene began to resemble a battle royal—with bats subbing for folding metal chairs—the cops were called in to make sure the boys didn't take the fisticuffs into the stands, clubhouses or parking lot.

1. Juan Marichal vs. John Roseboro, 1965. The same month as the Watts riots, the mother of all baseball fights occurred at Candlestick pitting the Dodgers catcher Roseboro vs. Giants ace pitcher Marichal and his Louisville Clubber . . . er, Slugger. Roseboro tried to intimidate Marichal by returning the ball to pitcher Sandy Koufax by throwing it close to Marichal's head. An enraged Marichal whacked Roseboro on his noggin, opening a severe gash. Although the pair later mended fences, the act delayed Marichal's entry into the Hall of Fame.

Bands need fans and venues, and that's why everyone plays San Francisco—because we got both in spades. Everyone who is anyone in modern music history has played one or more of these palaces, each its own little legend in rock lore. Most cities like to think they're cool. One look at this list and you'll see why San Francisco doesn't have to brag.

10. G.G. Park Drum Circle. Get out your inner hippy, kick off your shoes and find yourself back among the flower children. It's quintessential San Francisco. It's free. And what's that I smell burning?

9. Davies Symphony Hall. One of the most acoustically sound rooms in the city, and home of the San Francisco Symphony, Davies Symphony Hall sits at the feet of City Hall in famous Civic Center. Common folk like you and me are encouraged to come and taste high society.

8. Slim's 333. In the late Eighties, Boz Scaggs opened a new club that became an instant hit in San Francisco. Catering to every musical taste, and hosting national and local acts, Slim's is a regular stop for any local music lover.

7. Yoshi's in Oakland. One of the most famous Jazz clubs in the entire world, it's a unique Bay Area experience, and you'll have to get on the Bay Bridge to experience it. Even though there's a sister club with the same name that just opened in San Francisco, the original Yoshi's is in Oakland's Jack London Square. It's a great room that remains dedicated to America's purest musical art form.

6. Bimbo's 365. A famous façade that has become part of the fabric of North Beach, this City original has been operating on Columbus Avenue since 1951. A glamorous nightclub and great place to see a show, Bimbo's hasn't changed even though the music has.

5. The Paramount. Registered as a National Historic Landmark, Oakland's Paramount Theater is not only an amazing venue; it's regarded as one of the finest examples of Art Deco design ever created, operating since 1931. Forget about the show; go just to see the building.

4. Great American Music Hall. Opened in 1907, it's the Granddaddy of 'em all in San Francisco. The city's oldest operating nightclub is a lavish room decorated with ornate balconies, frescoes on the ceiling, with marble all around. They just don't make 'em like this anymore. Fans get up-close and intimate with artists who've ranged from the elegant Duke Ellington to the Grateful Dead. *One From the Vault* was recorded live at the Great American Music Hall on August 13, 1975—it's still my favorite Dead album.

3. The Warfield Theater. Opened in the roaring Twenties, it's my personal favorite place to see a show in San Francisco. Get on the floor or romp in one of the balconies—doesn't matter, because the room brings out the best of any artist on stage. Bands go out of their way to play this historic venue, which once boasted the Grateful Dead as the "House Band."

2. The Greek Theater, Berkeley. Built in 1903 under the direction and finance of media mogul William Randolph Hearst, this historic landmark sits in the middle of Cal's campus. Presidents have given speeches on a stage that has hosted a who's-who in music history. Home of the Berkeley Jazz Fest, graduation ceremonies and pep rallies, the Greek sets a perfect tone as the moon rises above the San Francisco skyline in the background. It's a venue that must be experienced to be appreciated. It's so cool to take in a great show in a place that would be right at home next to the Parthenon in Athens.

1. The Fillmore. This is music's original brand-name venue. There was really no need to build the Rock and Roll Hall of Fame in Cleveland when the original is standing right here. It was made famous by the bands that played here, and by Bill Graham, the most influential concert promoter in music history. Graham used his room to showcase new talent and weave his artists into the fabric of American culture. Home of acid tests, psychedelic artwork and some of the most important moments in popular music, it's an essential part of San Francisco and American history. It's safe to say that every important artist since the late Sixties has played the room.

A Dozen or So Favorite San Francisco Bands of a Certain Era :: by Ben Fong-Torres

NOTE: Ben Fong-Torres is a baseball fan, and was the former senior editor at *Rolling Stone* magazine in its San Francisco years. Featured as a true-to-life character in the movie *Almost Famous,* Ben has published eight books and is an Emmy-winning broadcaster with a Sunday radio show on KFRC. He is working on books on the Grateful Dead and Quincy Jones. It's an honor to have him contribute a list of the greatest bands of a bygone era in the history of the Bay; no one is better qualified.

Jefferson Airplane. The band that gave us Grace Slick, "White Rabbit," "Somebody to Love," Marty Balin, the Starship and "We Built This City." (Well, it can't be ALL good).

Grateful Dead. Bill Graham said it all: "The Grateful Dead are not only the best at what they do; they are the only ones who do what they do." Even in past tense, it's still true.

Country Joe & the Fish. Out of Berkeley, the Fish were more political, more acidic, and more comic than most, even pantomiming a baseball game on stage. Give 'em an F!

The Charlatans. They created the San Francisco scene out of a western saloon in Virginia City, Nevada. They never had a hit, but ah, the misses. . . .

Steve Miller Band. A true blues pro in the midst of what he thought of as a "social scene," Miller made great albums from the start. He should be in the rock hall of fame, dammit.

Quicksilver Messenger Service. Led by guitar slinger John Cippolina, Quicksilver were an excellent concert act—and got even more mesmerizing with the arrival of Dino Valente.

Moby Grape. A marketing stunt—issuing about eight singles all at once—backfired. Still, Skip Spence and the gang were among the best of the bunch.

Creedence Clearwater Revival. Pure genius. CCR had one as its frontman, and John Fogerty led the band from one name and style to another, until they settled into the Bayou. What "San Francisco Sound"?

It's a Beautiful Day. "White Bird," with its ethereal lyrics and vocal duet (Patty Santos and violinist David LaFlamme), was their only hit. But it was a beautiful moment.

Sly & the Family Stone. One of the best bands of all time, led by Sylvester Stewart, teen wizard record producer, DJ, composer, performer and all-around game-changer.

Big Brother & the Holding Company. So, they were not the best musicians. Most of the bands weren't the best, come to think of it. But, then, along came that chick named Janis from Port Arthur, Texas.

Cold Blood. The vastly underrated Lyndia Pense and the hard-rocking Cold Blood could've been another Janis & Big Brother. If only there weren't already a Janis. . . .

Santana. Dragged from Tijuana into the U.S. by his immigrant parents, Carlos Santana snuck into the Fillmore and wound up topping the bills there.

Sons of Champlin. Blood Sweat & Tears and Chicago get the credit for fusing rock with jazz, but Bill Champlin and the Sons did it first—and with soul.

Frumious Bandersnatch. I never heard these guys, but I loved their name. Turns out, one member was Ross Valory, who'd join the soberly-named Journey.

. . . And, Just a Little Later

Mother Earth

Dan Hicks & His Hot Licks

Boz Scaggs

Stoneground

Tower of Power

. . . And, Just a Little Before

Beau Brummels

Vejtables

Mojo Men

Grass Roots

We Five

All that glitters is not gold. It's a proverb that came true for several caught-off-guard Bay Area General Managers. Here are ten sure-fire can't-miss prospects who missed anyway.

10. Joe Strain, Giants. The Giants traded perennial .300 hitter Bill Madlock in mid-1979 to make way for the freckle-faced supposed slugger, and immediately began working on a time machine so they could undo the decision. After two terrible seasons, Strain was traded to the Cubs and out of baseball the next summer.

9. J.R. Phillips, Giants. After Will Clark "slumped" to .283 in 1993, the Giants let the superstar walk via free agency with the confidence they had Phillips waiting in the wings. Three seasons, 12 long balls and tons of strikeouts later, Giants fans were "thrilled" by Phillips departure from Candlestick Park.

8. Andre Rodgers, Giants. Owner Horace Stoneham predicted superstar status for the athletic, former cricket player from the Bahamas. Problem was, he didn't hit very well and he was a butcher in the field. In 1959, Rodgers drove pitcher Sam Jones to tears after he booted a routine grounder that was ruled a hit, spoiling the Giants ace's no-hit bid.

7. Bill Bordley, Giants. After the Reds failed to sign Bordley in 1979, the Giants won the right to ink the USC hotshot. But after going 2-3 with the 1980 Giants, Bordley blew out his arm and never returned to the majors. He later became a secret service agent and guarded Chelsea Clinton during the First Child's years at Stanford.

6. Jesse Foppert, Giants. In 2003, Baseball America tapped Foppert, a USF and Marin County product, as the No. 1 pitching prospect in all of baseball. Whiff. Foppert, or "Floppert," went 8-9 with a 5.00 ERA before blowing out his elbow. Still trying to make his way back to the Bigs, Foppert began the 2008 season with the Fresno Grizzlies, the Giants AAA affiliate.

5. Bob Garibaldi, Giants. After leading Santa Clara to the College World Series in the summer of 1962, the Giants signed the flame-throwing right-hander to a $150,000 bonus and were forced to add him immediately to their big league roster. He soon reported a sore arm. Garibaldi stayed with the organization for eight seasons but never earned a win for the big club.

4. Ariel Prieto, A's. Oakland heaped a dump truck of cash on Prieto, one of the first prospects to flee Cuba in the mid-Nineties, then watched helplessly as their investment added up to just fifteen big league wins over five injury riddled seasons.

3. Ben Grieve, A's. Oakland fans had every reason to be excited when this former No. 1 pick whacked three doubles against the Giants in his 1997 big league debut. He'd go on to win the Rookie of the Year honors the next season, but that was the peak of his career, not the beginning. Grieve quickly proved he wasn't much more than a slap hitter who competed with the enthusiasm of a doorknob. He was traded to Tampa Bay, Milwaukee and finally Chicago where he played himself out of baseball by the end of 2005.

2. Rich Murray, Giants. When Willie McCovey retired in mid-1980 the Giants were convinced they were set at first base for the next decade with the powerful younger brother of Eddie Murray. However, the "Murray era" lasted barely three months and produced a grand total of four home runs.

1. Todd Van Poppel, A's. The Texas high-school hotshot told teams not to bother drafting him because he was headed to college in his home state, but the A's pulled a fast one and overwhelmed the kid with a major league contract. The money was not well spent. Rushed to the big leagues, Van Poppel never matured into a polished pitcher and bounced around pro ball for a decade, spreading joy to hitters everywhere. He retired from baseball in the spring of '05 after it became clear he would not make the Mets roster.

I'd love to be a GM. Slamming down the phone after dealing with a slimy agent, knowing I had just changed the fortunes of my franchise—it must be a great feeling. That feeling must've been coursing through the GMs who made the most of their free agent decisions.

10. Frank Thomas, A's. Of all the designated hitters the A's hired during the moneyball era—Mike Piazza, Ron Gant, Erubial Durazo—former White Sox slugger Frank Thomas was the best, crushing 39 home runs and driving in 114 runs for the AL West Champion Oakland club of 2006. In the first game of the '06 divisional playoff series vs. Minnesota, the "Big Hurt" got the A's off on the right foot, pounding two home runs in a 3-2 road win.

9. Omar Vizquel, Giants. Vizquel swiftly showed why he's baseball's version of Baryshnikov, making spectacular plays at shortstop daily, and displaying a graceful brilliance never seen previously in San Francisco. In 2008, Vizquel established a new record for games played at his position, eclipsing Hall of Famer and fellow Venezuelan Luis Aparicio.

8. Bengie Molina and Aaron Rowand, Giants. The Giants clubs of 2007-08 were not particularly memorable in terms of wins and losses. But think what they would have been without these two dugout rats. The only thing Giants fans knew about Molina prior to his inking was that he was member of the Angels club that sucker-punched the Giants in the 2002 World Series. They quickly discovered that Molina pours his heart and soul into every contest behind the plate and swings a clutch bat of Jeff Kent proportions. The gritty backstop was the clear choice for the Willie Mac Award, for most inspirational Giant in 2007. Rowand joined up in 2008 and also immediately displayed why he was voted the toughest player in major league baseball by his peers. Despite absorbing the type of physical abuse that Ronnie Lott used to live for, Rowand kept coming back for more while continuing to hit like an All Star in his Giants debut season.

7. Dave Stewart, A's. Maybe the reason why Stewart has always played baseball the correct way, battling like a wildcat every time he took the hill for Oakland, was the fact that he had literally seen what rock bottom looks like. On May 9, 1986, Stewart was released by the Philadelphia Phillies after compiling a 6.23 ERA in eight relief outings. These were the same Phillies who finished 26 games out of first place the previous season. But three weeks later, Stewart landed on his feet and was reborn as a pitcher in the town he literally was born in. Pitching for new A's skipper Tony LaRussa, Stewart found himself, going 9-5 with a 3.95 ERA, and would win 20 games or more the next four seasons, leading Oakland to three straight AL Championship and a world title in 1989.

6. Ken Norton, Jr., 49ers. The son of the heavyweight boxer, Junior took some getting used to. As part of the Cowboys, he helped whip the Niners in numerous big games. But before the 1994 season, San Francisco turned the table on Dallas, snapping up Norton to play middle linebacker. Even though he insisted on wearing a cowboy hat—the ten-gallon kind—fans turned the other cheek when he became the man in the middle for the team that won Super Bowl XXIX with a 49-26 drubbing of the Chargers.

5. Joe Morgan, Giants. After two bitterly disappointing seasons in 1979-80, the Giants opted for a strong character influx for 1981, hiring the no-nonsense Frank Robinson as manager and bringing in former two-time MVP and Big Red Machine mainstay Joe Morgan to play second base. Morgan, who grew up in Oakland rooting for the Giants, brought a defensive stability to the infield and a strong presence to the clubhouse. Morgan's career caught a second wind in 1982 when he hit .289, with 14 homers and 61 RBI for a surprising Giants club that was in the pennant race until the last weekend of the season. On the final day of the season, Morgan whacked one of the Giants most memorable long balls ever, socking a two run shot off Terry Forester to knock the Dodgers out of pennant contention.

4. Dave Henderson, A's. The Athletics have been one of baseball's most reluctant clubs when it comes to signing free agents. They've preferred to develop their own talent rather than overspend for big names. But in 1988, they stepped outside the company model and signed the popular "Hendu." The starting center fielder on the A's three consecutive pennant-winning clubs from 1988-90, he powered 20 or more homers in four of his six seasons and came up with countless clutch hits. He batted .308 with a team-leading two home runs in the 1989 World Series.

3. Deion Sanders, 49ers. In Eddie DeBartolo's last all-out bid to win a Super Bowl, in 1994 the 49ers loaded up on big-name free agents: Gary Plummer, Norton, Jr., Rickey Jackson and . . . drum roll please . . . "Neon Deion." Formerly a showboat, Sanders was able to rein in his histrionics and tone down his camera-hogging act a bit. But he still loosened up the sedate Niners. "Primetime" would have his best season as a pro in Scarlet and Gold, racking up six interceptions and returning them for a record 303 yards with three TDs, including a 93-yard return to pay dirt at the Georgia Dome against his former team. He picked a pass in the Super Bowl that season and was later named NFL Defensive Player of the Year.

2. Billy Beane, A's. You wouldn't think that a guy who hit .241 in 37 games would make this list. But where would the A's be now if Oakland hadn't signed this former top prospect to a free agent pact prior to 1989? After washing out as an A's player, Beane stayed on with the organization in the front office, learning the trade from GM Sandy Alderson. Eventually, Beane took over the A's front office, introducing his own brand of baseball management detailed in the best-selling book *Moneyball*. In 1999, Sporting News named Beane the Major League Executive of the Year.

1. Barry Bonds, Giants. It wasn't shocking that Bonds signed a pact to become baseball's all-time richest player before the start of the 1993 season. The shocking part was that it was the Giants who lined his pockets. It was expected that the Yankees, Dodgers, Mets or Braves would ink Bonds after his MVP season with the Pirates in 1992. Instead it was the freshly purchased Giants who lured Bonds with a $43.75 million, six-year contract to come home to play with a team that had employed his family in the past. Eager to make a splash with ticket buyers and kick-start a new stadium drive, S.F. shelled out the cash and got back more than they could have expected. Like him or not, Bonds has to be the best free agent signing in the history of sports, based on franchise impact and performance.

It's not the dollars you spend; it's how you spend them. In the case of these human money pits, the cash was not well spent.

10. Richard Dent, 49ers. A former Bears Super Bowl MVP, Dent earned his second Super Bowl ring with the Niners in 1994. "Earned" isn't quite the right word. He barely played all season. Injuries kept Dent on the sidelines most of the campaign, and he was gone before the 49ers got their rings.

9. Warren Sapp, Raiders. Sapp's reign of terror in the NFC after several Pro Bowl seasons in Tampa Bay gave him all the street cred the Raider Nation needed. Too bad the Raiders play their games in the Coliseum, not the streets. Sapp toiled for four completely forgettable seasons in Oakland after signing a seven-year, $16 million deal. He retired with three seasons remaining, having lost interest in the NFL's most dysfunctional franchise.

8. Kevin Bass, Giants. A former Astros All Star, the Peninsula-raised Bass came home to play as Candy Maldonado's right field replacement in 1990, and proceeded to string together three of the most forgettable seasons by a starting position player in Giants history. Does anyone even have any memory of Bass, good or bad?

7. Rennie Stennett, Giants. As a young man, Stennett was a dynamic offensive force, regularly hitting .300. In a 1975 game, he set a record, batting seven for seven in a game vs. the Cubs. Then the Panamanian suffered a serious ankle break and lost most of his effectiveness at the plate. Despite his batting less than .250 1978-79, the Giants were convinced Stennett was still a game breaker, signing a three-year deal. Stennett never got any better, hitting just .240 in 120 games in 1980. He made it into just 38 games in 1981 and was released.

6. Dave Righetti, Giants. A former All-Star closer with the Yankees, San Jose product Righetti came home to the Giants in 1991 amid much ballyhoo. But it quickly became apparent that his best stuff was spent in the Bronx. Righetti saved 24 games in 1991, but posted a 2-7 record. He increasingly got worse, saving just four games the rest of his Orange and Black career. After posting a 5.31 ERA in 1993, the Giants released the ineffective southpaw, who later became (and still is) the team's pitching coach.

5. Mark Portugal, Giants. For a stretch in the early 1990s, Portugal was a better-than-average starting pitcher, but against the Giants he pitched like the reincarnation of Cy Young, and obviously left an impression. When he became available as a free agent in 1994, the Giants couldn't wait to get him on their side, and leapt into action, handing the SoCal native a lucrative deal. The Giants soon realized that without S.F. as an opponent, he had nothing to look forward to and became a very ordinary hurler, going 15-13 in parts of two seasons.

4. Edgardo Alfonzo and Ray Durham, Giants. Initially, Alfonzo and Durham seemed to be more than adequate replacements for the departed free agents Jeff Kent and David Bell when they opened the 2003 season. Both players were near .300 career hitters for the Mets and White Sox respectively, but each seemed to age inexplicably once they donned the Orange and Black. Third baseman Alfonzo struggled to hit .250 in his three seasons by the Bay. While second sacker Durham hit well enough, hamstring and other leg injuries cost him. Never a gold-glove caliber player, Ray's defense became more porous with age. In the last year of his original deal with S.F., Durham was inspired by his walk year and hit much better, prompting the Giants to ink him to an extension. Suckers.

3. Jeff George, Raiders. Some dudes are leg men. Al Davis? He gets aroused when he sees a drop-back quarterback with a cannon arm. The way Davis saw it, George was born to be a Raider. He had a losing record when he became a free agent, but that fact wasn't something for Davis to dwell on—just look at that arm! Well, George fared no better in Silver and Black than he did in Colts blue and white and Atlanta black and red.

2. Barry Zito, Giants. In 2007, San Francisco forked over a then-record $126 million, seven-year contract, boasting that the ace had never missed a start in his A's career. That may be a problem, because what the Giants failed to notice was his effectiveness and most notably his velocity had gone into free fall since his Cy Young season in Oakland. After two seasons with S.F., Zito has turned in a record of 21-30 in 66 starts, only missing one with a temporary bullpen demotion. His career worst ERA in 2007 of 4.53 was toppled with a 5.15 in 2008, when he started 0-8, walked 102 batters, and had a minor-league WHIP of 1.60. So, why not number one on this list? Well, the book hasn't closed on him yet. Zito has a small chance at redemption with five more seasons to prove he isn't close to washed up. If he's part of a big postseason win, salvation could be his. No matter what Zito does, this deal will forever be regarded as one of the worst values in the history of sports. Want proof? Although he said Zito's signing didn't have anything to do with his decision, Giants Managing General Partner Peter Magowan, who pushed the Zito deal through, suddenly resigned amidst rumors investors had lost confidence in him.

1. Larry Brown, Raiders. Al Davis became obsessed with Super Bowl MVPs in the mid-1990s, signing a pair who immediately went MIA in Raider Nation. But the biggest miscalculation had to be signing Cowboys cornerback Larry Brown to a lucrative deal after he was awarded the Pete Rozelle Trophy for his two-gift-wrapped-interceptions game in Super Bowl XXX. In twelve games spread over two seasons in Oakland, Brown managed just one INT.

While "bigger, faster, stronger" is the battle cry of modern athletics, it's not a good idea to ignore the vertically challenged. Sometimes the little guy has big game, proving that good things—including world titles—can come in small packages.

10. Monta Ellis. Listed at 6-foot-3. I don't think so. I've stood next to Monta on the court at Warriors games, and there's no way. A second-round pick straight out of high school, he has emerged as one of the more explosive young talents in the NBA. After a rookie season in 2005-06 that was full of adjustments and a bad coach, Monta thrived in Don Nelson's offense, and was named the NBA's most improved player of the 2006-07 season. His three-year scoring average has gone from 6.8 to 16.5 to 20.2 points per game.

9. Mike Gallego. The scrappy Gallego overcame cancer to become a key cog in the A's powerhouse clubs of the Eighties and Nineties. The tiny 5-foot-8, 160-pound Gallego came up big in crunch time. A UCLA grad, he made big plays at second base to make up for his .239 lifetime average.

8. Tim Lincecum. Despite winning every major pitching award in his final season at the University of Washington, Lincecum was the tenth pick of the 2006 draft because of why he's on the list. Fearing his slight 5-foot-10, 170-pound frame couldn't hold up under the torque he creates with his unique delivery, teams went bigger. That appears to be a big mistake. Lincecum burst out of the gate, leaving all the big names picked ahead of him in the dust. He began his Giants career with a 16-5 record and some of the nastiest stuff around. Mark my words. If he stays healthy, he's very Cy-ish.

7. Tim Hudson. While hulking hurlers were gobbled up by teams in the early rounds of the 1997 draft, the A's scooped up Hudson in the sixth—and never had any regrets. Though he stood just 6-foot, 190 pounds, the Georgian product pitched like a monster, winning 92 games in his six seasons pitching at the Coliseum.

6. Tim Hardaway. The speediest member of the Warriors' Run TMC, Hardaway was also the smallest, at 6-foot, 170 pounds. It was quite a sight to watch the high-energy Timmy run the court along the looping strides of 7-foot-8 Manute Bol. Hardaway had his best season in 1991-92, filling up the hoop to the tune of 23 PPG.

5. Omar Vizquel. Though he was in his late thirties when he arrived in San Francisco, Omar immediately showed Giants fans and the rest of the NL why he's a lock for the Hall of Fame. Vizquel seemingly made a highlight-reel-worthy play every game. A true artist of the infield—and now baseball's all-time leader at games played at shortstop—Vizquel has won two of his eleven Gold Gloves with the G-men.

4. Bill Ring. The 5-foot-10, 200-pound Ring was a special teams bulldog for the first two Super Bowl winning clubs. Bill Walsh also took advantage of Ring's fine pass catching ability out of the backfield. He turned into a real fan favorite.

3. Bert Campaneris, A's. One of the core members of the A's three-peat championship clubs, Campy was one of, if not the most beloved Athletics player ever. Exceptional on defense, the Cuban was also a hotheaded little guy, and once flung his bat at Detroit's Lerrin LaGrow during the 1972 ALCS when the towering hurler came in high and tight.

2. Cliff Branch. The speedy Branch was a prolific pass catcher for the powerhouse mid-Seventies Raiders. The 5-foot-11, 170-pound wide receiver was a lightning-quick touchdown machine, snagging 67 pay dirt passes in thirteen Raiders seasons.

1. Billy Martin. To survive the hardscrabble streets of Oakland, Billy "the Kid" had to learn how to use his fists at an early age. The feisty little guy never dropped his dukes throughout a baseball career that stretched from the 1940s when he helped Casey Stengal win a PCL championship with the Oaks, to the Bronx when he was a member of several world championship clubs. In the early Eighties, Billy turned the A's around taking a 108-loss team and making them a winner in 1980.

Warm and fuzzy. Beloved and loathed. These are the ten best cartoon characters brought to life to root, root, root for the home team.

10. Oski the Bear. Before the 1941 season, Cal used real bears. But common sense squashed that, and gave birth to Oski. Cal's mascot made his debut September 26, 1941 vs. St. Mary's. The name comes from a turn-of-the-century Cal student-section cheer: "Oski-Wow-Wow." Kids don't cheer like they used to.

9. Stomper. With roots dating back to the turn of the twentieth century, the elephant is connected to Philadelphia businessman Benjamin Shibe, who considered himself a "white elephant." The less-than-graceful creature has been associated with the Athletics franchise ever since. Stomper has been entertaining kids since 1997, and has caused thousands of A's fans to wonder why their team's mascot is an elephant.

8. Saber Kittens. Technically, they're cheerleaders—scantily clad cheerleaders—for the three-time Area Football League Champion San Jose Sabercats. But who cares. They're on the list. I've been to a few games, and did two seasons of pre-game for the team. I'm not sure I saw a play, thanks to the best sideline eye-candy in the Bay Area.

7. Thunder. Can your mascot do a 360-degree reverse dunk? The Warriors mascot can. Even though he looks like a failed superhero, Thunder probably gave Warriors fans something to cheer during a horrible decade of basketball that coincided with his 1997 debut. However, I want his rubber outfit tested for performance enhancers.

6. Lou Seal. Since 1997, kids going to Giants games have been lining up for pictures with the team's loveable mascot, inspired by the seals at Pier 39. He'll bound around the park, dancing, getting into trouble and—to the delight of gutter-minded people—gets off nearly 500 hip thrusts per game.

5. Charlie O. Flamboyant Athletics owner Charlie Finley didn't think his elephant was inspiring his team, and replaced the elephant motif with a live mule. Charlie O., named after Finley, could be seen on-field before games, at cocktail parties and in the clubhouse after games.

4. Banjo Man. With a beard that Z.Z. Top would be proud of, Banjo Man can be seen walking around A's and 49ers games, strumming his—you guessed it—banjo. Adorned with his signature propeller beanie, Stacy Samuels picked up his banjo at the age of eight, and started bringing it to Bay Area sporting events in 1980 to help energize crowds.

3. Crazy Crab. Poking fun at the Seventies mascot craze, the Giants came up with Crazy Crab in 1984. That season, the G-men were terrible, losing 96 games with Crazy Crab at their side. In the history of baseball, there's never been a mascot as hated by a local fan base. Every now and then, the Giants dust him off and bring him out to a chorus of boos.

2. Sour Dough Sam. Having presided over five Super Bowl titles, Sammy gets more respect than any other mascot in the Bay. After appearing as a scruffy, gold-panning prospector for decades, the Sourman underwent a major facelift in 2006. He now looks like he could model underwear in the off-season. Along with a cleft-chin, Sam also got a flame throwing pickax, which he wields before kickoff. Not bad for a guy who's based on baking bread.

1. The Stanford Tree. The unofficial mascot of the Stanford Cardinal, this ridiculous costume has been shaking its limbs at Maples Pavilion since the 1975 season. Awash in political correctness, Stanford changed its mascot from the Indians to the Cardinal in 1981, but never came up with an appropriate image to go along with the new name. Leave it to the Stanford Band to come up with The Tree. Only kids this smart could come up with something so absurd. In March 2006, the Tree was suspended from the Women's NCAA tournament after fighting with security guards trying to stop him from dancing in an undesignated area.

You never get a second chance to make a first impression, but when these players and coaches got a second chance, they made the most of it. These guys prove life can be more fun the second time around.

10. Jose Canseco. After breaking into baseball in a big way with the A's, Canseco took his home-run-hitting, hot-rod-driving, Madonna-dating, juice-shooting rock star act to Texas and Boston. But in 1997 he was back in Oakland, signed as a free agent and teaming once again with Bash Brother Mark McGwire. This time around, Canseco made less noise, hitting 23 homeruns and 74 RBI in 108 games. The following season he was off to the Blue Jays where he threw a party that Roger Clemens may or may not have attended.

9. Chris Webber. After obtaining Webber in the 1993 NBA draft, the Warriors looked to be on the path to a decade's worth of playoff appearances. He lived up to the hype, blowing away all other candidates for 1993-94 Rookie of the Year honors. Then Webber's other reputation as a spoiled crybaby leapt from the hardwood and he demanded to be traded. For the next 10 years the Warriors were a pathetic mess. Then miraculously, in the later stages of the 2007-08 season, Webber reappeared on the Warriors roster like a rash with bad knees. In a bit of poetic justice for those Warrior fans who still resented his earlier act, Webber was an awful, out-of-shape mess. He made zero impact and soon announced his retirement from basketball. But man, it was good for my show.

8. OJ Simpson. Born and raised in San Francisco, where he set the rushing record at Galileo High and City College, OJ gained extraordinary fame and fortune at USC, and with the Buffalo Bills. Then in 1978-79 the Juice came home to squeeze two more seasons out of his surgically scarred knees for two dismal 49ers clubs. In 23 games with the Niners, Simpson gained 1,053 yards and scored four touchdowns before retiring to the broadcast booth and cruddy movies. Other interests included blondes.

7. Felipe Alou. An original 1958 San Francisco Giant, Alou was a groundbreaking player in his first go-around with the club. The first athlete born and raised in the Dominican Republic to play in the big leagues, Alou was the spokesman for the Latino ballplayer community. He raised awareness when he felt basic rights were being denied to players, such as with bans on speaking Spanish in the clubhouse. In 1962, Alou led the pennant-winning Giants in hitting and would return, four decades later, as the team's manager, leading the Giants to the NL West title in his first season.

6. Joe Kapp. The starting quarterback on Cal's 1959 Rose Bowl team, Kapp played in the NFL and in Canada, as well as appearing in a few Hollywood movies before winding his way back to Berkeley in 1982. Though he had no previous head coaching experience, Kapp was a master motivator and turned the fading program around. That year, Kapp was under the headphones when the Golden Bears won with seven laterals to score a last-second touchdown against Stanford and its band in the Big Game. "The Play" has gone down in college football and sports highlight history.

5. Reggie Jackson. Prior to his days as "the straw that stirred the drink" in the Big Apple, Jackson drove the A's to three World Series titles. After his more famous stint with the Yanks, and another five with the Angels, Reggie returned to Oakland to wrap up his major league career in 1987. In 115 games Jackson batted .220 with fifteen homers and 43 RBI.

4. Bill Walsh. Prior to ascending to genius status as coach of the 49ers, Walsh turned the Stanford football program around, leading the Cardinal to a Blue Bonnet Bowl win in 1978 with an offensive scheme that would be copied again and again over the next three decades. Walsh coached the Niners to three Super Bowl titles and then retired from the sidelines. Or so it appeared. After he seemed to be done coaching for good, Walsh returned to the Farm in 1992. In his first season back he led the Cardinal to a Pac 10 Co-Championship and a victory over Penn State in the Victory Bowl. He left Stanford in '94 to return to the Niners front office.

3. Rickey Henderson. Like a friendly ghost, the stolen base king came and disappeared from an A's uniform several times during his career of two-and-half decades. Rickey packed a career's worth of action into his first six seasons with the A's, breaking the single season stolen base record. Then at age 26, Henderson was dealt to the Yankees for five players. The A's re-acquired Rickey in mid-1989 after four, all-star caliber seasons in the Bronx. Already a powerhouse club, the defending AL champs put Henderson at the top of the order and got even better, winning the World Series. Henderson strung together four fantastic seasons, breaking the all-time stolen bases record as an Athletic. Then in mid-1993 Henderson was dealt again, this time to the contending Blue Jays who would go on to win the World Series. But on opening day 1994, Henderson was back in the A's lineup, inked to a new deal. This time he stuck around for two seasons, batting .300 in 112 games in 1995. Then he was gone again for two seasons before reappearing one last time in an A's uniform in 1998. Though he batted .248, Rickey led the AL in walks that season with 118.

2. Willie McCovey. After limping through a six-home-run campaign with San Diego and Oakland in 1976, Mac looked like he would finish his career 35 long balls short of 500. The Giants signed him to a look-see deal in spring training of 1977, and boy did they like what they saw. The gentle giant produced his biggest season in years, batting .280 with 28 home runs and 86 RBI while winning NL Comeback Player of the Year honors. One of the most popular Giants ever, McCovey socked homer No. 500 in 1978 wearing Orange and Black.

1. Don Nelson. After a highly successful run helming the Milwaukee Bucks, Nelson arrived in Oakland as Warriors general manager. In 1988, Nellie moved to the sidelines as coach, and the W's began one of the most exciting runs in franchise history. Using speed, athleticism and shooting ability, the Warriors began filling the arena as Chris Mullin, Tim Hardaway and Mitch Richmond began hitting buckets like nobody's business. After Webber was traded away, Nellie lost interest and departed, too. Then, more than a dozen seasons later, after stops in New York and Dallas, Nelson reappeared as if he'd never left. With an updated Run TMC cast headed by Baron Davis, Stephen Jackson and Monta Ellis, the Warriors were back as one of the most exciting teams in the league. Nellie appears to be the only coach out there who can get the Warriors to win.

Ten Most Extreme Outdoor Destinations
:: by Cyrus Saatsaz

NOTE: Host of one of the nation's longest running radio shows that deals exclusively with Action Sports, Cyrus Saatsaz was engulfed in the outdoor scene years before the X-Games brought the fringe into our living room. You can catch Cyrus chatting with a "who's who" list of extreme athletes on his show, "The Extreme Scene" on KNBR 1050, as well as working as an action-sports freelance writer. My man Cyrus lives life like a Mountain Dew commercial, and is more qualified to write this list than anyone I've ever met. As he says: "Northern California is home to anything and everything for the outdoor enthusiast. It's one of the many reasons why San Francisco's populace is considered one of the healthiest in the country, and why real estate prices never seem to drop. Surf? World class. Snow? A vast collection of resorts to choose from. Skate? The Mecca lies within. Trails? Hundreds, if not thousands of miles of terrain. There's something for everyone; beginner to advanced, fun or challenging, relaxing or straight extreme. Northern California has it all. And here are ten of the reasons why Northern California is considered the top destination for extreme outdoor enthusiasts."

10. Fort Point. There are very few places in the world where you feel like you're living in the land of giants. The Golden Gate Bridge looms massively large above, and mammoth container ships cruise by. Meanwhile, you're trying to avoid a huge rock protruding the middle of an amazing left that can peel forever. The locals here can be downright nasty and mean, but if you can handle yourself, and the feeling that you're an ant surrounded by elephants, Fort Point can be an exciting adventure with gratifying results.

9. Bicycle Trip Bike Park. Located across the street from the Santa Cruz Beach Boardwalk, this savvy bike park allows BMXers to practice all sorts of tricks, maneuvers and aerials within safe confines. Residents and tourists alike are dazzled daily by the insane stunts pulled by the BMX daredevils.

8. Mt. Tam. If your idea of having to take a boat or ferry to an island just to hike or mountain bike doesn't sound appealing, then a short distance away in Marin County lays Mt. Tam. Home to over 60 miles of hiking and bicycle trails (not to mention breathtaking views) Mt. Tam is both beautiful and challenging. An outdoor-lover's dream.

7. Mavericks. One of the top big-wave destinations in the world would rank higher on this list, except only the most advanced surfers can actually catch and ride these gigantic and very dangerous waves. Jeff Clark first discovered Mavericks and surfed it alone for 15 years before other surfers finally believed him and saw for themselves what Northern California's natural wonder had to offer. The Mavericks Surf Contest is held annually (unless ideal conditions fail to present themselves) and you can visit Jeff at his surf shop in Half Moon Bay, located just inland from the legendary big-wave surf location.

6. Angel Island. Once used as an immigration station, Angel Island today is home to over 13 miles of foot trails, and 8 miles of spectacular bike trails. Angel Island offers a wide array of difficulty levels, and is considered a favorite of many mountain bikers. Plus, the views of San Francisco are sensational.

5. Ocean Beach. With a stretch of land measuring approximately 3.5 miles long, one need never worry about crowds when surfing San Francisco's Ocean Beach. Rather, one must worry about nasty rip currents, cold weather and shore breaks. This is not the spot for the novice surfer. If, however, you desire a challenging spot with no one around to crowd your space, Ocean Beach is the place for you. And the waves, while heavy and large most of the time, can be amazingly perfect under the right conditions.

4. Squaw Valley USA. All Alexander Cushing, who opened Squaw Valley USA in 1949, had to present to the U.S. Olympic Committee in 1955 was "the idea of a California valley with an annual snowfall of 450 inches, and a downhill event with areas that had never even been schussed successfully." Cushing's words were enough for the committee, and in 1960, Squaw Valley USA was home not just to the Winter Olympics, but also the first televised Winter Olympics. Yes, Squaw Valley is that good. Wide, vast terrain, steep, crazy drops, amazing quality of snow—and history. This is one of the top snowboard and ski destinations in the world.

3. Downtown San Francisco. The "Mecca" for skateboarders, the entire downtown area of the city is, in essence, one enormous skate park. It's a concrete jungle of steps, rails, jumps and kickers. Novices beware: The steep hills of San Francisco are not for you. This is the ultimate destination for the core skater, and home of Thrasher Magazine.

2. Kirkwood Mountain Resort. Out of all the Lake Tahoe destinations, Kirkwood Mountain Resort offers the best snow, hands down. Coupled with smaller crowds and extremely challenging runs (there are plenty of blues and greens as well,) Kirkwood is numero uno among Tahoe's class of ski resorts. Because of the topography of the region, snow here falls heavier and is drier, thus creating the kind of powder snowboarders and skiers dream of. It's a little out of the way, but remains the top destination when looking for overall quality of snow and terrain.

1. Santa Cruz. During the summer the weather is outstanding, and after the morning marine layers burn away, even the winter can provide sunshine and warmth for everyone. Yet the weather isn't the reason why Santa Cruz tops the list of the most extreme outdoor destinations. It's the world-class surf. In fact, the City of Santa Cruz is embattled to this day with Huntington Beach, Calif., over the label "Surf City" because of the quality of surf, and the numerous different breaks surfers can choose from. If you want some of the most ridiculously perfect waves, you can go to the west side and surf Steamer's Lane, or head east and ride the appropriately named Pleasure Point. The local temperament isn't what one should be worried about when you're in the water—it's trying to actually catch waves. The locals are just that good, so much so that the challenge is simply paddling hard enough to get proper positioning. And if you're a beginner, Cowell's is one of the premier beginner spots with long, gentle waves anyone can catch.

The movie industry may be based in Los Angeles, but no California town offers a more beautiful movie backdrop than San Francisco. Some of the best filmmakers of our time are based in the city. Here are ten really good movies where San Francisco offers a supporting role herself.

10. *The Game* (1997). An over-the-top action thriller with a twist that's easy to see coming, it's a good movie anyway. The Palace Hotel is the setting for the movie, which offers tons of great shots of San Francisco.

9. *The Rock* (1996). One of the best summer popcorn crunching action movies ever, San Francisco's beauty is on full display. Alcatraz is pretty—from the outside. Sean Connery is doing a great Sean Connery impression through the entire flick. It also gives us Nick Cage's fantastic character name, Stanley Goodspeed.

8. *Mrs. Doubtfire* (1993). Very charming, and funny, and chock full of city window dressing. It's actually one you can watch with the kids in the room, and still laugh. What's more San Francisco than Robin Williams and cross dressing?

7. *Murder in the First* (1995). Clint Eastwood's 1979 *Escape from Alcatraz* is much better known. But the best movie about Alcatraz (and who doesn't like a good prison movie?) is *Murder in the First*. Kevin Bacon—yes, Kevin Bacon—gives an amazing performance. As his lawyer, Christian Slater runs around old San Francisco streets looking to set his client free.

6. *Zodiac* (2007). A dark and true story of the murders that shook the Bay Area in the Sixties and Seventies—trust me, it's creepy. It's based on former *San Francisco Chronicle* reporter Robert Graysmith's book about the infamous Zodiac killer, and captures the amazing growth of the city during those decades. On a personal note, it was very freaky to learn one of the murder sites is just a couple of blocks away from my place.

5. *Tucker: The Man and His Dream* (1988). Probably did the worst box office of all the movies here, but it's a great film, directed by San Francisco's own Francis Ford Coppola. Jeff Bridges gives his best performance as the maverick automotive engineer, with ideas that revolutionized the industry once his voice was heard.

4. *48 Hours* (1982). San Francisco's sleazy side is on full display in the movie that launched Eddie Murphy's career in Hollywood. Chinatown and The Fillmore neighborhoods are both major locations where Detective Jack Cates (Nick Nolte) and convict Reggie Hammond (Murphy) crack one-liners when not fighting with drug dealers or each other.

3. *Bullitt* (1968). Steve McQueen is a stud, and he tears up the city in what is regarded as the best car chase in movie history. Doing his own driving, McQueen uses San Francisco's hills to launch his `68 Ford Mustang all over downtown and Pacific Heights. In a day when action movies star guys named Shia LaBeouf, it's nice to have a look back to see when the genre offered us a real man's man.

2. *Vertigo* (1958). San Francisco through the eyes of master director Alfred Hitchcock, and through the fears of Jimmy Stewart—it's the psychological thriller by which all others are measured. Shot with a style that gives you a tour of the best locations in S.F., *Vertigo* may move a bit slowly, but the scenery sure is nice.

1. *Dirty Harry* (1971). Clint Eastwood in all his side-burned glory gives an iconic performance as San Francisco's own Inspector Harry Callahan, who chases the "Scorpio Killer" across the city's rooftops. It's hardly an educational film, but I did learn that the .44 Magnum is the most powerful handgun in the word, and can blow your head clean off.

Worst Pieces of Crap Filmed in San Francisco

Just because San Francisco is a great location for a movie, it can't save us from the endless stream of garbage Hollywood offers more often than not. Here are ten films—and believe me, there are many more—that should never be seen by anyone.

10. *ED TV* (1999). It's not that the idea is terrible; it's the editing. All kinds of mistakes are on display as Matthew McConaughey runs around a corner in one neighborhood to emerge in another neighborhood. If you're going to take the time to make a film in our city, at least get it right.

9. *A View to a Kill* (1985). Quite possibly the worst James Bond movie. Roger Moore delivered one bad line after another in between some of the campiest action ever filmed. Christopher Walken makes a good villain whose plans to flood Silicon Valley were just plain dumb. The Golden Gate Bridge is the only thing in the movie with more coats of paint than Tanya Roberts.

8. *High Crimes* (2002). Fifteen minutes in, you'll know who the killer is by process of elimination. Ashley Judd is a serious lawyer looking for the truth with a bad haircut. I believe it was around this time Morgan Freeman called his agent and said, "No more crime thrillers," or he just fired the guy. Just goes to show you, a formulaic thriller can't be saved with a great location.

7. *The Wedding Planner* (2001). The dreaded "chick flick." Getting hitched? Why not hire a smoking-hot Jennifer Lopez to plan your big day? What could go wrong? It's not that *The Wedding Planner* is the greatest crime against humanity—and I know it wasn't made for me—but I wanted something on this list to represent all chick flicks, too many of which are filmed here because it's pretty.

6. Every Chevy Chase and Goldie Hawn Movie. Chevy Chase was once funny, and Goldie Hawn was once hot, but put 'em together and you've got box office . . . what? Would some please tell me what we got? We got another bad Chevy Chase and Goldie Hawn movie shot in San Francisco, that's what we got.

5. *Interview with the Vampire* (1994). Hey, we got vampires—can we get some blood-sucking action? Well, no. Not in this very long and boring tale in which a *San Francisco Chronicle* reporter, you guessed it, interviews a vampire. Tom Cruise in ruffled cuffs. Enjoy.

4. *Pacific Heights* (1990). Renting the downstairs apartment has never been scarier! Actually, there's nothing that scary about renting an apartment. Hence, this movie sucks. Michael Keaton won't move out . . . oh, the horror. Honestly, Melanie Griffith is in this movie, and no nude scene? Congratulations, you'll never get those two hours back.

3. *The Net* (1995). Sandra Bullock versus the information super highway. Was the Internet that scary back in 1995? Nothing like building a suspense thriller around identity theft. Dennis Miller falls flatter here than in the *Monday Night Football* booth.

2. *Jade* (1995). The movie's tag line: "Some fantasies go too far," like David Caruso's fantasy about leaving *NYPD Blue* for a Hollywood movie career. Caruso's inability to act is matched only by the lack of fire in his love scenes.

1. *The Fan* (1996). Robert DiNiro can sure pick a bad script from time to time— this one, he knocked out of the park. Wesley Snipes does a bad Barry Bonds impression as a selfish, free agent signed to play for the San Francisco Giants. DiNiro is an obsessed fan who likes knives and yelling at baseball games. There isn't one aspect of this movie that works on any level, except for John Kruk's mullet. He plays one of the Giants.

Drop a big pass? Miss a huge shot? Strike out when it mattered most? Doesn't matter—that's some amazing hair.

10. Travis Buck, A's. Is he one of the A's top prospects, or a fan who just got out of bed and grabbed a uniform? Buck drives the women crazy with his just-got-out-of-bed tangles.

9. Jamie Williams, 49ers. Milli Vanilli had nothing on "Spiderman's" braids. He was one of the few 49ers of the button-down Walsh/Seifert era to veer from the pack and make a fashion statement with his locks. It may have been a bold statement, but in retrospect, a hard choice to defend.

8. Nick Swisher, A's. It wasn't pretty, but it was special. All spit-spot now he's a White Sox player, when Swish was in Oakland, he looked like he either couldn't afford a haircut, or just didn't want one. Was it a good look? Nope. But it had a big heart. Swisher's shag was grown for the purpose of donating it to "Locks of Love," a charity that makes wigs for cancer patients.

7. Josh Childress, Stanford. And you thought the Stanford Tree was the only untamed growth running around Maples Pavilion. It had been a while—and it may be a long time again before we see a retro-'fro like this down on The Farm.

6. Al Davis, Raiders. Heeeeeeeeeeeeey! It's the Fonz. He's the reason they still make Brylcream. Nah, I bet he's a Dapper-Dan Man. Honestly, throw in the sweat suits and Al was about three decades ahead of the Sopranos.

5. Ken Stabler, Raiders. Either the Allman Brothers were trying to look like "The Snake" or he was trying to look like them. Honestly, Kenny's still got it—white, flowing, majestic and beautiful.

4. Mike Ricci, Sharks. He became the face (and teeth) of Bay Area hockey thanks to his grunge mullet. It's still maybe the top-rated "Kentucky waterfall" in the NHL's past 20 seasons, and that's saying something.

3. Latrell Sprewell, Warriors. There was actually a time when cornrows weren't crowding NBA locker rooms—and a time when players didn't put their hands around the coach's neck. Spree brought an end to both trends.

2. Garry Maddox, Giants. One of the first Bay Area athletes to sport a full, blown-out Mod-Squad-style afro, Maddox undoubtedly needed the assistance of a few bobby pins to keep his Giants cap affixed to his head at breezy Candlestick Park.

1. Chris Mullin, Warriors. When Chris Mullin dominated at St. Johns, he did it with a flat top. He ripped up NBA nets with his sweet jumper for 15 seasons, and did it with a flat top. He's now the Warriors General Manager, and he does it with a flat top.

Worst Hairdos in Bay Area Sports History

Sometimes it's better to leave it on the barbershop floor than on top of your head. Here's a list of some of the competitors who challenged opponents and fashion trends through the years.

10. Tom Tolbert, Warriors. As a rookie with the Warriors, Don Nelson said Mr. T's New Wave haircut made him look like a badger was camped on his head—think bleached Bart Simpson as a power forward. I work with Tom, and he has proudly shaven it all off, but he'll be happy his, um, effort was remembered here.

9. Rod Beck, Giants. That right arm wasn't the only thing that dangled on the mound. Beck possessed one of the wickedest mullets this side of the Mason-Dixon Line. "Shooter's" hair and mustache combo made him look like an outlaw biker closer.

8. Jerry Rice, 49ers. One year the TD king arrived in camp with a high-top fade (think Cameo). Soon he was being called "Fe-Fe." Neither the regrettable style nor the nickname would last long.

7. Robert Gallery, Raiders. If Robert Gallery hadn't had long, snarled, jet-black locks that made him look like the "Undertaker," the Raiders might not have drafted him. Given his knack for missing blocks, I'll bet Oakland wishes Robert had got that cut before he graduated.

6. Fred Biletnikoff, Raiders. Anyone seen him and fruit-smashing comedian Gallagher in the same room together? I rest my case.

5. Jason Giambi, A's. His hair symbolized a simpler time for Giambi. This once-loveable MVP traded in his rocker style for big New York dollars and steroids whispers. I'll bet there are days when he wishes he was still playing in low-profile Oakland with his tangles—and his image—intact. His current mustache with the Yankees is enough for me to forgive him, even though he's not saying what he's apologizing for.

4. John Montefusco, Giants. You can include any other number of white-guy Giants from the mid-1970s (Ed Goodson, Charlie Williams) who permed their hair into artificial afros, but no one did it better than "The Count." We can only thank heaven the Caucasian-afro movement was short lived.

3. Dennis Eckersley, A's. With the flowing jet-black locks and mustache combo, Eck looked like someone who would strike you out then go back to his locker, where several gold medals and a sun lamp were waiting for him.

2. Luis Polonia, A's. When he wasn't getting the phone numbers of underage girls in the go-go Eighties, Polonia was spackling his hair with greasy-looking jeri-curl activator. Just let your soul glow, Luis; and pray no one picks up your batting helmet by mistake.

1. Rick Barry, Warriors. Rick was never a fan of losing on the court or on top of his dome. Male pattern baldness was all that could slow him down, and his personal fight with his receding hairline is documented through team pictures though the years. To this day, three decades after taking his last shot, Rick's hair is so infamous he's still doing endorsements for a local doctor who specializes in hair replacement surgery.

I've paid homage to hair, but it's the mustache that binds us. You'd think there would be a couple of Sharks playoff beards on the list, but until they get to the Stanley Cup, no facial hair can be recognized.

10. Jack Taschner, Giants. It's not on all the time, but when Taschner is looking to add MPH to his fastball he channels Fu Manchu or goes all Grizzly Adams and breaks out the beard. You have to like a lefty reliever who believes his facial hair can make a difference. His efforts have given way to one of my favorite nicknames: Jack Mustachner.

9. Dennis Eckersley, A's. Why hasn't the Salem cigarettes model ever sued for copyright infringement? On anyone else, Eckersley's mustache would have looked so refreshed and breezy.

8. Johnnie LeMaster, Giants. There are fifteen-year-old kids a few months short of puberty who have had more success growing a mustache than LeMaster. Honestly, is that dirt on his lip?

7. Ken Holtzman, A's. Someone cue the funky music. Kenny may be the Bay Area captain of the "All-Porn Mustache Team," which may or may not have called Oakland its base of operation.

6. Baron Davis, Warriors. Before growing "look at me" playoff beards in the NBA—Drew Gooden, I'm talking to you—the Baron had been tapping into "beard power" for years. People don't have carpeting this plush. Davis averaged 21 points last season, while his beard is credited with seven assists per game.

5. Al Attles, Warriors. Dressed in head-to-toe polyester, talking in a booming, deep, Grand Canyon voice, topped with a jet-black afro and Kimbo Slice beard? Can you say, ahead of his time?

4. Russ Francis, 49ers. When he wasn't playing tight end he was in Honolulu working as Tom Selleck's stand-in on the set of *Magnum P.I.*

3. Jeff Kent, Giants. There was a stretch when Kent was the only big leaguer to wear a mustache for about five seasons. But man, he wore it well. Instead of evoking a pornographic image, Kent's mustache is decidedly State Trooper.

2. Billy Martin, A's. Did Jimmy Buffet sing of a cool, calm lifestyle with a pencil-thin mustache? Guess Billy Martin wasn't a fan. His thinly dressed upper lip got in the faces of more umpires, owners and players than maybe any other single streak of hair in sports history.

1. Rollie Fingers, A's. Was there any doubt who'd take the top ranking? When A's owner Charlie Finley offered him $300 to grow the famed handlebars as a promotion, Rollie probably didn't think he'd never shave again. His iconic 'stache is still the standard by which all others will be measured.

What good is a rich winning history if you didn't look good while doing it? Luckily, the Bay Area never had to worry about that, as fans here have rooted for some of the best-looking laundry in sports. On a personal note, just so you know where I'm coming from, the simpler you keep it, the better it looks. My all-time favorite sports uniform is Penn State football's away uniform. In other words, flashy modern uniforms do not score highly with me.

10. Joe DiMaggio's #10, 1933 Seals Jerseys. His legend would grow when he trimmed his number in half and became a legend with the New York Yankees, but his baseball roots trace back to his hometown. One of the originals from the fabled Pacific Coast League, the button-down jersey featured pinstripes and capital letter "S," with the "e-a-l-s" woven into the letter's negative space.

9. Stanford. The Cardinal red-and-white color scheme is one to be envied. It just looks great on the field. From the simple block "S" on the football helmets, to the classic baseball jerseys, Stanford proves how smart it is by not changing what has worked for decades.

8. 1978 Giants Home Jerseys. Like an ugly puppy, they beg for your love with their homeliness, and you give it to them. Not something you'd want every day, but these orange pullover beauties with black and white stripes around the sleeves immediately bring us back to the days when disco set the trends. Black socks, pulled up to the knees, are a must.

7. Athletics Home White-On-Whites. They've rocked the emerald green. They've rocked the yellow pullovers. But the current Athletics have got it right, right now. The crisp-and-clean, head-to-toe, white-on-white uniform with script "Athletics" across the chest is a modern classic.

6. Warriors Blue City Jerseys. With "Warriors" spelled down the leg of the shorts, and the state of California running down the left side of circle on the front, the "Dubs" paid homage to their San Francisco past and incorporated their new "Golden State" classification in fine fashion. Worn from the time they moved to Oakland until the late Eighties. I thought one of the biggest mistakes was moving away from this design scheme for the block letters that defined the Run TMC era.

5. Niners Scarlet and Gold. Again, deep, dark red always looks good on a field, and the 49ers color scheme is one of the NFL's best. Classic helmets, golden pants and the simple all-white letters of the team of the Eighties automatically evoke memories of excellence—or humiliating defeats, depending where you're reading this book. Later, San Francisco would incorporate black highlights and shadows to their numbers and nameplates, but the good old days just can't be improved upon. Hold true in the uniform, and on the field.

4. Gigantes Jersey. *Vamos Gigantes!* Conceived for a Cinco de Mayo promotion, the Gigantes instantly had a hit on their hands—and backs—when they unveiled this *muy caliente* item. The jerseys pay tribute to the strong Latino heritage the team has always enjoyed, and were an instant hit with every fan at the ballpark.

3. Niners All Whites. Again, I got a thing for white-on-white uniforms. It's simple and it says, "We're not here to look cool; we're just here to whoop your ass." And in 1994, that's what the 49ers did. The team ran roughshod over the NFL, wearing white pants instead of the team's signature gold bottoms. Throw in the white tops for the road games, and you've got a look that marked a passage from the Bill Walsh era to George Seifert's reign. The pants worked well for Steve Young that season, as he won the regular season and Super Bowl MVP awards, when he threw a record six TD passes to bury the Chargers.

2. San Francisco Warriors City Jerseys. Designed on a cocktail napkin, the simple circle with the Golden Gate Bridge running across the bottom, and the words "The City" written above, proves that less is more. One of the NBA's all-time classic jerseys, fans can't wait for Hardwood Classic nights, when the yellow tanks get pulled out of mothballs. But if you loved the way they look coming at you, going away is even better. The player's number is displayed on the side of a cable car, with his name below—not above—his number.

1. Raiders Silver and Black. Dating all the way back to the franchise's AFL beginnings, all you need to do is say those colors out loud in any sports bar in America, and people will know who you're talking about. Al Davis doesn't change with the times, and thank God, neither have the intimidating uniforms that embody the Raiders spirit. Known for a colorful roster of world-class athletes, misfits and outright villains, the world wouldn't be the same if the Raiders ever dressed any differently. It's like lining up to play football across from Darth Vader.

Ten Great Quotes About San Francisco

With her views and her hills, San Francisco is a lady who has inspired several memorable quotes.

10. Senator Barbara Boxer. "Those who survived the San Francisco earthquake said, 'Thank God, I'm still alive.' But, of course, those who died, their lives will never be the same again."

9. Hinton R. Helper. "I have seen purer liquors, better segars, finer tobacco, truer guns and pistols, larger dirks and bowie knives, and prettier courtesans here in San Francisco than in any other place I have ever visited; and it is my unbiased opinion that California can and does furnish the best bad things that are available in America."

8. Rudyard Kipling. "San Francisco is a mad city; inhabited for the most part by perfectly insane people whose women are of remarkable beauty."

7. William Saroyan. "San Francisco itself is art, above all literary art. Every block is a short story, every hill a novel."

6. Oscar Wilde. "It is an odd thing, but everyone who disappears is said to be seen at San Francisco. It must be a delightful city, and possess all the attractions of the next world."

5. W.C. Fields. "I was married once—in San Francisco. I haven't seen her for many years. The great earthquake and fire in 1906 destroyed the marriage certificate. There's no legal proof. Which proves that earthquakes aren't all bad."

4. Herb Caen. "Isn't it nice that people who prefer Los Angeles to San Francisco live there?"

3. Will Rogers. "San Francisco . . . the city that never was a town."

2. Ashleigh Brilliant. "There may not be a Heaven, but there is a San Francisco."

1. Mark Twain. "The coldest winter I ever spent was a summer in San Francisco."

The great Willie Mays will always reside in the plaza that bears his name.

WILLIE HOWARD MAYS, JR.

"THE SAY HEY KID"

NEW YORK N.L., SAN FRANCISCO N.L., NEW YORK N.L., 1951-1973

ONE OF BASEBALL'S MOST COLORFUL AND EXCITING STARS. EXCELLED IN
ALL PHASES OF THE GAME. THIRD IN HOMERS (660), RUNS (2,062) AND
TOTAL BASES (6,066); SEVENTH IN HITS (3,283) AND RBI'S (1,903). FIRST IN
PUTOUTS BY OUTFIELDER (7,095). FIRST TO TOP BOTH 300 HOMERS AND 300
STEALS. LED LEAGUE IN BATTING ONCE, SLUGGING FIVE TIMES, HOME
RUNS AND STEALS FOUR SEASONS. VOTED N.L. MVP IN 1954 AND 1965.

PLAYED IN 24 ALL-STAR GAMES - A RECORD

Reproduced from Hall of Fame plaque (Cooperstown, N.Y.)
Inducted in 1979

One plaque says it all.

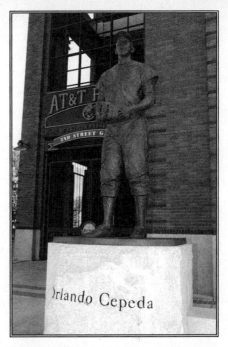

One of the best wind-ups in baseball history, frozen forever in bronze.

"The Baby Bull" has come to the corner of 3rd & King Street.

McCovey Cove provides the perfect backdrop for one of baseball's most respected sluggers.

Sitting on the dock of the bay, behind the park.

Blue sky above, blue water below, no Dodger Blue in site . . . it's going to be a beautiful day.

A gift to baseball fans everywhere . . . forget the name changes, the park is gorgeous.

Bonds launches his official assault on the HR record with #500.

When you haven't won a World Series, you remember things like division titles.

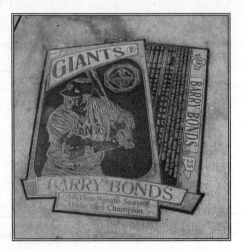

73 homers in 2001 . . . a lifetime of questions since.

Hello Mr. 600.

The parade of individual accomplishments pauses
briefly to mark the Giants' first World Series appearance since 1989.

Hello Mr. 600.

Bonds and Mays, forever linked.

Welcome to the 700 club.

Sing it Giants fans: "Smoke on the water . . . a fire in the sky".

Barry blew past the Babe, and as usual the milestone came at home.

Something tells me Mr. Schmidt will have Mr. Lincecum's company on this walkway soon

Although there were zero splashes on All Star weekend, the park never looked better.

The day Barry became king, 8/7/07.

Memories of Bill Walsh :: by Glenn Dickey

NOTE: Glenn Dickey is one of the deans of sports journalism in San Francisco. He has been writing about Bay Area sports since 1963. Among his 16 books is *Building a Champion*, with Bill Walsh. Glenn is now writing for *The San Francisco Examiner* and on his website, GlennDickey.com. Here are his Walsh memories, in reverse chronological order

10. I first met Walsh when he was named head coach at Stanford in 1977. After the press conference, we went to a coffee shop in the Town & Country shopping center, and he outlined some of his offensive concepts. I thought, "Wow. This guy is way ahead of the curve." From that point on, when Walsh and I were together, I mostly just listened to him—and I got a priceless education in football.

9. When Eddie DeBartolo fired Joe Thomas, he thought of finding a coach and then having him hire a general manager. I pushed for Walsh in my *Chronicle* column. Meanwhile, Stanford broadcaster Ron Barr, who had made friends with DeBartolo, was also pushing Walsh privately. DeBartolo, whose only time in the Bay Area then was at 49er games, told me later he had never heard of Walsh before I started writing about him.

8. Early in the 49ers first championship season, Walsh went on a tirade at his weekly press conference about ABC-TV ignoring the 49ers because they weren't on *Monday Night Football*. I always went up to his office after the press conference so we could talk privately. He told me he understood perfectly why the Niners hadn't been on the show but he thought this would help fire up his team. As always, he was right.

7. Walsh was always concerned about Bubba Paris' weight. One time when we were talking in training camp he said he was perplexed because he had the trainer supervising everything Bubba ate, but he was still gaining weight. Then he got a call from the maid. "What are we going to do with these chicken bones?" she asked. Bubba had been ordering out for KFC and putting the bones in his closet.

6. Late in the 1986 season, during which Joe Montana had had back surgery, Walsh told me that he needed to get a younger quarterback because he didn't think Montana's career would last much longer. He had a specific quarterback in mind: Steve Young. Though Young was struggling at Tampa Bay and most NFL people thought he'd make a better running back, Walsh said he was convinced that Young could be a very good quarterback. So, I wrote that the 49ers would trade for Young and predicted that he'd have a good career.

5. In the spring of 1988, I was playing in a celebrity tennis tournament at Silverado. At a dinner the night before, I was sitting at a table with Walsh and Cal coach Bruce Snyder. They started talking about offense and soon, both had taken out pens and were diagramming plays on the paper tablecloth. Maybe that's why Snyder was able to get Cal to a New Year's Day bowl a couple of years later.

4. In 1990, I was working with Walsh and Guy Benjamin on the book, ***Building a Champion.*** It was frantic. We would sit in Walsh's office and discuss a chapter, I'd write it and then Walsh would stand behind me and go through it line by line, often suggesting a word change. My wife, son and I had nonrefundable airplane tickets for a flight to Paris in June. The manuscript was finished the night before. Benjamin had to take it to the printer while we were in the air.

3. Walsh and I appeared in joint autographing sessions for the book and I learned how fans truly idolized him, but had no such warm feelings for me. Often, they'd approach him with reverence and ask him to autograph the book, and then they'd quickly snatch it away before I had a chance to sully it with my autograph.

2. One of Walsh's pet projects was developing an NFL program to help black assistant coaches get head coaching jobs. When he was back at Stanford as coach again in the early '90s, he held a conference on campus for black assistants, at which Dr. Harry Edwards spoke. Lowell Cohn and I were the only writers invited and, with Walsh, the only white faces. It was a fascinating insight into the thinking of the black coaches, who paid no attention to Lowell and me.

1. My last lengthy meeting with Walsh came in June 2006, when he was the acting athletic director at Stanford. We were slotted for half an hour and his secretary, Jane Walsh (no relation,) kept popping in to remind him of other appointments, but he just waved her off. We talked for an hour and a half, sometimes about current events, sometimes about shared experiences from the past. He was dying of leukemia, though I didn't know it, but he was tying up all the loose ends from his past. I treasure the memory of that meeting, and also the fact that I was privileged to be part of the huge list of his friends.**It's rare that the local football coach is also widely considered an intellectual, but that's exactly what Bill Walsh was: the smartest man in the room. Here are ten memorable quotes from the coach simply known as "The Genius."**

10. On being named Interim Athletic Director at Stanford. "I'm here, I've been here for a year, I'm of course familiar with the university . . . I know a lot of the people. It could be I was needed. It appears, and most people agree, I would be the logical person."

9. On furthering NFL interview standards for minority coaches. "This has turned out to be one of the most beneficial and helpful kinds of programs that any employer could ever have hoped to get in. It's on the leading edge."

8. On Steve Young. "I've always thought Steve could be mayor of San Francisco without too much of a fight. That's just the kind of man he is, and how highly he's regarded in that town. Everybody knows he didn't have an easy job following Joe Montana. The way he did it says all you need to know about him, and then he made quite a career for himself, too."

7. "It's gotten worse and worse, and the coaches and personnel people are more and more willing to take huge men that are grossly overweight, and just hope that size will take care of everything else."

6. "The running game in pro football has gotten so boring. There's just four or five plays they can run. I think the whole thing is headed in the wrong direction, and it's really unfortunate."

5. "You have to reinvent yourself each year . . . What helped us was that there was some turnover each year."

4. "The year we beat Miami in the Super Bowl . . . do you know how many defensive linemen were in our rotation? Nine and we used them all quite a bit. We just wore the Dolphins out."

3. "Joe might have been more active and quicker on his feet."

2. "There's so much to orchestrate."

1. "Nothing is more effective than sincere, accurate praise, and nothing is more lame than a cookie-cutter compliment."

To everything there is a season, turn, turn, turn . . . . In the case of these teams, turn out the lights, the party's over. Some are glorious reminders of days gone by, while others were massive failures.

10. San Francisco Demons. Did anything ever flame out as quickly as the XFL? After a successful first week, attendance and interest dwindled by the first down. In 2001, the Demons were the top-drawing team in the short-lived Vince McMahon creation, averaging 35,000 fans in their game at AT&T Park (at the time, it was called Pac Bell). Led by former Cal and 49ers quarterback Matt Barnes, the Demons went 5-5 and made the playoffs, but quickly evaporated along with the rest of the league.

9. Oakland Invaders. The Bay Area entry in the ambitious USFL was intended to fill void of the just-departed Raiders. Invaders/Raiders. Get it? Initially, they were a smash success, attracting more than 31,000 fans in 1983 and making the playoffs with a 9-9 record and a roster dotted with former Raiders (Ray Chester). However, just like the XFL decades later, the novelty soon wore off and the league folded after two seasons.

8. San Francisco Shamrocks. In the late Seventies, minor league hockey came to the Cow Palace in the form of the Shamrocks, one of a half dozen or so clubs that comprised the Pacific Hockey League. Though the Shamrocks won the league title in 1978, they never sold a single ticket. OK, they sold one, but that was it. The club folded halfway through the 1979 season.

7. Oakland Oaks (PCL). The Oaks and cross-bay rival San Francisco Seals played in the original Bay Bridge series, with a twist. On some Sundays the clubs would play a morning game on one side of the bay and a late afternoon contest on the other. Playing out of old Oaks Park, technically located in Emeryville, the Oaks—or "Acorns" as they were commonly known—were part of the PCL from 1903-55. Casey Stengal led the club to a league pennant in 1948 with a team that featured ex-major league stars Ernie Lombardi and Cookie Lavagetto as well as a young Billy Martin.

6. California Golden Seals. Originally a Western Hockey League franchise, the Seals joined the NHL as an expansion club in 1967 and played their home games at the Oakland Coliseum Arena through 1976. The Seals, who were never particularly successful on the ice or at the box office, had numerous ownership groups which, over time, included the likes of Charlie Finley, Pat Summerall and Whitey Ford. The team relocated to Cleveland prior to the 1977 campaign and would eventually become the Minnesota North Stars, who—in keeping with the theme of this list—no longer exist either.

5. San Francisco Spiders. Will they ever learn? Minor league hockey again tried and failed to make it in San Francisco with the debut of the Spiders of the International Hockey League. They could say "International" legitimately because the league included a couple of Canadian outposts. The Spiders, who did have a good logo, were 40-32, but still finished in last place. The ice melted for good after just one season.

4. San Francisco Golden Gaters. The sheer volume of drugs people took during the Seventies must have made any idea, no matter how outlandish, seem like a good one. That's the only way someone can justify coming up with World Team Tennis. Actually, the five-year run for the team was longer than anyone expected, but eventually the weed wore off and people realized they were watching a tennis team, and stopped.

3. University of San Francisco Football. You wouldn't know it now, but USF was a college football powerhouse, featuring such legends as Ollie Matson, Bob St. Clair and Gino Marchetti. In 1951, the team was undefeated and regarded as best in the nation, but didn't get a bowl invite because the team included black players. Because the school reaped zero bowl revenue, it had to fold the program due to lack of funding after the best season in school history. The legendary 1951 team boasted nine players who went on to NFL careers. Five of them would reach Canton. Football returned "to the Hilltop" as a Division II sport in 1965, but was dropped again, this time forever, in 1971.

2. Oakland Oaks (ABA). Not to be confused with the baseball-playing Oakland Oaks of the PCL, these Oaks were a charter team in the American Basketball League in 1967. Partly owned by goody-two-shoed singer Pat Boone, the Oaks immediately became a thorn in the Warriors side when they managed to convince disgruntled star Rick Barry to temporarily play with the red, white and blue ball. Though Barry would lead the Oaks to an ABA Championship in 1968-69, they were never able to harm the Warriors financially, and would have to leave town, unable to compete with the NBA team next door. Did they really think they could? The Oaks moved to Washington, D.C. the following season and became the Capitals before moving once again to Virginia, where they would rename the team the Squires.

1. San Francisco Seals. Old Schoolers who say things like, "Now you're on the trolley!" still rue the day the Pacific Coast League Seals were disbanded in 1957 to make way for the "big league" Giants. However, as far as the City was concerned, the Seals were big league enough with the notable stars they turned out, including San Francisco's own son Joe DiMaggio. Forget about hitting in 56 straight games with the Yankees, DiMaggio had a 61-game hitting streak as a member of the Seals. But alas, when the Giants arrived in 1958, the Seals disappeared—but not Seals Stadium, which the Giants called home for two seasons before moving to Candlestick in 1960.

Ten Greatest Moments in Bay Area Tennis History
:: by Ted Robinson

NOTE: In a world of sports screamers, the calm, intellectual voice of Ted Robinson is an oasis of professionalism, lost in a desert of loud mouths. The lead announcer of NBC's tennis coverage, Ted is one of the most versatile broadcasters in TV and radio history. Along with nine years broadcasting the Giants, Ted does the Olympics and playoff baseball, and can frequently be found elevating sports conversation on KNBR. Sure, he went to Notre Dame, but not everyone is perfect. Ladies and gentlemen, prepare to be smarter. Here's Ted Robinson: "The Bay Area is a tennis paradise. Courts are full with players young and old. It's a vibrant area of growth in a sport that has a firm foothold in our lifestyle. But it isn't just participatory; television ratings are tremendous and attendance at events both pro and amateur have made the Bay Area a must-stop home for competitive tennis."

10. Suzi Babos, 2006. Babos, a Hungarian native, became the first Cal women's tennis player to win the NCAA singles title. To further the pride, she won the title in the first NCAA Championship held at Stanford.

9. John McEnroe and Jimmy Connors meet at the Cow Palace for the Transamerica Open championship, 1986. McEnroe wins 7-6, 6-3. They would only play three more times in their storied careers.

8. World Team Tennis, 1974. A pioneering attempt to marry American team sports concepts with tennis comes to the Bay Area with the San Francisco Golden Gaters. In that era, virtually every top pro played WTT. The Gaters played for the WTT title in 1975 and 1976.

7. Rosie Casals, 1988. The 39-year-old born in San Francisco wins the last of her 112 double titles, partnering with Martina Navratilova for the Oakland WTA championship.

6. Billie Jean King wins the Virginia Slims event in San Francisco, 1972. She was at the peak of her game, and in the year in which she won all three Grand Slams in which she played.

5. Fourteen-year-old Venus Williams wins her first professional match, 1994. Defeating Shaun Stafford at the Oakland Coliseum.

4. Stanford goes 28-0 and lost only 3 points all year, 1998. Bob and Mike Bryan, Paul Goldstein and Ryan Wolters anchor what is considered the best collegiate men's tennis team in history.

3. Dick Gould retires after a 38-year run as men's tennis coach at Stanford, 2004. His final tally: 17 national titles and 10 individual singles champions.

2. John McEnroe at Stanford, 1977. Having made the Wimbledon semis as a qualifier, he bypasses the pro tour and arrives at Stanford University where the next spring he would win the NCAA singles title.

1. Barry MacKay, a pioneering pro, starts the men's professional tournament that nearly 40 years later lives on in San Jose, 1970.

Mays and McCovey. Montana and Rice. Silver and Black. All are quintessential Bay Area icons. Here's an offering of a few more household or nearly household names whose ties to the Bay Area aren't as obvious.

10. Alice Marbel. As a young girl, she honed her swing on the tennis courts of Golden Gate Park. She would grow up and hold four U.S. Women's singles titles, and split eight more titles evenly as a doubles and mixed doubles partner. In 1939, she captured the Wimbledon singles title along with five more doubles and mixed doubles championships.

9. Vada Pinson. He developed his skills as a student athlete at Oakland's Mc-Clymonds High School. Pinson would flourish in eighteen Major League seasons with the Reds, Cardinals, Indians, Angles and Royals. A two-time All-Star and two-time NL hits leader, Pinson is in the top 75 in several Major League hitting categories.

8. Gino Marchetti. Named the top defensive end of the NFL's first fifty years, the Hall of Fame lineman guided the now defunct University of San Francisco football team to an undefeated season in 1952. Playing the majority of his career for the Baltimore Colts, Marchetti had his number 89 retired by the franchise.

7. Tony Lazzeri. Born in the San Francisco the same year as the great quake (1906) it didn't take any more evidence than a 60 home run season with the Pacific Coast League's Salt Lake City Bees for the Yankees to come calling. He would go on to win five World Series in the Bronx before playing with the Cubs, Dodgers and eventually the New York Giants.

6. Max Baer. Remember when Russell Crowe whooped that guy at the end of *Cinderella Man*? Well, that guy was this guy—Max Bear, who in 1934 knocked down Primo Carnera twelve times on the way to claiming the heavyweight champ. Born in Livermore, an East Bay suburb, Baer was one of the first major American-born sports stars that proudly displayed his Jewish heritage.

5. K.C. Jones. Everyone knows that Bill Russell guided the USF Dons to back-to-back NCAA basketball titles in the Fifties, but did you know that K.C. was on that team, too? Never able to step out of Russell's shadow, (what guy would want to?) Jones and Russell won eight more titles together to cement the Celtics dynasty. Jones attended San Francisco's Commerce High School and would also win gold at the 1956 Olympics.

4. Willie Stargell. Not short for William, Wilver Dornell Stargell would become "Pops" during his 21-year career with the Pittsburgh Pirates. Raised in Oakland, where he went to Encinal High School, Stargell won two world titles to go along with seven All-Star selections with an MVP and World Series MVP in 1979.

3. "Gentleman" Jim Corbett. Owner of one of the great nicknames in boxing history, the city-born native would win the heavyweight title after a 21-round bout with John L. Sullivan in 1892. A member of the famous San Francisco Olympic Club—which meant he was a gentleman indeed—Corbett was the first national champion of any kind born west of the Mississippi River.

2. Dan Fouts. A two-time NFL MVP, Fouts began his mastery of the passing attack as an All-City quarterback at St. Ignatius High School before heading to Oregon, where he would shatter school and Pac 10 records. Spending fifteen season with the San Diego Chargers, Fouts would be named to six Pro Bowls, lead the league in passing four times and set a new NFL record for passing yards in a single season.

1. Frank Robinson. Another product of Oakland's McClymonds High School, Robinson became the first player to win MVP honors in both the American and National Leagues. One of the game's most prolific sluggers—and often overlooked—Robinson, best known as a member of the Reds and Orioles, played in five World Series, winning two. One of the game's all-time, underrated icons, Robinson won the AL Triple Crown in 1966, and became the first African-American manager in baseball history.

Ten Greatest Athletes to Attend Stanford University

More than just a collection of big brains, Stanford has a long tradition of excelling in student athletics. Ninety-five NCAA titles give the Cardinal the second most won by any university. Since 1980, Stanford has won more team and individual NCAA titles than any other school in America. Further, Stanford has been represented in every Olympics since 1908. Here are the ten best who ever called Palo Alto their home.

10. Candice Wiggins, Basketball. Named the best female collegiate basketball player in 2008, she scored more points than any other woman in Pac 10 history.

9. John Lynch, Football and Baseball. A starter in two sports who got drafted by the Florida Marlins, the hard hitting safety made the right choice when he decided to hand out big hits for a living. Lynch, regarded as one of the NFL's most ferocious tacklers has been selected to nine Pro Bowls.

8. John McEnroe, Tennis. After a strong showing at Wimbledon, an eighteen-year-old McEnroe decided to go to Stanford instead of turning pro. He won the 1978 NCAA singles title, and led the tennis team to a national championship. He would win the first of seven career Grand Slam titles at the 1981 U.S. Open.

7. Darrin Nelson, Football. The former All-American and four-time all-conference running back became the first player in NCAA history to rush for over 1,000 yards with fifty receptions, which he would do in three of four seasons on "The Farm." Nelson went on to an eleven-year NFL career, and now works in the Stanford Athletic Department.

6. Ernie Nevers, Football. The NFL Hall of Famer ran for more yards than Notre Dame's famous Four Horsemen in the 1925 Rose Bowl, in which he played the entire sixty minutes. Nevers is regarded as one of the greatest players in the history of NCAA football.

5. Tim Azevedo, Water Polo. The kid from Southern Cal came to Palo Alto to study International Relations, and became the Michael Jordan of water polo. Azevedo won national player-of-the-year honors as a freshman and again as a sophomore and a junior, before being named the youngest player on the 2000 Olympic team. He is considered the best American-born water polo player ever.

4. John Elway, Football and Baseball. A standout on the baseball diamond as well, Elway would become one of the most prolific passers in football history, although he was never able to lead the Cardinal to a bowl game. His final game in a Stanford uniform culminated in "The Play" where any dreams of beating Cal in the big game went running through the Stanford Band.

3. Jim Plunkett, Football. The man who ushered in the pass-happy attacks we're now used to in the Pac 10, Plunkett rewrote record books in Palo Alto before going on to NFL fame. In 1971, he led the Cardinal to the Rose Bowl, where they upset Ohio State 27-17.

2. Hank Luisetti, Basketball. One of basketball's most innovative players ever, Luisetti is credited with the advent of the running one-handed shot. He finished second to the legendary George Mikan in a polling of the greatest players from 1900-1950. At Stanford, he became the first player in NCAA history to score fifty points in a game on January 1, 1938. The school record still stands—an astonishing achievement considering most teams didn't get to fifty points in those days.

1. Eldrick "Tiger" Woods, Golf. With fourteen Major titles to his name, Tiger Woods has already established himself as the most dominant golfer ever. It's only a matter of time before he has enough trophies to make the declaration official. At the age of 20, Tiger became the first golfer to win three consecutive Amateur titles and the NCAA individual golf championship. Doubt there are any regrets about leaving "The Farm" after just two years to join the PGA Tour.

Tucked away in the Berkeley Hills, the University of California is a beautiful place that has long marched to its own drummer; it was the site of radical student protests in the Sixties. The student athletes on this list used their physical prowess to call attention to their causes. Here are the ten best athletes to wear the blue and gold.

10. Natalie Coughlin, Swimming. From Concord, California, this little woman left a big impression in the Berkley pool, and then took the entire world by storm. Decorated with numerous NCAA awards, Coughlin won five medals in the Athens Olympics—two gold, two silvers and a bronze.

9. Shareef Abdur-Rahim, Basketball. He was the first freshman in the history of the Pac 10 to be named Conference Player of the Year, averaging 21 points and 8 rebounds. But after setting four school freshman records, Shareef was off to the NBA, where he was the third pick overall in the 1996 Draft. Currently with his fourth NBA franchise, Abdur-Rahim's minutes and career are nearing an end. He'll be remembered as a good-not-great pro who helped the U.S. take the gold medal at the 2000 Sydney Olympics.

8. Tony Gonzalez, Football and Basketball. This communications major had no trouble translating his athletic gifts on two fields of play. Along with being an All-American Tight End, Gonzalez was a better-than-average D-1 power forward on Cal's Sweet Sixteen team. A nine-time Pro-Bowler with the Kansas City Chiefs, Gonzalez owns the NFL records for most touchdowns and most receptions as a TE. However, he may have saved his biggest play for Fourth of July weekend, 2008, when he saved a choking man with the Heimlich maneuver.

7. Michelle Granger, Softball. An Olympian power pitcher, she threw in the low Seventies—the baseball equivalent of 110 MPH. In her storied career, Granger recorded 1,640 strikeouts and 94 shutouts—both are NCAA records. She threw 25 no-hitters, with five perfect games. A goddess in her sport, Granger would rank higher on this list if her teams had been more successful. Michelle's teams never won a conference title or finished higher than fifth in the College World Series.

6. Steve Bartkowski, Football. After splitting time with Vince Ferragamo, Bartkowski became a consensus All-American in 1974, leading the nation with 2,580 passing yards. The next year, he became the first and only Golden Bear to be drafted #1 overall by the Atlanta Falcons.

5. Kevin Johnson, Basketball. When K-J graduated, he left Berkeley as the school's all-time leader in assists, steals and scoring. Although some of his records have fallen, his number (11) will never come down from the rafters at Haas Pavilion. Johnson was the first player in Pac 10 history to record a triple double, and was named first-team all-conference twice. After being picked seventh overall in the NBA draft, he'd help lead the Phoenix Suns all the way to the NBA finals, before falling to Jordan's Bulls. A major player in the history of West Coast basketball at the high school, college and professional levels, Kevin Johnson is looking to make a bigger impact—he's running for Mayor of Sacramento.

4. Jackie Jensen, Baseball and Football. Born in San Francisco, Jensen would become an All American in both sports. As a pitcher and outfielder, he helped Cal win the inaugural College World Series in 1947. The next season he became the first Cal running back to gain 1,000 yards in a single season. After leaving school, he decided on a baseball career, and was named the American League MVP in 1958 with the Red Sox. He is the first athlete to ever play in the Rose Bowl and a World Series.

3. Harold "Brick" Mueller, Football. Known for having freakishly large hands—which allowed him to throw the larger football used in the 1920s—he quarterbacked the team that put the West Coast on the national football radar, although radar had yet to be invented. A two-way player on Cal's historic 1921 squad, Mueller's team outscored the competition 424-14 on the way to a 10-0 season, including a 28-0 victory over Ohio State in the Rose Bowl. His legend is one of the pillars upon which the program has been built.

2. Joe Capp, Football. With enough pure talent to play all 22 positions on the field, Capp would become a football icon in Berkeley. After a 1-9 season in 1957, Cap turned the Golden Bears misery into a Pacific Coast Conference title—leading the league in rushing as a QB—and a Rose Bowl berth the next year. The first team All-American proved his worth as a pro in the Canadian Football League before taking the Vikings to the Super Bowl. Capp famously refused to be named the team's MVP because he didn't believe in individual awards. Capp the player would become Coach Capp at Cal, but his teams never enjoyed much success. However, they did manage to send him off the field as a winner in his final game on the sidelines with a little something known as "The Play."

1. Jason Kidd, Basketball. He's ranked #1 on the list because he's likely the most identifiable Cal Alum. After breaking the NCAA steals-by-a-freshman record, and setting the school's assists record, Kidd was named All-Pac 10 in his first season. His team reached the Sweet Sixteen that season after an upset of two-time defending champion Duke. The next season, he broke his own assists record and was named Pac 10 Player of the Year and First Team All-American, becoming the first basketball player from Cal to win the award since 1968. After just two seasons in Berkley, he left for the NBA, where he was named Co-Rookie of the Year, establishing himself as one of the game's elite point guards. He would win gold with the Olympic team in 2000, and was tapped to represent the United States again in 2008. A triple-double machine, Kidd is now winding his days down with the Mavericks, and will be making his way to Springfield for enshrinement in the Basketball Hall of Fame when it's all over.

Sports fans fall in love with stadiums, arenas and parks even when they're dumps. No current Bay Area team calls the Cow Palace home, but several franchises have leaned on this ugly, lovable, local legend. The old building just south of San Francisco's city limits has seen more than 50 million people pass through its doors, but finds itself on the endangered species list. Officials are considering razing the arena, built in 1951, to make room for condos. Too bad. Just look at the historic events that have passed through its doors.

10. Gate to the Pacific Theater. Two weeks after the doors at the Cow Palace swung open, the Japanese attacked Pearl Harbor. All events were put on hold, and the building served as a staging area for troops headed to fight World War II until the job was done.

9. Concerts Galore. The list of bands and artists who have come through the Cow Palace reads like the roster of the Rock and Roll Hall of Fame. The Stones, Beatles, Dead, Doors, The Who, U2, Pink Floyd, Elvis and, of course, Journey have all rocked the Cow!

8. Home of the San Jose Sharks (1991-93). Can hockey work in the Bay Area? It had failed before with the short-lived Oakland Seals, and looked to get off to a rocky start after the Sharks made their NHL debut, following it with a record 71 losses in 1992-93. But after that season, the team left for their new arena in San Jose, where they were embraced as the "only game in town" for the rapidly expanding South Bay population. Now a clear expansion success, the Sharks are thriving, despite their humble beginnings at the Cow Palace.

7. 1956 and 1964 Republican Conventions. They "liked Ike" in 1956 and he rode his Cow Palace nomination all the way back to the White House. For Barry Goldwater in 1964, things didn't go so well; the senator from Arizona was nominated, but didn't get elected President. However, the irony of the "conservative movement" being born in liberal San Francisco is just too precious not to be mentioned.

6. Home of the Bay Area Bombers. It's big women on roller skates, and it's coming to you from the Cow Palace! If you ever caught it on TV, chances are the derby you watched took place in San Francisco. If the Bay Area Bombers were the Yankees of the Roller Derby circuit, Ann Calvello was Derek Jeter. A graduate of San Francisco's Presentation High School, her career spanned seven decades. She actually made this wacky sideshow a niche thing to do for the city's hip crowd for a short time in the Seventies.

5. Home of the San Francisco Warriors (1962-62; 1966-71). When the team moved to the West Coast from Philly, the Warriors landed at the Cow Palace. In the 1967-68 season, the Warriors led by Rick Barry went to the NBA finals and lost to the team that replaced them in Philadelphia, the 76ers. After 1970-71, the Warriors moved to Oakland and adopted their "Golden State" moniker, but returned to the Cow Palace due to a scheduling conflict with the new Oakland Arena . . . to sweep the Bullets in the finals.

4. Exotic Erotic Ball. For the last three decades, San Francisco has been unleashing its kinky side at the annual event billed as the "world's sexiest party." I think this is why liquid hand sanitizer was invented. Anyway, shave your balls and come on down to the Cow Palace! Get your lady those leather boots she has always wanted, 'cause you'll blend in fine during the annual October fetish-fest.

3. 1960 Final Four. When the University of California, coached by Pete Newell, reached the Final Four, it only had to travel across San Francisco Bay to get to the Cow Palace. However, waiting for Cal on the visitor's bench was Jerry Lucas and the Ohio State Buckeyes. OSU won the game 75-55. Lucas was named Most Outstanding Player, while Cal had to settle for runner-up and a short ride back to Berkley.

2. Grand National Rodeo. For over 60 years, the Cow Palace, complete with its built-in stables and staging areas, has been the home of the Grand National Rodeo. Cowboys and cowgirls have been hanging on for their dear lives in the event that has always made the posh Bay Area its home, not some dusty field in Texas.

1. 1967 NBA All-Star Game. Jerry Lucas returned to the Cow Palace as a member of the 1967 Eastern Conference All Stars, one of the greatest collections of basketball talent ever. Along with Lucas, the East featured Wilt Chamberlain, Hal Greer, Oscar Robertson, Bill Russell, Willis Reed and John Havlicek—seven of the NBA's Fifty Greatest Players. The Western Conference team was completely outmatched on paper, despite dressing: Rick Barry, Elgin Baylor, Jerry West, Nate Thurmond, Darrall Imhoff, Lenny Wilkins, Dave BeBusschere and Jerry Sloan. When it had ended, youth was served, and one of the biggest All-Star Game upsets had occurred. West beat the East 135–120. Just to prove the game isn't what it used to be, Red Auerbach was ejected that night. Do you know what the chances of a coach being tossed from an All-Star game today? Zero.

Greatest Quotes in Bay Area Sports History

In a time when a ten-second sound bite can come back to haunt an athlete for days, weeks or an entire career, I understand why there is less and less reason to open up to the media. But on a rare occasion when athletes or coaches bare their inner souls, it can be insightful, funny or just plain moronic.

10. Jeff Kent. "Enjoy the Game."

9. John Madden. "The road to Easy Street goes through the sewer."

8. Bill Walsh. "We have a lot of players in their first year. Some of them are also in their last year."

7. Barry Bonds. "They're not trading me . . . I'm staying."

6. Jerry Rice. "I feel like I'm the best, but you're not going to get me to say that."

5. Joe Montana. "In sports . . . you play from the time you're eight years old, and then you're done forever."

4. Barry Bonds. "This record is not tainted at all, at all. Period. You guys can say whatever you want."

3. Al Davis. "Once a Raider, always a Raider."

2. Willie Mays. "It isn't hard to be good from time to time in sports. What is tough is being good every day."

1. Rickey Henderson. "Rickey don't like it when Rickey's limo is late to pick up Rickey." OK, this may be more local legend than fact, but this quote can usually be overheard while someone is standing waiting for the next train on the Coliseum BART platform. Knowing what we know about Rickey, and what Rickey has always said about Rickey, we'll just assume it's fact.

Sometimes the biggest stars come from funny places. Here's a list of guys who no one thought would reach the big time—no one except the Bay Area teams that drafted or signed these players.

10. Joe Montana. Despite his Notre Dame pedigree, Montana dropped to the third round of the 1979 draft, where the 49ers nabbed him with the 82nd overall pick. Two seasons later he was fitted with his first of four Super Bowl Rings. Known for his mental focus and football I.Q. as much as his physical tool set, Montana manufactured countless 49ers drives, always staying cool under pressure.

9. Bob Brenly. An undated free agent out of Ohio University, he spent five-and-a-half seasons in the minors before he got a sniff. His hard work paid off. Brenley was the Giants' starting catcher for five seasons and was named to the All-Star squad in 1984.

8. Terrell Owens. The 49ers' draft luck continued when they snagged Owens in the third round, 89th pick overall out of Tennessee-Chattanooga in 1996 draft. He was initially a soft-spoken, physically dominating pass grabber. It took a few seasons before his megalomaniac tendencies showed through, and "T.O." was unleashed upon an unsuspecting public—and the Eagles.

7. Jim Plunkett. After getting cut by the 49ers in 1978, Plunkett rode the bench for two seasons in Oakland before finally getting another shot and writing one of sports' most remarkable comeback stories. The 33-year-old former Heisman winner from Stanford led the 1980 wild card Raiders to a shocking Super Bowl championship, winning MVP honors after throwing for three scores in the big game. Three seasons later he did it again in Super Bowl XVIII.

6. Charles Haley. Selected by San Francisco in the fourth round of the 1986 draft out of James Madison, the volatile Haley was an intimidating pass rusher on the 49ers back-to-back Super Bowl championship clubs of 1988-89. After getting kicked off the Niners in part for peeing on George Seifert's car, Haley went on to three more Super Bowl titles with Dallas. Finished with 100.5 career sacks.

5. John Taylor. Although he scored 42 touchdowns at Delaware State, the 49ers managed to snag Taylor in the third round of the 1986 draft. He was deployed perfectly by Bill Walsh as both a fabulous secondary receiver and as a punt return specialist, using his blazing speed to eat up yardage after catching the ball. Of course, San Francisco might have been shy one of their five Super Bowl titles if Taylor hadn't grabbed Joe Montana's 10-yard TD pass on the winning drive in waning moments of Super Bowl XXIII.

4. Kenny Stabler. Stabler wasn't the first quarterback taken in the 1968 NFL draft. He wasn't even the first quarterback the Raiders selected. Al Davis took Eldridge Dickey in the first round before taking the Snake in the second round with the 52nd overall pick. By the early Seventies, Stabler had become a Silver and Black icon, leading the Raiders to numerous come-from-behind victories and a victory in Super Bowl XI.

3. Jeff Garcia. Garcia was stranded in the Canadian Football League when Walsh pulled him from obscurity in 1999. He would make three Pro Bowl squads and set the 49ers all-time single season passing yardage record in 2000—no minor accomplishment considering his predecessors. A decision to run Garcia out of town left the team without a top-notch quarterback since his departure.

2. Lester Hayes. He joined the Raiders as a fifth-round pick in 1977, and exited the NFL nine seasons later as one of the league's all-time greatest corner backs, recording 39 career interceptions. The stickum enthusiast was named 1980 NFL Defensive Player of the Year. After beating a debilitating stuttering problem, Hayes became a quote machine, labeling himself the "only true Jedi" in the NFL prior to Super Bowl XVIII.

1. Dwight Clark. Bill Walsh was scouting a Clemson teammate—quarterback Steve Fuller—when Clark caught his eye. Ten rounds into the 1979 NFL draft, there he was, and the 49ers took him. Great "catch." Clark would nab 506 passes and 48 touchdowns during his career, including the most famous sports moment in Bay Area sports history, in the 1982 NFC Championship game.

A beautiful city, tradition-rich teams, fans who care but who won't ride you into the ground if you struggle. . . . Life for a professional athlete can be pretty good out here. But it doesn't always work out. Sometimes it's a wrong fit. For these guys, it was obvious this just wasn't where they wanted to be.

10. Warren Sapp. To have a Hall-of-Fame caliber career, you have to love what you do. Sapp loved playing football until he decided to do it for the dysfunctional Oakland Raiders. With at least a season or two of solid, well-paid football left in him, Sapp decided to retire rather than continue to deal with the Silver and Black.

9. Tom Gugliotta. Looking to capitalize on the Chris Webber debacle, the Washington Bullets traded Tom Gugliotta to the Warriors for the NBA's Rookie of the Year, after Don Nelson and Webber decided they couldn't be in the same gym together. "Googs" didn't like playing for Nelson or in Oakland either, and was gone after just one season with the Warriors after averaging only ten points per game.

8. Dan Pastorini. After proving himself a dependable quarterback with the Houston Oilers, Dan Pastorini found himself back in the Bay Area—he had played college ball at Santa Clara, which no longer even has a football team—playing for the Raiders. Five weeks into the 1980 season, Pastorini broke his leg. Jim Plunkett assumed the starting role, and led the Raiders to a win over the Eagles in the Super Bowl. Needless to say, the writing was on the wall for Pastorini, who was an L.A. Ram the next season.

7. Tracy Jones. Tracy Jones and Cincinnati just go together; Tracy Jones and San Francisco did not. Now a Queen City sports broadcaster, he wasn't happy anywhere else but there. After being shipped to the Expos, Jones came to San Francisco for one forgettable season when he played in just 40 games before leaving the Giants and the California coastline behind him.

6. Rony Seikaly. In 1994, the Miami Heat traded Seikaly to the Warriors, and wouldn't you know it, yet another slow, white center didn't work out. He averaged twelve points and seven rebounds in his two, injury-shortened seasons before being traded to Orlando, where he averaged 17 points and nine rebounds in the very next season. Thanks for trying, Ron.

5. Bobby Murcer. Murcer enjoyed being a Giant, but not as much as he enjoyed being a Yankee. The man who wanted to be the next Mickey Mantle came to the San Francisco in 1975 after eight seasons in New York. He had good numbers but never felt right, far away from the Big Apple. After 1976, he was traded to the Cubs before winding down his career with his beloved Yankees. At one time, Murcer was the highest paid player in Giants franchise history when he signed for $175,000 in 1976.

4. A.J. Pierzynski. When you knee your own team trainer in the nuts in the first week of Spring Training, you're not going to be around too long. Well, that's what A.J. did after being traded to the Giants in 1993. He didn't endear himself to the fans, either, by becoming a human double play. Not only did Pierzynski want out, the team felt the same way and didn't put up a fight when he left for a free agent deal with the White Sox, where he helped them win the World Series in his first season.

3. Terrell Owens. Doing my best T.O.: "Trade the quarterback! No, trade me. No, don't. Wait. Yes, trade me. The quarterback may be gay. Trade him. No, trade me! Baltimore? Hell no. You don't have the rights. My agent screwed up the paperwork. T.O. don't want to be a Raven. Don't trade me. Wait, trade me to Philly." And then he became the Eagles problem.

2. Baron Davis. He loves the Bay Area, but not as much as the prospect of being a L.A. Clipper. Enjoy Hollywood, Benedict Dizzle. After letting it be known he was not opting out after three-plus career- and franchise-changing seasons with the Warriors, Davis walked away from $17.8 million for a long-term deal with the fucking Clippers. A good business decision for Baron, but a complete 180-degree change in his position—post draft day, no less—leaving Golden State wondering if it would have drafted a guard instead of two forwards if they had known.

1. Randy Moss. The biggest dog in the history of Bay Area sports, Moss mailed in his time in Oakland so shamelessly, he can never be considered among great NFL players. Vikings fans know of what I speak. Patriots fans, pipe down, you'll eventually find out. I don't care how many records he breaks or how many Super Bowls he wins (career total still stands at zero) his time with the Raiders was pathetic, and properly defines his career. After battling injuries in his first season, Moss mailed in more than just a couple of routes; he personally addressed and stamped an envelope with a big middle finger for Raiders fans in year two. The fact he went from "not trying" to All-Pro after being traded to the Patriots shows what a true front runner he really is, and how bad the Raiders really were.

Every story needs a villain, and these players and coaches played the part perfectly. Watching the home team win wasn't enough for Bay Area fans, who took extra pleasure in the failures and shortcomings of the following gentlemen.

10. Mike Piazza. Not only was he the hated Dodgers' best player for a number of years, he was also somehow related to Tommy Lasorda . . . a fourth cousin? Case closed. He's evil, and will probably end up in the Hall of Fame someday. Giants fans thought it was a blessing when he was traded away from Los Angles.

9. Ozzie Smith. Viewed by many Giants fans as a cowardly punk because of a flurry of cheap shots, the Wizard of Oz could drop the "lovable" moniker when he got to Candlestick. In 1988, Will Clark began mixing it up with Cardinals second baseman Jose Oquendo. Out of nowhere, Smith ran in and peppered Will with blind cheap shots to the noggin. Smith, famous for his pre-game back flips, was the recipient of many a flipped bird from the hands of Giants fans.

8. Armando Benitez. Unlike the rest of the players on this list, 'Mondo became public enemy number one while he was a Giant. Blowing save after save when he wasn't injured, Armando kept cashing big paychecks while his skills on the mound shrank as quickly as his ERA, and his waistline expanded. In his third and final season in San Francisco, it got to the point where Benitez was balking in runs and saying, "I did my job" after a blown save against the Nationals. Giants ate millions on the contract and traded him back to Florida after bowing to overwhelming hatred from season ticket holders.

7. Reggie Smith. The muscular Dodgers right fielder was not shy about his dislike for the Giants, and Giants fans weren't shy about their feeling for him. It all came to a head at Candlestick in 1981. Smith ventured into the stands to dole out punishment with his fists on a drunk who had thrown a souvenir batting helmet at him.

6. Mike Marshall. The fact Marshall once famously dated Go-Gos lead singer Belinda Carlisle didn't help the heckling he took from Giants fans. In 1988, he'd had enough. After clubbing a home run and rounding the bases, Marshall stood at home plate and screamed obscenities at the Giants dugout, and in particular at the lovable skipper Roger Craig. Hey, Mike's got the beat!

5. Jason Giambi. A's fans took it as a personal affront when the much-loved Giambi traded his scraggily hair and rock and roll persona, for Yankees pinstripes and the corporate image that comes with the uniform. He's booed out of the Coliseum whenever he's back in Oakland. When Giambi became ensnarled in a steroids scandal, A's fans took delight in the fact they benefited from his choice, and didn't have to deal with the disgrace that Giambi is trying to shake off to this day. And now to the final four—all Dodgers, of course:

4. Steve Garvey. This guy was just soooo Dodger-like it was sick. The crisp uni-form, the lantern jaw, pearly white smile, hair that looked like it was painted on, the Popeye forearms. Garvey was just too easy to hate. He represented everything Gi-ants fans hated about the Los Angeles Dodgers. Involved in dozens of dramatic mo-ments in the best baseball rivalry on the West Coast, Garvey is forever enshrined in the darkest spot in the hearts of Giants fans.

3. Jeff Kent. After a half-dozen Hall-of-Fame worthy seasons with San Francisco, Giants fans began turning on Kent in 2002 when he fell off his motorcycle and lied about how he had injured himself. Fast forward into the season, and there's Kent and Barry Bonds in a dugout altercation during a game. Kent left for Houston but eventu-ally ended up in L.A., erasing all he had done, including an MVP season, in the minds Giants fans. He's easily the most despised visiting player in the history of AT&T Park.

2. Don Drysdale. This Dodgers power pitcher (see antichrist, here in S.F.). was the Giants headhunter. Drysdale made no attempt to make anyone believe otherwise. He'd say he was going to drill anyone wearing black and orange, and then go do it. In 1968, Giants fans got really pissed off when they thought a run had plated to end a long, Drysdale scoreless-innings streak when Dick Dietz was hit by a pitch with the bases loaded. Not so fast, the umpire said. Dietz never tried to get out of the way of the pitch. Most Giants will tell you, there was no getting out of the way of Drysdale's bullets.

1. Tommy Lasorda. If there is a Hell, Tommy Lasorda will be there to greet sinful Giants fans as they enter. Let it be known from coast to coast, Tommy Lasorda and his Dodger-blue bullshit are not welcome in San Francisco. Lasorda was Hollywood, pompous, fat and, to make matters worse, a baseball genius. When "Tommy Spaghetti" took over the Dodgers in 1977, he single-handedly rekindled the rivalry by building his club into an annual contender, while the Giants dwelled in mediocrity. A prototype for the "guy you love to hate," Lasorda is now retired, but delights in tweak-ing Giants fans late into his years, still billowing his Dodgers propaganda. No one in San Francisco would ever admit it, but they miss the man they rooted against for all those years. He was great for the Dodgers, and without him, the greatest baseball ri-valry on the West Coast wouldn't be the same.

After enduring seasons in the cold and wind at Candlestick Park, the Giants moved into their plush downtown digs just in time for the 2000 season. Originally called Pacific Bell Park, it then changed to SBC. The name was finally settled when the damn phone company stopped changing its name. Sure, the name still stinks, but it's a reality of our new corporate-sponsored world. Perfect in design, the park only lacked memories, which the Giants wasted no time providing.

10. Opening Day. Although the Giants had played a couple exhibition games, the "House that Barry Built" was officially unveiled to rave reviews on April 11, 2000. Fans were awestruck by the picturesque park's unique features, and by then Dodgers second baseman, Kevin Elster, who hit three home runs and ruined a perfect day with a Dodgers win. As a matter of fact, the Dodgers swept the Giants, who lost the first seven regular season games played in their new home.

9. Bonds Gets #500 Wet. With McCovey Cove inviting sluggers to swing for the water beyond the right field wall, Giants fans, players and visiting teams quickly realized was how hard it was to record a "Splash Hit." Of course, Bonds made it look easy. On April 17, 2001, Bonds delivered on the park's watery promise by hitting his 500th career homerun into McCovey Cove. To make it even better, it was a two-run shot in the eighth inning, powering the Giants to a 3-2 win over the Dodgers.

8. J.T.'s Pinch-Hit Homer. Making his first appearance on this list, J.T. Snow may have unleashed the loudest roar in AT&T Park history when he tied Game Two of the NLDS on October 5, 2000. After Bonds drew a walk and Jeff Kent singled, J.T. Snow came to the plate with one out in the ninth inning, and sent a three-run, pinch-hit homer down the right field line into the arcade, off Mets closer—and future Giants mistake—Armando Benitez. New York would win the game in extra innings, but because of Snow's clout, San Francisco had its first downtown, October memory.

7. Home Runs number 71, 72, and, 73. If watching Mark McGwire become baseball's single-season homerun leader inspired Barry to turn to BALCO, he didn't waste much time putting Big Mac back in the natural pecking order of greatness. According to Barry, that place is behind him in the record books. Bonds made a mockery of the new HR plateau with three dingers in his final two games of the season, which would see him break five major league records and be named MVP. To make it even sweeter for Giants fans, the three shots were against Dodgers pitching the weekend of October 5-7, 2001. Chan Ho Park served up two on Friday, with Dennis Springer coughing up number 73 on the final day of the season.

6. Jason Schmidt K's Sixteen. There was 101 years of Giants baseball in between sixteen strike performances. The first was by Hall of Famer Christy Mathewson, who recorded sixteen strikeouts all the way back in 1904. Fast-forward to June 6, 2006. There stood Giants ace Jason Schmidt, striking out the heart of the Marlins lineup in the ninth inning to finish off his franchise-record-tying masterpiece.

5. #660. April 12, 2004. Barry Bonds had a knack for hitting milestone homeruns in San Francisco, and proved it time and time again with 500, 600, and 700 all coming at AT&T Park, or whatever it was called at the time. But for Giants fans, his 660th shot is their warmest memory, because it offers a rare, pure moment in Bonds' epic home run chase. It's the homer that tied him with his Godfather Willie Mays for third place on the All-Time homer list. The two embraced at home plate, and despite the fact the world was watching, had an honest family moment that not even Barry's harshest critics could condemn.

4. 78th All-Star Game. The Midsummer Classic washed upon the shores of Mc-Covey Cove for the first time on July 10, 2007, and it was a beauty. A pre-game ceremony for Willie Mays was a touching tribute. But fans really remember it because, of all things, a baseball game broke out in the final frame. The NL scored three times with two outs in the ninth inning, before finally falling to the American League by one run. Ichrio Suzuki was named MVP, and recorded the first inside-the-park HR in All-Star Game history.

3. Game Five of the 2002 NLCS. October 14, 2002. For the first time since 1989, the Giants punched their ticket to the World Series with a 2-1 win over the Cardinals. After Barry Bonds tied the game with sac-fly in the eighth, San Francisco loaded the bases in the bottom of the ninth. Journeyman Kenny Lofton singled to right-center field, scoring David Bell from third, giving the Giants the NL Pennant, and fans a chance to dream about being a world champion.

2. J.T. Snow rescues Darren Baker. One of the most beloved players in team history saved his best "golden-glove play" for a scoop at home plate, to keep manager Dusty Baker's three-year-old son out of harm's way. Darren was the team's batboy that evening, and was in the wrong place at wrong time—Game Five of the 2002 World Series. As J.T. scored, he pulled the toddler off the plate, avoiding a near disaster as David Bell charged in behind him to beat the throw home. San Francisco routed the Angels 16-4, and the park rocked while the Giants took a three-games-to-two World Series lead. Six career Gold Gloves, and it's still the play that J.T. gets asked about the most.

1. Bonds Passes Henry Aaron. August 7, 2007. Years of accusations, thousands of whispers, hundreds of pissed off pitchers, gobs of critics . . . all rendered silent for just a moment, a moment that belongs to Bonds and San Francisco forever. Was 756 worth it? Only time will tell, but for one moment, Bonds became the only man on the planet who mattered. The home run throne was his after Bonds deposited a pitch from Washington Nationals lefty Mike Bacsik 435 feet away into the centerfield bleachers. Someday the Giants will win the World Series, and that day will be very special, but not as historically significant as the most memorable moment in AT&T Park history.

Someone call a sleep specialist because counting sheep won't help quiet the thoughts that keep Bay Area sports fans up at night.

10. Where have all the icons gone? With Barry out of the picture, with the 49ers' and Raiders' glory days in the rearview mirror, with the A's turning their team over like restaurant tables. . . . Who is going to be the next face of the city? Patrick Willis, it could be on you.

9. Is JaMarcus Russell really 300 pounds? Forget the "tuck rule;" can JaMarcus tuck it in? Oakland has pinned its hopes to return to NFL respectability on the big—sometimes very big—quarterback from LSU. His future in the pocket may depend on the size of his pants, printed on his back pocket.

8. Can the Sharks win the Stanley Cup? San Jose has finished first or second in their division in six of the last seven seasons. Still, Lord Stanley eludes them. In fact, the Sharks, despite being one of the NHL's most successful regular season teams over the last decade, have never even advanced out of the Western Conference Finals.

7. What if Mike Montgomery had waited? After eighteen amazing seasons at Stanford, Monty left for the Warriors and the NBA dollars. That's all he got after two terrible seasons. Fast forward to April 4, 2008, and he's being introduced as the new basketball coach at Stanford's archrival, Cal. Not even a week later, Trent Johnson left Stanford. What if Monty hadn't jumped? Second thoughts? He says no. He's lying.

6. Is Alex Smith a bust? 49ers fans should have their answer by the end of 2008. The number-one overall pick of 2005, he signed for big bucks but hasn't produced big numbers. The doubts are out on Smith, who has thrown only 19 touchdowns against 31 interceptions in three disappointing seasons.

5. The Fremont A's? Despite winning season after season with gobs of young talent, the A's couldn't draw ants to a picnic. Al Davis ruined the Coliseum, and going to a game in Oakland is like attending a small family gathering. Enter plans for a new stadium. But wait. That's not Oakland; it's Fremont. Yup, could happen if owner Lew Wolf gets to realize the thoughts that keep him up at night.

4. Will Bonds get a statue? He's the greatest player in franchise history. Now move along, there's nothing to see here. Mays, McCovey and Marichal have theirs, but will the controversial Home Run King be immortalized in bronze . . . or behind bars? It will be very interesting to see if the Giants try to put some distance between themselves and Mr. Bonds.

3. What if there's an earthquake at a Cal game? The most serious question, and the only on one on the list that's life threatening. The University of California's Memorial Stadium sits in Strawberry Canyon, tucked away in the Berkeley hills. It's defiantly one of the most beautiful venues in college football. Opened in 1923, the historical bowl was unfortunately built on top of the Hayward Fault, which runs almost directly from goal post to goal post. While there's never a good time for an earthquake, a major seismic event would be especially catastrophic on game day.

2. Would the 49ers move to Los Angeles? Speaking of stadiums, San Francisco has a problem of its own. Candlestick is a dump, the worst stadium in the NFL. With San Francisco making it hard to build within city limits, it looks like a move to a new state-of-the-art venue in Santa Clara could be on the horizon. But wait. The NFL wants a team in L.A. more than L.A. wants a team. Could the Bay Area's reputation for grinding construction to a halt, along with ownership's frustration, make the 49ers a candidate for relocation? It wouldn't be the first time Los Angeles plucked an NFL franchise from the Bay.

1. Will the Giants win the World Series? Why own a wedding dress when you're always the bridesmaid? The Giants moved to San Francisco 50 years ago and are still looking for their first World Series. They've been to the Fall Classic three times since coming West but have never won it all. The parade down Market Street is ready. Fans are waiting . . . and waiting . . . and waiting.

For decades, baseball fans assumed that the Hank Aaron HR mark of 756 would stand for all-time, and why not? Hammerin' Hank held the record for 12,173 days. But in 2007, we learned once again: All records are made to be broken. Well, maybe not all records. Here's a list of numbers that will forever be safe because of the way the game, players and structure of baseball has changed.

10. 4,256 career hits. No one is going to touch Pete Rose. Want to bet on it? A player would have to average 200 hits for the better part of 21 seasons to get in the neighborhood. The only thing more astonishing than Rose's record is watching how far he has fallen. No trip to Vegas would be complete without checking to see if Pete is signing autographs at the Forum Shops in Caesar's.

9. Rickey's record of 1,406 stolen bases. Get a runner aboard and wait for the long ball—that's how the game's played now. Well, it's a good thing that Rickey Henderson played then. Speed was the name of the game for baseball's most dangerous leadoff man—that, and referring to himself in the first-person at all times. What makes this record doubly hard to imagine anyone breaking is that it comes in two parts, first; you have to get on base, than perform than theft.

8. 5,714 strikeouts. We've witnessed two of the great strikeout artists in baseball history, thanks to Randy Johnson and Roger Clemens, who rank second and third on the all-time list. Well, neither is close to the Ryan Express, who averaged better than nine punch-outs per nine innings pitched for his entire career. Ryan is still more than 1,100 strikeouts ahead of second place. If you assume that Clemens was juiced out of his mind—which I think we're all safe to assume now—that just shows you how long this record will stand. Steroids obliterated home run records, but Roger still couldn't get close to Ryan. Even if Randy Johnson has a huge schlong that gives him power, it isn't enough, either.

7. 56-game hitting streak. Does this seem a little high on the list for such a hallowed record, even with Bay Area ties? For shame! DiMaggio is one of San Francisco's most revered sons. Actually, I doubt anyone will ever stay as steady as the "Yankee Clipper" did in 1941, but at least it's a record in play, and could conceivably be broken. The rest of these records are, as they say in Vegas, "off the board."

6. The Real Iron Man. Robert Downey, Jr. would need a ton of blow for the energy to stay in the lineup for 2,632 consecutive games like Cal Ripken, Jr. did. . . . Seriously, how much of a stud was Ripken? After famously passing Lou Gehrig's record of 2,130 games in a row, Cal stayed in the lineup for another 502 straight days and nights before taking a seat.

5. Hitting over .400. If someone ever approached hitting .400 again, the media pressure would likely be enough to crush the man in the final weeks. Now, can you imagine then if you had to hit .438? That's the record, set back in 1894 by Bill Duffy of the Boston Beaneaters. How great of a name was that?

4. 74 complete games in a season—or 680 innings pitched in a single season. Take your pick. The records belong to Will White, who pitched (an understatement) for the 1879 Reds. Considering Barry Zito signed the richest deal in pitching history before the 2006 season and can't make it out of the seventh inning, both records should be safe forever.

3. Two World Series records. Thanks to how much harder it is to reach the Fall Classic now, ain't nobody going to sniff Yogi Berra's 71 career World Series hits. His Yankees teams went to fourteen Series in eighteen seasons. No slugger will ever get the chance to match Yogi's teammate Mickey Mantle's 18 career World Series home runs.

2. 751 career complete games. And you wonder why it's called the Cy Young Award? Pretty safe to say that no one is going to touch Cy's 7,356.2 innings-pitched record either. That, sports fans, is an innings eater.

1. 60 victories for a pitcher in a single season. Come on, now? A pitcher sees about 60 starts over the span of two years, much less has a chance to win 60! But that's just what Charles "Old Hoss" Radborn did back in 1884, when he set the mark for the Providence Grays. Seventy-four appearances, sixty wins, eleven shutouts and a whopping 679 innings? And we now live in the day of 100-pitch counts. Doesn't anyone else remember when men were real men?

It isn't always pretty—and when it came to these guys, it was downright ugly. The Bay Area has a strong tradition of winning teams, but these guys have nothing to do with that.

10. Art Shell. Between his first stint coaching the Raiders in L.A. and his return engagement in Oakland in 2006, Shell seemed to turn into a block of granite, standing emotionless on the sideline as the Raider Nation crumbled around him. When he did open his mouth, Shell got into bitter feuds with his players, and embodied the dysfunction that has become the team's calling card.

9. Jim Davenport. Leo Durocher's quip, "Nice guys finish last," applied to Davenport, who skippered the dismal 1985 Giants. An original San Francisco Giant and longtime company man, Davy was given the reins of the club in 1985, but didn't last the season. Roger Craig replaced him, and his omnipresent tobacco spittoon.

8. Pete McCulley and Fred O'Connor. Besides leading to the hiring of Bill Walsh, nothing good came out of the one season these two guys shared the headphones for the 49ers in 1978. After starting the season 1-8, McCulley was dumped and assistant O'Connor took over for the remainder of the season. He went 1-6 before Bill Walsh was brought in. Pro football has never been the same since, or as bad as it was in San Francisco during the McCulley/O'Connor era.

7. Joe Bugel. The quintessential Al Davis yes man, he even shared Al's ducktail hairdo. Bugel set the Raiders back a few seasons with his bungled game plans, going 4-12 in 1997. Mr. Davis than said "no" to his yes man, canning Bugel after one season.

6. Steve Boros. On the heels of Billy Martin's 1982 flame out, the A's brought in the New-Agey Steve Boros. Toting a degree in literature from the University of Michigan, the cerebral Boros brought a civility to the dugout, and predictably zero respect from his players. Boros and his bookshelf were gone after one-and-a half seasons.

5. Tom Sheehan. Horace Stoneham's search for the successor to original S.F. Giants manager Bill Rigney in mid-1960 began and ended in the lounge at Candlestick Park when he tapped his rotund drinking partner Sheehan. A former catcher, Sheehan was so large that he managed his first few games in a coat and tie until a tent—er, uniform—could be stitched together. His teams were as shoddy as his attire.

4. Dave Bristol. The things best remembered about Bristol's stint with the Giants in 1979-80 are his fits of anger, which led to a punch-up with star pitcher John Montefusco. The Count lost, as did the Giants most of the time Bristol was making out the lineup card.

3. P.J. Carlesimo. A prime example of why college coaches don't fly in the NBA. He brought his screaming and sour-faced act to the Warriors in the mid-1990s and was immediately tuned out. After bellowing at the edgy Latrell Sprewell to "put a little mustard" on his passes one day, Carlesimo ended up with welts the size and hotdogs around his neck. Worse yet, most of Carlesimo's players came to the defense of the loony Sprewell at a press conference, inferring that P.J. may have had it coming for long time. The scandal relegated the W's to an NBA also-ran for nearly a decade after it happened. Golden State's list of coaches reads like a list of failed coaching careers, but Carlesimo was the only coach who was ever assaulted, so he gets to represent all of them.

2. Jim Marshall. In Marshall's lone season helming the A's in 1979, Oakland began the campaign by losing nine of its first ten games, and concluded the season dropping 12 of the final 14 contests. In between that, the green and gold mixed in a lot more losing, finishing an all-time Bay Area big league worst, 54-108. In 1980, Billy Martin had essentially the same cast of characters and produced a winning team.

1. Dennis Erickson. Maybe it was his Miami pedigree or arrest for drunk driving, but Erickson always appeared too sleazy to be the head coach of the regal 49ers. He roamed 49ers sideline looking like a disgruntled parks-and-rec playground supervisor. Also, he had the play-calling creativity of a garden gnome. He followed a seven-win debut season with only two victories in 2004, after which he and the horrible GM Terry Donahue were both sent packing.

Worst Pro Quarterbacks in Bay Area Football History

Despite being the birthplace of the West Coast Offense, and Al Davis' coveted, vertical passing game . . . not all the gunslingers who called the Bay Area their NFL home found success, or the end zone. Here's the list of ten quarterbacks who never lived up to their billing. One more thing: if you're wondering why Todd Marinovich isn't on the list, it's because he was a Los Angeles Raider.

10. Giovanni Carmazzi, 49ers. Technically, Carmazzi never played in the NFL. The 49ers thought enough of the Sacramento native to use a third-round draft selection on the prospect, passing on San Mateo product Tom Brady in the process.

9. Alex Smith, 49ers. Expectations assigned to the first pick of the 2005 NFL draft were high, but patience is officially wearing thin with not just the fans, but the team as well. With his six-year, $49.5 million dollar deal, Smith will enter 2008 fighting for not only his starting job, but his NFL career. Although circumstances have made it difficult for anyone to succeed, Smith's bright moments have been few and far between.

8. Steve Spurrier, 49ers. The "Old Ball Coach" won the Heisman at Florida and would go on to staggering coaching success at the NCAA level, but the NFL and Spurrier never meshed. His failures as coach of the Redskins are well documented. Forgotten was how terrible he was as an NFL quarterback. Spurrier, while backing up local legend John Brodie, managed just 33 touchdowns with 48 career picks as a Niner.

7. Steve DeBerg, 49ers. The quarterback who was just good enough to lose, DeBerg was the man before "The Man." Montana's predecessor was competent, throwing for nearly 8,000 yards as the 49ers lead man, but inaccuracy would be known as one of his calling cards. DeBerg threw 60 interceptions from 1978-1980.

6. Marc Wilson, Raiders. The Raiders ushered in an era of mediocrity and, eventually, moving vans when they spent their No. 1 pick of the 1980 draft on Wilson. The squeaky clean kid from BYU had a big arm, and that was it. He hated contact, and two years later, most Raiders fans hated the team when they moved to L.A.

5. Jim Plunkett, 49ers. After Al Davis picked him off the scrap heap, Plunkett led the Raiders to two Super Bowls championships. But it was his crash-and-burn effort with the 1976-77 Niners that forced the former Heisman winner to take up residence in S.F.'s quarterbacking scrap heap.

4. Jeff George, Raiders. George fit the Raider criteria to a tee. He was chased away by other teams, had a massive ego and leased his right arm out as a fireworks launcher in the fall. However, George failed to read the most vital chapter of the Raiders playbook, the one that begins with: "Just Win, Baby." George airmailed 29 scoring plays in 1997, but the team went just 4-12. After struggling in 1998, he announced he was done for the season with a balky groin, which he told the media about before he informed the team.

3. Kerry Collins, Raiders. Loose cannon with a good cannon, Collins signed with Oakland after going to the Super Bowl with the Carolina Panthers, and two forgettable stops in New Orleans and with the N.Y. Giants. Hoping he'd lead the Silver and Black back to the Super Bowl, Raiders fans watched horrified as Collins misfired time after time, backing up Rich Gannon. In 28 games as a Raiders starter, Collins compiled a 7-21 ledger.

2. Dan Pastorini, Raiders. Not only did he fail with the Raiders, he later took the team to court after Al Davis failed to pay him $1 million in an arbitration ruling. Who can blame Al for holding back the funds? Pastorini was so disappointing that Raiders fans actually cheered when he broke his leg against Kansas City and was carted off the field. He never played for Oakland again.

1. Jim Druckenmiller, 49ers. Drafted with the Niners first pick in 1997, "Drunken-Miller" played as if he'd been drinking all Sunday morning. A career QB rating of 29.2, Druckenmiller played in just six games, completing 21 of 52 passes, 1 TD, 4 INT. He was traded to Miami and released by the Dolphins. His last gasp in pro sports was as quarterback of the XFL's Memphis Maniax. Legend has it, the 49ers brass ignored Bill Walsh's suggestion to select Arizona State's Jake Plummer over Druckenmiller. It always pays to listen to a genius.

You can't always get what you want—but sometimes you do. While some of these deals only added big-time talent, others created the foundation to a title. Here are the ten best decisions made by Bay Area GMs and owners. Nice job boys.

10. Warriors get guard Baron Davis from Hornets for guard Speedy Claxton and forward Dale Davis, 2005. The Warriors' decade-long bout of bad luck and mismanagement grinded to a halt when new GM Chris Mullin pulled off this steal. Baron's a high-maintenance kind of guy, but when he's on, he's one of the most dangerous playmakers in the NBA. He's the heart and soul of the Warriors and he drove them to the biggest upset in NBA playoff history when he bounded MVP Dirk and the number one seeded Dallas Mavericks in 2006-07. Boom-Dizzle!

9. Giants acquire 3B/OF Kevin Mitchell, pitchers Dave Dravecky and Craig Lefferts from San Diego for third baseman Chris Brown and pitchers Keith Comstock, Mark Davis and Mark Grant, 1987. This blockbuster deal on the Fourth of July, 1987, lit the fuse on a remarkable Giants revitalization. After the seven-player pact was completed, the Giants shot from the middle of the NL West to first place, winning their first division title in 16 seasons. Mitchell matured into one of the game's elite sluggers and won an MVP. The inspirational Dravecky, who came back from cancer in 1989, was brilliant down the stretch and into the playoffs that year. Lefferts had a rubber arm, and ate up innings for three years. The only guy to make a name going out the door was Mark Davis, who earned Cy Young Award honors in 1989.

8. Giants acquire pitcher Rick Reuschel from Pittsburgh for pitchers Jeff Robinson and Scott Medvid, 1987. San Francisco wasn't finished with the Mitchell deal. Weeks later, GM Al Rosen shipped two arms to Pittsburgh in exchange for former 20-game winner Reuschel. "Big Daddy" responded, going 5-3 the rest of the season. In 1988, he went 19-11 and in 1989 was 17-8, as the Giants won the pennant.

7. Sharks get center Joe Thornton from the Boston Bruins for Marco Sturm, Wayne Primeau and Brad Stuart, 2005. When Thornton asked out of Boston, the Sharks jumped at the chance to add one of the NHL's best centers. The decision was easy to make, and paid off instantly. While the three players traded for Thornton are all enjoying solid careers, Joe showed up to San Jose, led the league in scoring and immediately won the Hart Trophy, hockey's MVP award. A contract extension—another easy decision for the Sharks—will keep "Big Joe" in teal until 2011.

6. Giants get pitcher Vida Blue from the A's for pitchers Phil Huffman, Alan Wirth, Dave Heaverlo, John Henry Johnson, catcher Gary Alexander, infielder Mario Guerrero, outfielder Gary Thomasson and $300,000, 1978. In a real shocker, cross-bay rivals Giants and A's completed the biggest swap ever between the two clubs as San Francisco received 1971 MVP and Cy Young winner Vida in exchange for a bus load of serviceable vets and untested prospects. Blue was a major force on the mound (18-10) and in the clubhouse that season as S.F. led the NL West for much of the summer. The players the A's received soon became less serviceable—and tested, they received middling grades. If you root for the A's, this isn't on your Top Ten list.

5. Giants get pitcher Jason Schmidt from Pirates for outfielder Armando Rios and a spare pitcher, 2001. The Giants have snookered the Pirates in trades so many times over the last 25 years that it's easy to lose count. This one was arguably the best. The Giants literally gave two spare parts for one of the most dominating starters of the early 2000s. Schmidt would win 78 games for the Giants and was, at times, simply unhittable. In 2003, Schmidt led the Giants to the NL West title with a 17-5 ledger and league best 2.34 ERA. Schmidt holds San Francisco's single season (251) and single game (16) records for strikeouts—before the Giants passed on the chance to re-sign him after 2006, fearing he had a dead arm. He signed a big deal with the Dodgers (ouch, Schmidty) and has been on and off the DL ever since.

4. Giants get infielders Jeff Kent and Jose Vizcaino, pitchers Julian Tavarez and Joe Roa from Indians for Matt Williams, 1996. Following this mega-swap that sent one of the most popular Giants ever out of town on a rail, there was such furor directed at Giants GM Brian Sabean that Sabean was forced to proclaim that he was more than mentally fit to be GM of a big league club, infamously saying, "I am not an idiot. . . ." Once the dust settled, the new players proved their boss right. Kent's career took off in Orange and Black, as he swatted 29 homers and drove in 121 RBI in his first season here.

3. 49ers get defensive tackle Fred Dean from San Diego for No. 2 draft choice, 1981. Dean was a pass rushing legend in his own right, and once acquired mid-season, kept the pressure on in Super Bowl XVI, and again in Super Bowl XIX. Dean had just one sack with the Chargers before Bill Walsh plucked him midseason. Twelve more sacks that season caused Steve Sabol to call it the last "meaningful mid-season trade" that altered the course of the Lombardi Trophy. The Chargers, by the way, became the San Diego Chargers after this trade.

2. A's get pitcher Dennis Eckersley and infielder Dan Rohn from Cubs for David Wilder, Brian Guinn, Mark Leonette. Oakland received Eckersley from the Cubs for two players who never played a game in the majors. Though initially reluctant to move to the bullpen, the former 20-game winner was masterful as a closer, writing his ticket to Cooperstown.

1. 49ers acquire QB Steve Young from Tampa Bay for No. 2 and No. 4 Draft Picks, 1987. This hits the top of the chart because of the vision and balls this trade really took. Instead of using his draft picks to get more weapons or defense for Montana, Walsh traded them for an eventual H.O.F quarterback that he decided to put away for a rainy day. Wow. He saw through Young's troubles and bumbles with the L.A. Express and Tampa Bay, and made the move. Further examination into the psychology of the trade is, however, the true genius of the deal. Not only did Walsh get Young, he got the best out of Joe Montana until the switch was made. Nothing pushes a quarterback like a quarterback, and Walsh knew that.

Sometimes a deal goes bad. In that regard, Bay Area franchises have laid some whoppers in their days. Here are some of the worst decisions to come out of front offices and land with a thud.

10. 49ers trade Y.A. Tittle to the Giants for G/LB Lou Cordileone, 1961.
Apparently the 49ers made the Giants an offer for Cordileone they just couldn't refuse. The rugged Tittle was a fixture under center for the 49ers for a decade, racking up more than 16,000 yards and 108 touchdowns in the air. The future Hall of Famer was also an innovator, teaming up with receiver R.C. Owens for the groundbreaking alley-oop pass. But an NFL title always evaded the Tittle-led Niners. They got close in 1957, but lost a 31-27 heartbreaker to Detroit at Kezar Stadium. A couple more seasons that ended too soon, and Tittle time was over. The 49ers turned the starting quarterback reins over John Brodie in 1960 and dealt the 35-year year old Tittle to New York in 1961. The change did Tittle good as he was named MVP in his first season with the Giants. He was MVP again in 1963, setting a then-NFL record with 36 TD passes. Cordileone meanwhile played just one season with San Francisco.

9. Giants trade pitcher Gaylord Perry and infielder Frank Duffy to the Indians for pitcher Sam McDowell, 1972.
The old greaseballer had just "slipped" to 16-12, with a 2.76 ERA for the NL west champion Giants in 1971 when he was shipped to Cleveland for big right-hander Sam McDowell, a pitcher known for his blazing fastball and the ability to drink everyone under the table. Perry would win the Cy Young Award during his first season in Cleveland and be called Cy again in 1978 with San Diego. McDowell won his first five San Francisco decisions then promptly took a nosedive, going 11-10 in parts of two Giants campaigns.

8. Warriors trade forward Chris Webber to the Bullets for forward Tom Gugliotta and three first-round draft picks, 1994.
Pampered his whole life, Webber decided he was above Don Nelson's coaching rants and demanded that either he or Nellie would have to go. Webber indicated he would exercise his one-year escape clause if he ever saw Nelson again. Instead of letting Webber cool his jets, the Warriors overreacted and swapped the 1993-94 NBA Rookie of the year to Washington for Gugliotta, who couldn't rip off his warm-up pants without straining something. The Warriors proceeded to blow all three of the picks they got in the trade, and went straight down the toilet for the next dozen years.

7. A's trade outfielder Rickey Henderson and pitcher Bert Bradley to the Yankees for outfielder Stan Javier, pitcher Eric Plunk, pitcher Jose Rijo, pitcher Jay Howell and pitcher Tim Birtsas, 1984. It must be written in stone somewhere that the A's must trade or let every one of their stars walk before he hits the prime of his career. They did it with Reggie, Vida and Rollie and again with the 26-year-old homegrown Henderson, shipping him to the Yankees at the end of the '84 season. The stolen base king would spend four-and-a-half of his best seasons in pinstripes. Besides Howell, the five players Oakland received never amounted to much while wearing Green and Gold. Oakland saved a little face by reacquiring Rickey in mid-1989.

6. Warriors trade guard Mitch Richmond to the Kings for forward Billy Owens, 1991. Yet another great idea from the minds of the Golden State Warriors, trading the best shooting guard not named Jordan at the time, in the prime of his career. Fans were eating up the fast-paced excitement generated by 1988-89 Rookie of the Year Richmond and his Run TMC partners Tim Hardaway and Chris Mullin. Then, just before the start of the 1991-92 season, like Coca-Cola they fiddled with the winning recipe, swapping Richmond for Owens, the Kings' first-round draft pick (third overall) out of Syracuse. While Owens averaged a respectable 15 points in three seasons with the W's, Richmond blossomed into an All-Star Game regular. To make matters worse, Warriors fans only had to drive 90 minutes to Sacramento to see what might have been.

5. Giants trade outfielder Willie Mays to the Mets for pitcher Charlie Williams, 1972. Mays was 41 years old and finished, but he should have finished in San Francisco, and that's why this one hurts. Unlike the Joe Montana trade to Kansas City—which although painful, could be justified because Steve Young was ready—Willie shouldn't have been dealt. In his first game in a Mets uniform, he let the Giants know how he felt by hitting a homer against his old club. Williams meanwhile stuck around for five forgettable seasons, none of which would have been better than hanging onto Mays, if for only one more season.

4. Giants trade outfielder George Foster to the Reds for infielder Frank Duffy and pitcher Vern Geishert, 1971. From 1969 through 1971, Foster rode the Giants bench saying little and hitting less. So there were no shock waves to be felt when he was swapped to the Reds in mid-1971 for a couple of fellow no-names. But after riding the pine in the Queen City for a couple of seasons, Foster blossomed into a home run machine, mashing a staggering 321 home runs from 1974-86. In 1977, when he slugged fifty long balls, Foster took home the NL MVP award. Duffy meanwhile hit .179 in 21 games for the Giants, while Geishert never made it into a single game with the Orange and Black.

3. Giants trade first baseman Orlando Cepeda to the Cardinals for pitcher Ray Sadecki, 1966.

Unlike Foster, the Giants knew Cepeda could play, but lost confidence as knee injuries mounted. Manager Herman Franks thought Cepeda was a big baby, not a Baby Bull, for being cautious with his rehab, and practically demanded that the slugger be dealt for a starting pitcher in mid-1966. The deal immediately embarrassed San Francisco. The Giants, leading the NL by two-and-a-half games at the time of this mid-May swap, sorely missed Cha-Cha's booming bat and lost the pennant to the Dodgers by one-and-a-half games. Meanwhile, Cepeda hit .303, swatted 17 homers and drove in 53 runs the rest of the way for the Redbirds. To grind salt into the wound, Cepeda won the MVP in 1968 and led St. Louis to a world title. Former 20-game winner Sadecki was a sub-500 hurler in parts of four seasons with S.F.

2. Warriors trade center Wilt Chamberlain to the 76ers for guard Paul Neumann, center Connie Dierking, forward Lee Schafer and $150,000, 1965.

Though Chamberlain loved San Francisco's cosmopolitan ambiance, and the ladies, as we've learned, City basketball fans expected a 100-point game every night, making for a rocky two-and-a-half seasons in the Bay Area. In 1963-64, Chamberlain poured in a NBA-best, 36.9 points per game, leading the W's to the finals against Boston, but lost four games to one. Chamberlain was in the middle of his third season with S.F. when the financially strapped Warriors decided to trade the Big Dipper back to his hometown of Philadelphia for a trio of players and $150,000. A Stanford product, Neumann played for the W's for three seasons. Dierking averaged eight points in his 30 games. Schafer retired and never even reported to San Francisco. By the way, "Wilt the Stilt" went on to win three consecutive MVP awards with Philly and was MVP of the NBA finals for the Lakers in 1972.

1. Raiders acquire wide receiver Randy Moss from the Vikings for linebacker Napoleon Harris along with first- and seventh-round draft picks, 2005.

Number one with a bullet because Randy gave it to the Raiders both coming and going. You can just see Al Davis salivating at the thought of Moss running scissor patterns in Silver and Black. The Raiders would've been better off if it were left as a daydream. Randy reported to the Raiders with a massive chip on his shoulder and did nothing to shake it off with his play. Not only did Moss refuse to talk to the local media and pretty much acted like a total jerk, he admitted he didn't try all the time and said he smoked weed every "once in a blue moon." Did I mention he was team captain? Wait, it gets better. Not only did Moss mail in his two seasons in Oakland, he ruined his trade value, leaving the Raiders just a fourth-round pick when he finally got dealt to the Patriots. So Oakland traded a starting linebacker, two picks including a first rounder, and got nothing from Moss in terms of on-field production, then got nothing of any real value when he was traded away. Yeah, that's as bad as it gets. At least he didn't set a new NFL single-season TD record as soon as he got to New England. Oh wait, he did. What a dick.

Things About Bonds' HR Record You Didn't Know

The historic number of 756 was passed at 8:51 pm PDT, on August 7, 2007. It was a 435-foot solo home run to center field in front of a wild, sold-out home crowd. Bonds and Giants fans shared a long and often difficult-to-defend relationship, so it was only fitting they got to share the moment. The number 756 was the most important number in sports—and in many eyes, it still is. Here are some other numbers Barry accumulated along the way.

11. Bonds hit eleven grand slams and eleven home runs in extra innings. These are the only numbers that seem a little small considering Barry's body of work.

10. He hit 22 homers as a center fielder. Of course, the vast majority of Bonds' HR total (725) came as a left fielder where he spent most of his career. He hit one more from a start in right field, ten as a designated hitter and four more homers coming off the bench as a pinch hitter.

9. It took Bonds 7,774 days to pass Hank Aaron. That's the amount of time between his first career home run—served up by Atlanta Braves pitcher, Craig McMurty, on the night of June 4, 1986 when Bonds was a skinny rookie for the Pittsburgh Pirates—and the historic home run off Washington Nationals hurler Mike Bacsik.

8. The eighth month of the year. Barry loved August, the month when he went deep 149 times, the most of any other month in the season. It's nearly 20 percent of his career total. He liked Fridays, too—129 of his blasts helped Giants fans ring in the weekend. And like the rest of us, he hated Monday, when he hit just 81 homers.

7. Along the way Bonds totaled 13 consecutive, 30-home-run seasons and 14 seasons with 100-or-more walks. Both are major league records.

6. There are 449 different men that served up a home run to Bonds. Don't worry, good chances are you're not one of them.

5. Bonds became the only player in Major League history to hit 500 home runs and steal 500 bases. Not impressed? Okay, he's the only member of the 400/400 Club, too. Only five others are in the 300/300 Club and Barry is related to two of them. One is his father, and the other his Godfather, Willie Mays. Safe to say, Barry was born with some amazing baseball DNA—it wasn't all BALCO.

4. Barry loved swinging early and, chances are, he was going to get to your pitcher in his first or second at-bat. Bonds hit 133 homers in the first inning, 102 more in the third, and 100 in the fourth.

3. Of all the homers Barry hit, he had to pump his legs and work really hard for his three inside-the-park home runs.

2. **Bonds finished with 71 multiple home run games, leaving him in second place on the list.** It's one home-run record Babe Ruth wouldn't let go of; Ruth still leads all with 72.

1. Quick . . . what's the all-time home run record? It's the best way to stump almost every hardcore fan who can't replace the number 756 in their mind with the new all-time total: 762.

Seven Quotes from the Seven-Time MVP

It's sad that Barry Bonds grew up with such a negative perception of the media and rarely gave us a chance to learn more about him. As complex an athlete as has ever been covered, he sometimes did offer a nugget or two, revealing his obsession with the game, his sense of humor, and the contradiction that was Bonds' way of life.

7. "They can say whatever they want to say.... To me, anybody who has to go out of their way to say something negative about somebody else, they're in a lot more pain than I am. I'm not in that kind of pain. You've got to be miserable to go out of your way just to be negative about somebody all the time."

6. "It's good when you win. It just makes it a little more gratifying, that's all it does. . . . I can hit a baseball. I've never had any problems doing that. I'm trying to do it when we win games."

5. "I went to jump and the wall hit me in the shoulder."

4. "All my baseball stuff I keep. . . . I keep every home run bat and put it in one of my vaults. Maybe down the road I'll get rid of it."

3. "Boos. You're supposed to boo me, shoot. They ain't mad at you, they like you, man. They're supposed to boo you—because I'm good, that's why. I'm coming to get them. . . . I don't care, bring it on, baby. You're supposed to [boo]. It's all good."

2. "You've just got to go with what's in front of you. That's why you all should turn the page on me. You guys keep bringing back old crap. Just turn the page, move on."

1. "I've been hearing wild fans my whole career for 20 years. Why should that bother me?"

With a home run in his first game in a Giants uniform, Bonds began his one and only love affair with a fan base. Despised in Pittsburgh after leaving to sign the most lucrative deal in baseball history at the time, Bonds began a process of alienating the entire outside world—except for Giants fans, for whom he delivered over and over again. If you don't like Barry Bonds, that's fine. But blame baseball and the powers-that-be who allowed the record to fall, not Giants fans for rooting for their slugger.

10. If Giants fans feel any guilt about cheering for the man, they should only feel about 77 percent guilty when it comes to dethroning Henry Aaron—586 home runs, or 76.9 percent of Bonds round-tripper total, came wearing a Giants uniform. He hit 176, or 23.1 percent, in Pirates black and gold. But I don't think there was ever guilt in Pittsburgh, or San Francisco for that matter, to begin with.

9. Along the way, Barry became the San Francisco Giants all-time leader in Batting Average (.312) runs (1,555) hits (1.951) doubles (381) RBI (1,440) walks (1,947) and of course, home runs. Trust me, you would root for anyone who produced like that for your team.

8. Eight different 40-home-run seasons. That's a NL record he still shares with Hank Aaron.

7. He hit a home run every 12.90 at-bats. That's staggering. That means you can't miss this guy hit. That means drop what you're doing, whatever it is, because Bonds is coming to the plate. No one man could grind San Francisco to a standstill for two or three minutes at a time like Barry.

6. In 2004, Bonds left the yard 45 times, while striking out just 41 times. That just the fifth time in Major League history a player went deep more times than he struck out. In other words, this guy could hit.

5. Five Most Valuable Player awards won by Bonds while playing left field in San Francisco. He had a total of seven, four more than anyone else who ever played the game.

4. The number of post-season appearances the Giants made while he played for San Francisco. The Giants are not used to frequent trips to October, but Bonds lead the team there in 1997, 2000, and 2002, and again in 2003.

3. Look at the company he's in. Including Mel Ott, who played in New York, the Giants boast four 500-plus HR sluggers, with Bonds, Mays and McCovey.

2. His march to the single-season home run record in 2001 was staggering. This could have brainwashed anyone. Seventy-three homers? Come on, that's insane. Pure? No. Insane? Yes. Oh, one more thing: Why aren't Cardinals fans chastised for their adoration of Mark McGwire when he broke the record?

1. His one and only World Series appearance in 2002. After developing a reputation for not coming through under post-season pressure, Bonds silenced his critics by hitting .356 (16 for 45) that October with 18 runs, two doubles, a triple, eight homers, 16 driven in with 27 walks. He slugged .978 and had an on-base percentage of .581. Four of those homers—one is still traveling somewhere above Anaheim— came in the World Series, which, of course, the Giants did not win. Karma's a bitch.

From Orange and Black to Green and Gold—or the other way around—here are ten players who only had to pay the auto toll on the Bay Bridge to reach another chapter in their major league careers.

10. Joe Morgan. The Oakland-raised Hall of Famer is a San Francisco fan favorite for knocking the Dodgers out of contention with a HR on the final day of the 1982 season. He's less vividly remembered in the Bay as an Athletic after batting .244 in his final big league season with the 1984 A's. He also complained that his younger Oakland teammates should have treated him with more respect, which probably would have happened had he not hit .244.

9. John Johnstone. A fairly decent reliever for eight big league seasons, Johnstone did something in 1997 that will likely never happen again. He started the season with San Francisco crafting a 2.16 ERA in 16 innings. The Giants tried to sneak him through waivers, but he was claimed by Oakland. He pitched in five games, was released then reclaimed by the Giants, who handed him back his old jersey and watched him pitch in three more games that season.

8. Ray Durham. The A's managed to get around playing Durham at second base in his brief stay with Oakland in 2002, using him 43 times as a designated hitter. Giants fans however were subjected to six seasons of choppy infield play and inconsistent hitting from Durham from 2003-08. He was a monster in a contract year but not much else in any other season. San Francisco finally said goodbye to "Ray by the Bay" when he was traded to the Brewers at the deadline in 2008.

7. Barry Zito. With its laid back clubhouse, a Zen-preaching pitching coach and a GM who didn't wear socks, Oakland was the perfect spot for Zito, winner of the 2005 Cy Young Award. Then the Giants gave Zeets 126 million expectations he could never live up to and took away his surfing privileges. Essentially, they have paid for the success A's fans enjoyed, and Giants fans are still waiting for.

6. Dave Kingman. All-or-nothing Kingman broke into the majors with San Francisco, crashing 77 home runs from 1971-74 and striking out 422 times. He returned to the Bay Area to wrap up his career with Oakland in the mid-Eighties, socking 100 more long balls while fanning on 359 occasions, and sending one live rat in a box to a female sports writer.

5. Dusty Baker. The Giants manager from 1993-2002, Baker played one season with San Francisco in 1984, batting .292. He ended his playing career with Oakland in 1985-86, batting .256 with 18 homers in his only American League experience.

4. Orlando Cepeda. Giants fans still curse the day in 1966 when exceedingly popular Cepeda was dealt to the Cardinals for hack pitcher Ray Sadecki. But unless you eat, breathe and sleep Green and Gold you may not realize that a sore-kneed Cha-Cha returned to the Bay to make three pinch-hitting appearances with Oakland in 1972.

3. Felipe Alou. One of the few hitters to perform admirably for both sides of the Bay. An original 1958 S.F. Giant, Alou led the 1962 NL Champion Giants in hitting. After spending several seasons with the Braves, Alou returned to the Bay Area with the A's in 1970 to help a young A's club learn how to win just before their World Series three-peat.

2. Willie McCovey. One of the most popular Giants ever, Willie Mac spent more than a decade with San Francisco before a shocking trade to San Diego in the mid-Seventies. He returned to the Bay Area as a limping DH in Oakland in 1976, batting just .208 in 11 games. He revived his career the next season in Orange and Black, winning the NL Comeback Player of the Year award with a 28 home run season. Who says you can't go home again?

1. Vida Blue. The 1971 MVP and Cy Young Award winner in Oakland, Blue was a member of three World Champion clubs in the East Bay. A blockbuster 1978 deal moved him to Candlestick Park. Blue helped breathe life into a flagging Giants franchise, winning 18 games and whipping Orange and Black fans into frenzy with his relentless, energetic pitching performances.

The San Francisco 49ers and the Oakland Raiders are two of the most iconic franchises in football history, and they couldn't be more different. One symbolizes the class of the NFL—a regal franchise that fancies itself as football royalty. The other is an outlaw, pushing the boundaries of decorum and civility, and loving every minute of it. That's why it's so jarring when a player turns in one uniform for the other. Here are the ten best who wore both the Red and Gold, and the Silver and Black.

10. Ted Kwalick. The tight end out of Penn State went to three straight Pro Bowls with San Francisco in 1971-73 before playing three seasons with Oakland. He once commented that he never heard a Raider booed at a home game. Not the case when he was a Niner.

9. Kevin Gogan. The chippy, 6-foot-7, 325-pound offensive lineman—a product of the city's Sacred Heart High—was All Pro with both of his favorite childhood teams, going to Honolulu as a Raider in 1994 and as a Niner in 1997-98.

8. Tom Rathman. The crew-cut-sporting fullback from Nebraska personified the stiff-upper-lip 49ers of the Bill Walsh era. In his only season as a Raider in 1994, his car was broken into during a home game.

7. Jamie Williams. Braided "Spiderman" was a popular blocking tight end with the 49ers from 1989-93, and then he went on to do his thing with the Raiders in 1994. He used both experiences as background to score a technical consultant gig on the film *Any Given Sunday*, the only movie I've ever walked out of before it was over. Sorry Jamie.

6. Roger Craig. The high-stepping running back, the epitome of the classy 49ers, never looked right to most fans in an eye patch during his lone season with the Raiders in 1991.

5. Cedrick Hardman. The two-time Pro Bowler was a relentless pass rusher and was one of the more popular Niners of the mid-Seventies. He missed San Francisco's glory decade of the Eighties, but earned a Super Bowl ring with the 1981 Raiders.

4. Matt Millen. The Raiders' second-round pick in 1980 went from the spartan environment of the Raiders facility to the plush 49ers locker room in 1989. The hard-nosed linebacker is the only player to earn Super Bowl rings with both clubs.

3. Jim Plunkett. After a couple of sub-par seasons with the Niners, he was a backup in Oakland for a couple of seasons before he led the Raiders to a couple of Super Bowl titles.

2. Ronnie Lott. It was clear that the Niners gave up too soon on the man who once had the tip of his finger chopped off so he could play in a game. Lott debuted with the Raiders in 1991 with 93 tackles and NFL-best eight interceptions.

1. Jerry Rice. The best there ever was as a 49er. When San Francisco chose Terrell Owens over him, Rice defiantly signed with Oakland. Hard to say it ended pretty for Jerry, who played in Seattle and Denver before hanging it up. But during that first year in Silver and Black, he reminded the 49ers what they were missing, with 83 catches and nine touchdowns in 2001. The next season he was even better and helped Oakland reach the Super Bowl, where he caught a touchdown, of course.

San Francisco, Oakland, San Jose and all points in between are decidedly pro towns when it comes to rooting interests. However, the Bay Area is ready to go toe-to-toe with any other locale when it comes to training or producing some of the greatest athletes to represent the United States. Golden Gate? Gold medals? Coincidence? Let's just be happy it's not the Bronze Gate Bridge.

12. John Naber. Out of Woodside H.S. in Redwood City, Naber became a powerhouse swimmer at USC before winning four golds and one silver medal at the 1976 Olympics.

11. Summer Sanders. Hands down, the hottest lady ever to take a competitive dip for her country. A six-time NCAA champion and two-time Pac 10 Swimmer of the Year at Stanford, Summer won a pair of gold medals in Barcelona along with a silver and a bronze. Speaking of nice pairs . . . uh-hum.

10. Don Schollander. The first American to win four gold medals in the pool at the 1964 Olympics in Tokyo, the kid who moved to Santa Clara during his high school years would come back for another gold and a silver medal in Mexico City.

9. Donna de Varona. She stunned all the ladies back at the Santa Clara Swim Club when she was named to the 1960 Olympic team at the tender age of thirteen. By the time she matured, she set 18 world records during her career, and won gold twice in 1964.

8. Kristi Yamaguchi. Before she won "Dancing with the Stars" (kill me now) Kristi perfected her moves on a much slipperier surface. One of the most-decorated figure skaters in U.S. history, the little girl from Mission San Jose High School won Gold in Albertville.

7. Lee Evans. Winner of two gold medals at the 1968 games in Mexico City, Evans was best known as the anchor of the 4x400m relay team that shattered the world record with a time of 43.86 seconds, a mark that stood for 20 years. A San Jose native, he also ran San Jose State University to the 1969 NCAA Championship.

6. Peggy Fleming. Oh, what a cute haircut, and the little girl could skate too! Born in San Jose, she took the skating community for a spin by winning the first of five National Titles at the age of fifteen. Peggy's good looks were no match for her talent, which blossomed to win gold at the 1968 Winter Games in France. *Mon Dieu!*

5. Bruce Jenner. Before making some questionable plastic surgery decisions, Jenner's move to San Jose laid the groundwork that made him one of the most iconic athletes of the Seventies. He set a decathlon world record at the 1976 Montreal Games, won every single amateur award you could think of and graced nearly every magazine cover the nation had to offer. Unable to find peace with a fading spotlight, Bruce is now infamous for showing his stretched face and his stepdaughter's big ass on *Keeping Up with the Kardashians*. Oh, how the mighty have fallen.

4. Bob Mathias. The first iconic track-and-field star from the Bay, Mathias was declared "World's Greatest Athlete" when he took gold in the decathlon in the 1948 London Olympics. He became the first to repeat the feat four years later, in Helsinki. As a Stanford student and two-time varsity football player, Mathias returned a 96-yard kickoff for a TD that helped beat USC and earn Stanford the 1951 Pac 10 title. Excelling in all avenues, Mathias worked for the State Department as a Good Will Ambassador to the world, served four terms in the U.S. House of Representatives, and became the first director of the U.S. Olympic Training Center.

3. Tommie Smith. Didn't take long for his basketball scholarship at San Jose State to turn into track-and-field history. He's the only man to ever hold eleven simultaneous World and Olympic records at the same time. Beyond that, Smith is the centerpiece of one of sports' most memorable images. His defiantly raised fist, the symbol of black power—along with teammate Jon Carlos at the 1968 Mexico City games—is forever etched in sports history.

2. Matt Biondi. Born in Palo Alto, Biondi was the second coming of the guy who holds the number one ranking. A member of three U.S. Men's National teams, Biondi took gold in Los Angeles, captured five more gold medals in Seoul—he set four world records in Korea—and two more gold in Barcelona. Three-time Swimmer of the Year at Cal, Biondi won eight individual NCAA titles and played some mean water polo before his date with Olympic fame.

1. Mark Spitz. Born in Modesto and a graduate of Santa Clara High School, Spitz dove into Munich's Olympic pool unknown outside swimming circles. He emerged from the water world famous and drenched in gold. He swam to a record seven gold medals in 1972, the single greatest individual performance in Olympic history (until Michael Phelps broke the record in 2008). Spitz—who also attended my alma mater, Indiana University (Go Hoosiers)—would go on to set 33 world records, and set millions of mustaches in motion.

25. Willie Mays. "It isn't hard to be good from time to time in sports. What is tough is being good every day."

24. Willie Mays. "In order to excel, you must be completely dedicated to your chosen sport. You must also be prepared to work hard and be willing to accept destructive criticism. Without 100 percent dedication, you won't be able to do this."

23. Willie Mays. "I think I was the best baseball player I ever saw."

22. Jerry Rice. "I feel like I'm the best, but you're not going to get me to say that."

21. Jerry Rice. "The one thing about T.O. is that T.O. is very defensive."

20. Jerry Rice. "I enjoyed the hard work and the dedication and the preparation I had to make to try to be one of the best receivers to ever play the game. The first 10 years, my wife and I, we never took a vacation."

19. Jeff Kent. "That's not an excuse. Me and Barry fought all the time and we went to the World Series. Just because we can't all always get along doesn't mean we shouldn't win. It still shouldn't have affected the way we played." On the "slug-out in the dugout."

18. Jeff Kent. "I feel sorry for you Bay Area people. People out here are so dumb, pay so much money for property, it's crazy. I'm happy I made money on my property, but they're stupid. I don't get it."

17. Wilt Chamberlain. "Everybody pulls for David; nobody roots for Goliath."

16. Wilt Chamberlain. "They say that nobody is perfect. Then they tell you practice makes perfect. I wish they'd make up their minds."

15. Former General Manager Terry Donahue. "I tell everybody that my time at the 49ers was a great flight...except for the crash landing."

14. Steve Young. "The principle is competing against yourself. It's about self improvement, about being better than you were the day before."

13. Art Shell. "I don't know. I got to the point where I kept telling people they couldn't ask me that. Ask the people doing the hiring."

12. Joe Capp. "They say football is America's greatest game, but it's not. The greatest game in America is called opportunity. Football is merely a great expression of it."

11. Charles Haley. "If you sacrifice early, you'll win late."

10. O.J. Simpson. "The day you take complete responsibility for yourself, the day you stop making any excuses, that's the day you start to the top."

9. Leo Durocher. "Baseball is like church. Many attend, few understand."

8. Reggie Jackson. "The will to win is worthless if you don't get paid for it."

7. Barry Bonds. "This is nothing. I've got nine writers standing here. McGwire had 200 writers when he had 30 home runs."

6. Johnny Miller. "Sports are 90 percent inspiration and 10 percent perspiration."

5. Charley O. Finley. "Sweat plus sacrifice equals success."

4. Bill Russell. "Heart in champions has to do with the depth of your motivation and how well your mind and body react to pressure."

3. "Gentleman" Jim Corbett. "You become a champion by fighting one more round. When things are tough, you fight one more round."

2. Bruce Jenner. "I learned that the only way you are going to get anywhere in life is to work hard at it. Whether you're a musician, a writer, an athlete or a businessman, there is no getting around it. If you do, you'll win. If you don't, you won't."

1. Peggy Fleming. "The first thing is to love your sport. Never do it to please someone else. It has to be yours."

You know the fans love you when they take you into their hearts and give you a nickname.

10. The Say Hey Kid—Willie Mays. Even with the loveable nickname, his career numbers still speak for themselves.

9. Dominican Dandy—Juan Marichal. He high-kicked himself into Cooperstown.

8. The Mad Bomber—Daryle Lamonica. Three words come to mind: vertical passing game.

7. T.O.—Terrell Owens. More than a nickname, it's now a brand name for sports selfishness. He may have become sports tabloid fodder in Philly, but T.O. was born in San Francisco.

6. The Fighting Hydrants—F.P. Santangelo, Marvin Bernard, Armando Rios. Small in stature, big on effort. It's the name given to the Giants diminutive outfield by longtime broadcasters Duane Kuiper and Mike Krukow.

5. The Assassin—Jack Tatum. One of the fiercest hitters in football history, he embodied all the Raiders stood for, causing pain and intimidation. His alma mater Ohio State awards the "Jack Tatum Hit of the Week Award" to the player who does the most damage.

4. Joe Cool—Joe Montana. Only number sixteen and Snoopy can get away with it.

3. Run TMC—Tim Hardaway, Mitch Richmond, Chris Mullen. One of the best group nicknames in sports history, it paid tribute to changing times and culture, and the iconic Run DMC.

2. Jim "Catfish" Hunter. You know you got a cool nickname when Bob Dylan writes a song about it. Dylan did, in 1975, but the song wasn't released until his box set in 1991. Joe Cocker also released the song on his 1976 album, Stingray.

1. The Snake—Kenny Stabler. The nickname was born in a `76 playoff game vs. Pittsburgh better known for its "Immaculate Reception." Before Franco Harris made his amazing catch out of nowhere, Stabler had scrambled thirty yards for the go-ahead score late in the fourth quarter. His ability to wind his way around trouble led to the birth of "The Snake."

Sometimes a nickname lets you know they love you; sometimes, it has the opposite effect. In a sports town as forgiving as this, you have to go out of your way to earn a bad nickname.

5. DunMurphy—Mike Dunleavy and Troy Murphy. A hybrid of Warriors' mediocrity, both Dunleavy and Murphy played with exactly the same lack of passion. They became hard to tell apart, so why not put them together? Now, without patting myself on the back too hard, I must claim ownership. It was I who created "DunMurphy." On post-game shows, I just started combining their line scores, as in: "With Mike going for five points, and Murphy scoring six . . . DunMurphy had himself an eleven point night."

4. Johnny Disaster—Johnny LeMaster. For more than ten years, LeMaster was the whipping boy for Giants fans who never stopped riding this career .222 hitter. The sixth overall pick of the 1973 draft, he never lived up to expectations, and never even came close. Secure in his status as the team goat, LeMaster did win lots of Giants fans over when he took the field with "Boo" on the back of his jersey instead of his last name.

3. Buffy—Mike LaCoss. Mike LaCoss was a decent pitcher for the Giants who just happened to look a lot like one of the kids on the long-running sitcom, A Family Affair. He looked like Jodie, the oldest son. Unfortunately, when a writer referenced the similarity, he got the character name wrong, calling him "Buffy," the name of the daughter. Needless to say, Mike was not happy the gaffe was made and less happy when it stuck.

2. Old Penitentiary Face—Jeffrey Leonard. Also known as the "Hackman," this nickname was reserved for the surly Leonard, who sometimes was about as warm and charming as a prison cell.

1. Joe Barely Cares—Joe Barry Carroll. With the number-one overall pick of the 1980 NBA draft, the Warriors selected an indifferent, slow center out of Purdue. Actually, Joe suffered from a perception of not caring, more than true indifference. He did average over twenty points on four different occasions, but all Warriors fans could see was what he wasn't. He wasn't Robert Parrish, who the Warriors traded to Boston with their pick for the number one overall. And he wasn't Kevin McHale either, who the Celtics ended up taking with the W's pick.

Five Ways to Remember Willie Mays

If you love baseball, you have to love Willie Mays. Mays had style and grace. It showed on the field. It showed on TV . . . and radio. Here are five fond memories and ways to jump on the waaaay back machine.

5. "Willie, Mickey and The Duke" by Terry Cashman. Although it's more commonly known as "Talking Baseball," this 1981 classic has endured the test of time and may be the most beloved baseball song this side of "Take Me Out to the Ball Game." It made fans remember why they loved the game during a strike-shortened season. Cashman famously declares, "If Cooperstown is calling, it's no fluke. They'll be with Willie, Mickey and the Duke."

4. *The Knickerbocker Beer Show.* Yes, it dates back to New York, but it speaks to me, since I date back to N.Y. myself. In 1954, Mays appeared on Steve Allen's *Knickerbocker Beer Show*. There's a better chance of a show named *Chugging Gin* being released these days.

3. Blasting Caps! Just trust me. Look up "Willie Mays, blasting caps" on YouTube and you'll see what I mean. When was this a big problem? Either way, Willie cared. "Remember, now, don't touch them."

2. Syndication, Baby. Willie will always live on as long as they're showing sports highlights. Beyond that, you can check out his walk-on appearances on Nick at Night. Willie has been on *The Ed Sullivan Show*, *The Donna Reed Show*, *The Jack Paar Show*, *Bewitched*, *My Two Dads* and the immortal *Mr. Belvedere*.

1. "Say Hey" (The Willie Mays Song). With the legendary Quincy Jones conducting, the Treniers laid down one of the most swinging baseball songs ever recorded. Willie himself sings backup. It takes you back to days gone by, and it's a big reason why Mays is so adored—he's instant nostalgia. Talk to someone who had the pleasure of watching Mays play, and they'll turn 24 years younger instantly. It's beautiful.

Len Eshmont Award Winners

Established in 1957, the Len Eshmont Award is the most prestigious honor the San Francisco 49ers bestow upon a player. It acknowledges the teammate who best displays "inspirational and courageous play" most reflective of Eshmont's career. A two-way player on the original 1946 Niners, Eshmont died in 1957 at the age of 40 after contracting hepatitis. It's one of the few individual team awards to garner routine national attention.

One-time winners:

QB—Y.A. Tittle (1957)

FB—J.D. Smith (1959)

S—Dave Barker (1960)

DT—Leo Nomellini (1961)

T—Bob St. Clair (1963)

DT—Charlie Krueger (1964)

QB—John Brodie (1965)

LB—Matt Hezeltine (1968)

S—Roosevelt Taylor (1970)

LB—Ed Beard (1971)

DE—Tommy Hart (1972)

T—Len Rohde (1974)

DE—Tommy Hart (1976)

DT—Archie Reese (1980)

TE—Charlie Young (1981)

TE—Dwight Clark (1982)

RB/ST—Bill King (1983)

LB—Keena Turner (1984)

NT—Michael Carter (1987)

DE—Kevin Fagan & LB Charles Haley (1990)

WR—John Taylor (1991)

WR—Jerry Rice (1993)

FB—William Floyd (1995)

DT—Dana Stubblefield (1997)

RB—Garrison Hearst (2001)

S—Tony Parrish (2002)

OLB—Julian Peterson (2003)

Two-time winners:

HB—John David Crow (1966, 1967)

S—Mel Phillips (1973, 1977)

CB—Jimmy Johnson (1969, 1975)

RB—Paul Hofer (1978, 1979)

RB—Roger Craig (1985, 1988)

QB—Joe Montana (1986, 1989)

QB—Steve Young (1992, 1994)

Nine-time winner:

DT—Bryant Young (1996, 1998-2000, 2004-08). If the 49ers ever decide to rename the award (they never will, and never should) it would be renamed after B.Y.

NOTE: Rich Lieberman's experience in radio goes back as far as his experience at the deli counter. He's a media critic, gossip columnist, political hack, social observer, pizza salesman, and does a mean Al Davis impression to boot. Rich "Big Vinny" Lieberman has had his ears and eyes on the radio scene for a long time, and here's his list of top ten all-time favorite Bay Area broadcasters. Since my arrival in San Francisco, he's been one of the most vocal supporters of my show, and clearly has great taste.

10. Mike Krukow, S.F. Giants color commentary. It's common knowledge that San Francisco is not known for "homer" announcers, but former Giants pitcher Mike Krukow is a beloved figure in the team's pantheon of color commentators. Krukow and his sidekick, another Giants ex-player, Duane Kuiper, managed to become almost as popular as Barry Bonds and Willie McCovey. Krukow's commentary, sort of a credible S.F. version of Ron Santo, albeit with less vocal and contrived "outrage," was a combination of "right on" plaudits to semi-corny putdowns of the opposition. "Grab some pine, meat!" His jock status made him lovable in the clubhouse and in the stands. It didn't hurt that "Kruk" was around for Barry Bonds' milestones and the first decade of S.F.'s beautiful waterfront stadium.

9. Don Klein, 49ers play by play, Stanford football, KCBS. If Joe Starkey's call of "The Play" was one of college football's most listened-to renditions, then Don Klein's version of one of the most memorable plays in Bay Area football lore has to be right up there. Klein's thrilling, no-nonsense call of the Joe Montana to Dwight Clark touchdown in the NFC Championship game in January 1982 will go down as perhaps the most awe-inspiring calls in Bay Area sports history. He also did Stanford football for 20 years and called John Elway's last college game at the Big Game in Berkeley in 1982.

8. Joe Starkey, Cal Football, 49ers, KGO Radio. Starkey is the voice of Cal Football dating back to 1975, and now his voice is heard forever as the voice of "The Play," the bizarre, most compelling play from the 1982 Big Game between Cal and Stanford. Starkey's shrill, unconventional description of one of college football's most "amazing" endings will forever be enshrined in broadcast history. It has been re-aired on ESPN literally thousands of times. Starkey also called hockey for the old Oakland Seals and began doing radio sports in 1979 for KGO and became the radio voice of the 49ers in 1989. His work is steady, professional and informative to the max.

7. Monte Moore. Monte Moore was the head play-by-play man for the Oakland A's in the early Seventies and mid to late Eighties. He worked for the Charlie Finley A's of the World Series teams of 1972, '73, and '74, and was the first Bay Area announcer to be labeled a "homer." But Moore had a distinct, Midwest, semi-southern style that many fans liked and some detested. Monte coined the term "dingers" for homeruns, and often called the Athletics the "Swingin' A's." Many players and fans often stated that Charlie Finley dictated how Monte Moore was to call the game, a charge that Moore vigorously denied.

6. Gary Park, KTVU-Channel 2. Park, like Wayne Walker was one of the early pioneers of Bay Area TV sports. His no-nonsense sports anchoring at Channel 2 was admired and respected. He did the color on TV for the S.F. Giants in the Seventies and mid-Eighties. Park had a reputation as a perfectionist and also an innate ability to infuse his play-by-play with a healthy dose of restaurant references. That's right, restaurant references. Gary liked good wine and food and on occasion would let viewers know about the "excellent restaurants in Montreal." A fixture.

5. Hank Greenwald, S.F. Giants. Greenwald broadcast Giants baseball from the late Seventies until the mid-Nineties. A very distinct voice, almost an East Coast vibe with a bravado that was uniquely baseball-laden. He was a great storyteller and often embellished his own Brooklyn childhood with baseball stories in the broadcast. Like King and Simmons, he was not afraid to rip the locals. One of the few voices who preferred radio over TV, his baseball oratory was a Bay Area staple with the Giants.

4. Gary Radnich, KRON-TV/KNBR. Radnich came to the Bay Area in 1986; a little known TV sports anchor from Columbus, Ohio, who grew up in San Jose and worked in Sacramento and other small markets before hitting S.F. His offbeat, hilarious delivery and performance was received with initial hostility from a critical Bay Area TV market, but as Radnich became established and went from the weekend to daily reporting, his style of irreverence became extremely entertaining for viewers. Gary has a unique style of mixing everyday news into the sporting realm and began doing so in his radio gig at KNBR, where he performs every morning in addition to his TV duties.

3. Wayne Walker, KPIX-TV, Channel 5 Sports Anchor. Wayne Walker was one of the first successful ex-athletes to go from the gridiron to the TV studio—in this case, from the Detroit Lions to the Bay Area in the early Seventies. Walker also was the color analyst for the 49ers, working with Lon Simmons, Don Klein and Joe Starkey. His anchor duties at KPIX transformed Bay Area local TV. Walker was one of the highest paid broadcasters in the business and most influential. His straightforward delivery was both relished and admired by his peers, and was consistently #1 with viewers.

2. Lon Simmons, S.F. Giants and 49ers. Lon Simmons was one of the most professional, powerful voices in Bay Area radio. He did the sports reports at KSFO, the unofficial "voice of San Francisco," working with a distinct baritone voice and provocative sense of humor that was a staple of his work with the Giants and 49ers. Simmons had a most hilarious sense of humor, which he placed in many of his broadcasts; often so subtle you had to listen very closely. Lon worked with Russ Hodges in N.Y. when the Giants moved west to S.F. in 1958. He also teamed with Bill King in the early Eighties for over 20 years with the Oakland A's. He also had a very independent style and was not afraid to criticize the home team.

1. Bill King. A major force in Bay Area sports play-by-play, he was one of the few guys who did three sports, including the Oakland Raiders, the Oakland A's and Golden State Warriors. King, befitting his name, was indeed the "King of Sports." His delivery and style almost transcended the sport in which he broadcast. He was particularly great on basketball, with an almost flawless, verbally intense style. Those who had the pleasure of listening to Bill felt as if they were right at the Oakland Arena when Bill did his play-by-play. He had the most incredible vocabulary and was fond of showing it. King was fantastic with his rapid-fire delivery on football, too; his vivid call of the famous "immaculate reception" and stellar call on the "holy roller" play have been re-broadcast numerous times on ESPN and local broadcast outlets. King's biggest asset was his professionalism and intense desire to remain independent to the core, often doing today what most announcers do not: he'd criticize the home team when the situation merited. A gem of a guy and a true legend, King died in 2005.

Top Ten 'Krukowisms'

The broadcasting team of Mike Krukow and Duane Kuiper has entertained Giants on radio and TV going on a quarter century. It doesn't take long for new listeners or viewers to realize that Krukow and Giants fans have a language all their own. Here are the top ten "Krukowisms" to come from the broadcast booth.

10. "The Shin Burger." A meal fit for anyone who takes a bad hop or foul ball on their lower extremities.

9. "Ha-Ha-Ha Laugher!" A pressure filled extra-innings game that the Giants pulled out the bottom of the 14th inning? Just another "Ha-Ha-Ha Laaaaaaugher!"

8. "Non-Chance." A foul ball back into the stands. The fat guy eating a hotdog and popcorn, and drinking a beer all at the same time had a "non-chance" of getting to the ball.

7. "Hey Big Boiiiiiii." Typical greeting for a player who may be pulling more weight than his frame should carry. Also the greeting I usually get.

6. "Atta-Babe." Any sentence in the world can be properly punctuated with an "atta-babe." Used in agreement or sarcastically, it always works.

5. "Eliminate." Telestrator justice never came so swiftly. If you wear anything blue to a Giants game when the Dodgers are in town, don't expect to be caught on camera for long. Krukow will cross you out, or "eliminate" you on sight. Some Giants fans however, consider it a badge of honor, and bring signs to the game begging to be eliminated.

4. "Ugly Finder." Hey, that fat guy finally got his foul ball, must have been an "ugly finder."

3. "Ownage." Hitter has a lifetime batting average of .335 with two homers off a pitcher in 20 at-bats—that's some "ownage."

2. "Serious Ownage." Hitter has a lifetime batting average of .405 with four homers off a pitcher in 20 at-bats—well, that's "serious ownage."

1. "Grab Some Pine, Meat." Kevin Costner may have popularized the nickname "Meat" in the movie *Bull Durham*, but Mike Krukow has perfected its execution. Now take your 0-4, with three strikeouts and "grab some pine, meat."

The rest of baseball uses the A's as their farm team. The same can be said for the A's broadcast booth. Here's a list of ten broadcasters—some locally famous, some nationally known—who honed their chops doing play-by-play in Oakland before moving on to careers elsewhere.

10. Hal Ramey. The voice of KCBS sports, San Jose State football, San Jose Earthquakes soccer and longtime 49ers PA announcer, he spent 1979 announcing oh-fers for the likes of Mario Guerrero and Jungle Joe Wallis. Hal was able to coax 54 wins out of the team. Nice job, Ramey.

9. Jimmy Piersall. He's more famous for running around the bases backwards on his 100th career home run, and climbing the backstop (played by Tony Perkins) during a mental meltdown in Fear Strikes Out, but he was also in the A's radio booth (KEEN) when the club won its first Oakland World Series title in 1972.

8. Wayne Walker. The extremely popular former Detroit Lions LB was best known for his color work on 49ers radio broadcasts, and outrunning cable cars up Hyde Street in his days as sports anchor at KPIX. He also did A's games on channel 5 from 1976-82.

7. Curt Flood. He was shunned by baseball's higher-ups for challenging the reserve clause when Charlie Finley—the man free agency hurt the most—hired Flood to do A's games on KNEW and KPIX radio in 1978.

6. Ted Robinson. Now John McEnroe's partner for Grand Slam tennis tournaments on NBC, Robinson teamed with the likes of Dom Valentino and Red Rush on A's radio broadcasts beginning in 1980 on KDIA. He returned to call more than a few Bash Brothers homers on KPIX from 1985-87

5. Dick Stockton. The A's have always been known for the unnatural brightness of their uniforms, but Dick Stockton's fire-engine-red hair brought an entirely new hue to A's fans living rooms on KPIX from 1993-95. Fans never identified with Stockton who, despite being a solid PxP guy, seemed less than thrilled to have the gig.

4. Reggie Jackson. OK, so he was famous for something else before doing A's games, but he makes the list. Despite doing most of his damage at the plate with Oakland, Reggie chose to enter the Hall of Fame as a Yankee. That didn't stop him from collecting a check from the Green and Gold as an awkward analyst on KPIX and KICU in 1991-92.

3. Hank Greenwald. Lon Simmons, Ted Robinson and Jon Miller—typically known as Giants voices—were all A's play-by-play men during their careers. Nobody seemed more deflated to be broadcasting Oakland action than former iconic San Francisco voice Greenwald, calling select TV games in 2004-05. Going from the Giants on KNBR to the A's, wherever they are, is like being sent down to the JV team in your senior year.

2. Harry Carey. After he was run out of St. Louis and before becoming a national icon in Chicago, Carey got a chance to bellow "A's Win! A's Win!" 89 times in 1970 on KNBR, then-radio-home of the Green and Gold. Yes, the A's once had Harry Carey and KNBR to themselves, but parted ways over—you guessed it—money.

1. Jon Miller. The baritone voice of the Giants and ESPN's Sunday Night Baseball received his big break in baseball with the 1974 World Champion A's, calling games with Monte Moore and Bill Rigney on radio (KEEN) and TV (KPIX). Charlie Finley fired his young broadcaster after just one season. Miller recovered from the career setback and went on to become, in my humble opinion, the greatest baseball broadcaster of his generation.

NOTE: Beyond being a sports broadcasting icon in the Bay Area, Gary Radnich is the #1 personality in all San Francisco media, period. He's been on KNRON TV for nearly a quarter century, and has been broadcasting on KNBR for 15 years as well. I'd continue to compliment the guy, but as Radnich would say himself, "nobody cares." Here's Gary's list of the greatest high school athletes to ever come out of his hometown, San Jose. "Where'd you grow up, punk?"

10. Dennis Awtrey, Blackford H.S. South Bay's first hoops big man at six-foot-ten-inches. All American at Santa Clara and 12-year NBA career. Awtrey once punched Kareem Abdul-Jabbar in the face.

9. John Albanese, Bellermaine H.S. Prep All-American and Northern California player of the year. Leader in San Jose charity work.

8. Donna Devaronna, Santa Clara H.S. Olympic swimmer and ABC broadcaster.

7. Carney Lansford, Wilcox H.S. American League batting title in 1981 with the Red Sox before becoming an All Star with the A's. Lead his Santa Clara Little League team to the 1969 LLWS, where they lost to Taiwan.

6. Bud & Ralph Ogden, Lincoln H.S. The brothers led Santa Clara University to a 29-1 season, losing in the NCAA tournament to Lew Alcindor and UCLA.

5. Drew Gordon, Archbishop Mitty H.S. Two-time prep All-American and ticketed to replace Kevin Love in Westwood.

4. Steve Bartkowski, Buchser H.S. NFL #1 draft choice, Atlanta.

3. Dave Righetti, Pioneer H.S. Yankee no-hitter on the Fourth of July vs. Boston.

2. Jim Plunkett, James Lick H.S. Only Bay Area Heisman winner at Stanford, two Super Bowls with the Raiders.

1. Mark Spitz, Santa Clara H.S. Seven gold medals at the 1972 Olympics.

Since this book is about the Bay Area, time to pay some attention to the area in between the cities of San Francisco and San Jose. Some of the most expensive land in the United States, along with an abundance of athletic talent can be found right there.

10. Barry Bonds, Serra High School. Since he's #1 just about everywhere else in this book, I'll start with him here. Ask any of his classmates, they all knew he was going to be great (and a huge prick) all the way back then.

9. Nick Vanos, Hillsdale High School. No telling what would become of the 7-foot-1 center had his life not ended so early. Born in San Mateo, he was drafted by the Phoenix Suns out of Santa Clara University with the 32nd overall pick in 1985. Just two years later Vanos and his fiancée, along with 152 others were killed in a plane crash.

8. Jim Harbaugh, Palo Alto High School. While his father was the defensive coach at Stanford, young Jimmy went to high school directly across the street from Stanford Stadium. He'd go on to quarterback the Michigan Wolverines and become "Captain Comeback" with the Indianapolis Colts before coming all the way back to Palo Alto, where he is now the head coach of Stanford Football.

7. Gary Beban, Sequoia High School. The Redwood City native mastered the pass at the prep level and became a Heisman-winning QB at UCLA soon after. To this day, he's the only Bruin to win college football's top prize. He would score both Bruins TDs in the 1966 Rose Bowl win over top-ranked Michigan State. A very short NFL career would follow before he joined the business world.

6. Eric Brynes, St. Francis High School in Mountain View. He sprayed hits and his own body over the field going after balls all over the Western Conference Athletic League when he played in high school. Broke into the Bigs with the Oakland A's in 2000. Now with the D-Backs, he's the engine that drives the team, and one of the most personable and coolest pro athletes I've ever had the pleasure of meeting.

5. Kurt Rambis, Cupertino High School. The kid with the funny sports specs now can clearly see his retired number hanging in the gym. After a quick trip overseas to play pro ball after a solid career at Santa Clara University, it wasn't long before the hard-working power forward found a home with the Lakers.

4. Keith Hernandez, Capuchino High School. Born in San Francisco, Hernandez was a standout start just south of San Francisco before going on to catch the eye of MLB at San Mateo Junior College. Known for his good looks and great glove, Hernandez won the 1979 NL MVP in St. Louis before joining the Mets and going down in Seinfeld-reference history.

3. Lynn Swann, Serra High School. Born in Tennessee, he was raised in Foster City and attended the high school with a reputation for producing great athletes. Swann is now a big part of that reputation after spending his entire Hall of Fame career with the Steelers. His big game reputation was as well known as his graceful, leaping catches.

2. Greg Jeffries, Serra High School. A two-time All Star and all-around good guy, Greg Jeffries raked in the runs so often that the Mets picked him right out of high school as the 20th overall pick of the 1985 amateur draft. Although his Major League career never returned home, Jeffries did; he now lives in Pleasanton.

1. Tom Brady, Serra High School. Born in San Mateo, Brady went from being a good high school quarterback who got a full ride to Michigan, to an All-Pro quarterback who owns the NFL single-season TD record with three Super Bowl rings, twice being named the game's MVP. The kid who grew up worshiping Joe Montana has become a football god himself.

The number of game-changing, record-breaking and history-altering athletes to come from Oakland/Alameda is staggering. Here's a list of ten high school kids who went on to rewrite sports history.

10. Gary Payton, Skyline High School. One of the greatest point guards in NBA history, the "Glove" was teammates at Skyline with another NBA player, Greg Foster.

9. Dave Stewart, Saint Elizabeth High School. 1989 World Series MVP, 168-129 career record with a 3.95 era and 1,741 strikeouts. Wonder if he was ever caught smoking in the boys' room?

8. Joe Morgan, Castlemont High School. Twenty-two years in the major leagues with Houston, Cincinnati (1975 and 1976 World Champions) San Francisco, Philadelphia and Oakland. The Hall of Famer remains well known as one of the best baseball analysts on television.

7. Jackie Jensen, Oakland High School. Born in San Francisco, he would pursue his education on the other side of the Bay, where he attended Cal. Jensen would be named American League MVP in 1958, before deciding to retire in large part due to his fear of flying.

6. Willie Stargell, Encinal High School. 475 home runs, 1979 NL MVP (with Keith Hernandez) and 1979 World Series MVP. The city of Pittsburgh wouldn't be the same without him.

5. Jason Kidd, St. Joseph Notre Dame High School. Everyone who saw him play knew they were watching someone special. Kidd guided his team to back-to-back state championships averaging 25 points, ten assists and seven rebounds the season he was named the 1992 Naismith High School Player of the Year.

4. Frank Robinson, McClymonds High School. Only player to win MVP in both the American and National Leagues, he also became the first African-American manager in baseball. With 586 career home runs, it's hard to understand why he remains baseball's most underrated player of all time.

3. Rickey Henderson, Oakland Technical High School. Simply put, he's the greatest leadoff hitter in the major league history. Henderson was also a standout basketball and football player, garnering two dozen scholarships to play tailback in college. Seems to me he made the right choice.

2. Bill Russell, McClymonds High School. Teammates with Frank Robinson (what a class) Russell was cut once and nearly twice from the basketball team before blossoming his junior and senior seasons. Back-to-back NCAA titles at the University of San Francisco, followed by 11 NBA Championships with the Boston Celtics, and I think we can all agree he got the hang of it.

1. Curt Flood, McClymonds High School. How is it I came to rank Curt Flood as the most important athlete from an Oakland high school? Well, it's simple really. While the rest of these players had a huge effect on their own sport, Flood's decision to challenge for a player's right to file for free agency caused a ripple effect felt by everyone. Not a league, team or player in the world of sports escaped Curt Flood's impact. Bill Russell never changed major league baseball, international soccer, hockey and football; he just changed the NBA. Flood's decision to refuse a trade in 1969 was appealed all the way to the U.S. Supreme Court. Although he lost the decision legally, it created solidarity among players who eventually got their way.

Ten Most Important High School Athletes from San Francisco

Like Rome, the City of San Francisco sits on seven distinct hills. They provide the background for the daily beauty we enjoy. And like every great sports town, the background of High School athletics also serves as a setting for greatness. Here are ten of the best High School standouts the city has ever seen.

10. Dan Fouts, St. Ignatius High School. An All-City QB, Fouts was offense on the West Coast before there ever was a West Coast offense. He'd go on to shatter Pac 8 passing records, and throw for more than 43,000 yards in the NFL with the Chargers. He spent several seasons as a 49ers ball boy before becoming a Hall of Fame QB, and a very good broadcaster.

9. Jerry Coleman, Lowell High School. The man who would proudly serve his country in World War II would go on to have a solid major league career with the Yankees, and become a Hall of Fame broadcaster with the San Diego Padres. "You can hang a star on that, baby."

8. Ollie Madson, Track and Football, Washington H.S. With blazing speed and toughness, Madson turned his outstanding gifts into an undefeated season for the USF Dons when he led the nation in rushing. A Hall of Fame football career soon followed along with a silver medal for the 4x400-meter relay team at the 1952 Summer Olympics.

7. Tom Meschery, Lowell High School. Books like this are written to teach kids about players like Meschery. A rock-steady prep player in the late '50s, his high school, college, and pro careers all touched San Francisco. He was a banger before becoming a gentleman with a Master of Fine Arts degree and an interest in poetry.

6. Fred LaCour, St. Ignatius High School. During his senior season at Ignatius, LaCour dropped 40 points on the Stanford Frosh team and is considered one of the great cagers San Francisco courts had ever seen. With three straight City "Tournament of Champions" titles and All Northern California Player of the Year, his short NBA career doesn't tell the story of this San Francisco great.

5. Hank Luisetti, Galileo High School. A native of San Francisco, he would travel south to Palo Alto to stake his claim to fame. Credited with inventing the running, one-handed shot, he took the game he developed on the streets of S.F. and turned himself into a three-time All American at Stanford.

4. K.C. Jones, Commerce High School. He would revolutionize the attacking defensive style of guard play, and would team up with Bill Russell at the University of San Francisco to win back-to-back NCAA titles and eight NBA Championships in nine seasons with the Celtics.

3. Bob St. Clair, Polytechnic High School. Played in every phase of football right here in the city. From back yard, two-hand touch as a child, to the field at Kezar Stadium, where he starred in college and with the 49ers. He's a living legend, and was an all-around bad-ass back in his day.

2. O.J. Simpson, Galileo High School. Broke city records as a back, running behind an undersized offensive line, before setting records at City College of San Francisco and transferring to USC, where he'd become an icon. Enshrined in the Pro Football Hall of Fame, it's very difficult to think of O.J. as just an athlete now.

1. Joe DiMaggio, Galileo High School. Born in San Francisco; buried here, too. The Great DiMaggio had a 61-game hitting streak for the Pacific Coast League's Seals before gaining glory in Yankee pinstripes. Although he gained his fame New York, DiMaggio never forgot his true hometown. During the 1989 earthquake, there he was, an ordinary citizen on a bucket brigade, trying to help fight fires and rescue people in the Marina.

NOTE: Born in Fremont, there is no one who has tasted Bay Area football quite like the bold and brash linebacker who played in high school, college, USFL, NFL and works in the broadcast booth—all right here. A Super Bowl Champion turned critical color analyst, Gary Plummer is on the radio every Sunday when the 49ers play, or on his bike doing 50-mile rides around his home in San Diego, wearing an extra-medium shirt.

10. High school in Fremont. At Mission, San Jose HS, I was on the undefeated, North Coast Champion team that averaged more than 40 points per game. We finished 12-0, and ten guys from my team were given major scholarships. I wasn't one of them.

9. Ohlone College. Since I wasn't good enough to get a look from a major program, I enrolled and became a two-way starter, playing 60 minutes per game. I won every school tackling record for a program that no longer exists. That's when I got noticed by bigger schools. Letters came in from hundreds of schools, but I really wanted to get a good education, and was interested in Stanford. At the time, the Cardinal defensive coordinator decided to come and see my 6-foot, 200-pound frame in person. He laughed in my face and said, "You're Gary Plummer? You can't play in the Pac 10."

8. Walked on at Cal. With that Stanford coach's words ringing in my ears every day, I took a year off to do nothing but work, workout and eat. I grew two inches and gained 28 pounds in 11 months. I walked on at Cal, for one reason only: to stick it to Stanford and the coach who told me I would never play in his conference. Motivated by revenge, all I saw was his face laughing at me during every drill and rep. With two All American LBs, I was moved to nose tackle. A 228-pound nose tackle? I thought they were setting me up to quit or fail. One month later, I was starting. Cal's coaches had promised if I contributed, they would give me a scholarship. They never did. It was yet another example of life slapping me in the face. Good. More motivation.

7. Oakland Invaders of the USFL. Undrafted by the NFL, I found myself on a rainy field at Menlo Atherton College with 200 other guys getting a workout for USFL scouts. By the end of the day, I had survived, and was signed to the Oakland Invaders for $25,000 on the spot. Our camp was in Arizona, and if there were 24 linebackers, I was 25th on the depth chart. I sat and watched others get chances for nearly six weeks. They also got hurt. On the last day of camp, I made four tackles on five plays and finally made believers out of those who yet again underestimated me. I was told that day, I'd be starting for the Invaders. I made the USFL based on one goal-line drill in practice, and would go on to be the franchise's all-time leading tackler. That's when the NFL finally noticed me.

6. The Chargers. The dissolving USFL put me in contract limbo. I found myself at Chargers camp in 1986, watching practice, unable to participate because of my Invaders deal. Finally, when the lawyers stopped arguing, I got my chance. I made two open-field tackles in two drills, and made the roster, again, on the final day of practice. Two weeks later, I was a starting NFL linebacker and would lead the team in tackles that year, and four of the next five seasons. But still, San Diego was constantly trying to replace me. Good. More motivation. Long before it was fashionable, I hired trainers, practiced yoga and martial arts, anything to gain an edge. Through discipline alone, I turned myself into a 255-pound tackling machine, but my days in Southern California were numbered.

5. Facing the Niners and my past. Despite playing the best football of my career, I was told by the Chargers they wanted to cut my deal and pay me less. Thirty-four years old, and being elbowed out, I refused. My agent, Lee Steinberg, was good friends with Carmen Policy, who needed help stopping the run in San Francisco, so I returned to the Bay for a "little workout" that turned into a two-hour audition while not just a couple of scouts, but the entire franchise looked on. After that, I walked into Head Coach George Seifert's office, where he looked me in the eye, took my hand, shook it, and said, "You're not good enough to play in the Pac 10, but you're good enough to play for the 49ers." The man who had lit my fire by telling me I wasn't good enough was now the head coach of my childhood team, and giving me a job. My life had come full circle.

4. 1994 team. I was the first who signed . . . after that, Ken Norton, Rickey Jackson, and I restructured my deal so we could sign Deion Sanders. It was football Shangri-La. In our locker room there was no doubt who was going to be the team to beat. We not only had high expectations, but we had the team to reach them. And it was family. All those years in San Diego, and never once did the owner know my name. In less than one month, Eddie DeBartolo not only knew my name, but my wife and my children. He sent us flowers to welcome us into the 49ers family. Never once was I treated like a player just filling pads.

3. Super Bowl XXIX. Not one ball hit the ground in practice for two weeks leading up to the game. It was the most amazing offense I had ever seen, precision at its finest. Steve Young was on fire; it was the most amazing thing I've ever seen. Still, I was nervous. I'd never been to the Super Bowl. I was sitting near my locker before the game, next to Ricky Jackson, both our stomachs full of butterflies. That's when Jerry Rice came up to us, tapped both our pads and said, "Tonight I'm going to get you your Super Bowl rings." A wave of confidence came over me. Before we left the locker room, I called my wife and told her to have the boys close to the 50-yard line with two minutes left, because we were going to "kick San Diego's ass." I always wanted my sons with me on the field for the winning moments of a Super Bowl, and I knew it was going to happen that night.

2. The Monkey. Standing on the sideline, the game was all but over. Steve had set a Super Bowl record with six TD passes, and now Elvis Grbac was mopping up. Growing up a family of 49ers fans, I knew more than anyone what Steve Young had gone through. Playing in the shadow of Montana, he was never appreciated for the great quarterback he was before that night. That always made me sick. And out of nowhere, he said, "Someone get the monkey off my back." Without thinking, I said "Dude, it's not a monkey, it's a gorilla" and pulled the imaginary animal off his back. Steve regrets the words, but I knew how hard he had worked, and he deserved that moment of recognition. People ask me about that moment all the time.

1. Into the Booth. After all these years, what means the most to me is that I'm still part of the 49ers family. I played football and have been a fan all my life. To call the 49ers my family is the icing on the cake of my life. To still be associated with this great organization, well, it doesn't get any better.

The 'The' List

The city lays claim to "The" moments. One is better known locally, while the other two can be referred to in any sports bar in America, and people will instantly know what you're talking about. Can any other city in the United States boast three, "The" moments? I don't think so.

3. The Dunk. In the 2006-07 Western Conference Semi-Finals, Baron Davis turned "YouTube" into a verb—as in "Baron just YouTubed Andrei Kirlienko." Although the Warriors would fall in the series, it was a moment to punctuate an unexpected play-off appearance and caused what could be the single loudest roar to ever be unleashed by a California sports crowd. Go ahead. Just say "the dunk" here in the Bay Area. It can only mean one thing.

2. The Play. The greatest highlight in the history of NCAA football was born in the Big Game, Cal vs. Stanford, on the field of Memorial Stadium on November 20, 1982. John Elway, in his final game with the Cardinal, stormed down the field to give Stanford a late FG and a 20-19 lead with four seconds left. Five laterals later on the ensuing kickoff, and a mad dash through the Stanford Band, Cal wins 25-20. Long-time play-by-play announcer Joe Starkey summed it up with one of the most classic calls in the history of sports: "We've heard no decision yet. Everybody is milling around on the FIELD—AND THE BEARS! THE BEARS HAVE WON! The Bears have won! Oh my God! The most amazing, sensational, dramatic, heart-rending...exciting, thrilling finish in the history of college football! California has won the Big Game over Stanford! Oh, excuse me for my voice, but I have never, never seen anything like it in the history of I have ever seen any game in my life! The Bears have won it! There will be no extra point!"

1. The Catch. The moment the 49ers' Dynasty was born, January 10, 1982. After a classic 59-minute struggle with the Dallas Cowboys in the NFC title game, San Francisco was down by six points. With just 58 seconds remaining, Joe Montana scrambled to his right from the Dallas 6-yard line, pump-faked to freeze the defense, and tossed a pass high in the back of the end zone, where it found the outstretched fingertips of Tight End Dwight Clark. The 49ers scored the winning TD with 51 seconds left, and punched their ticket to the team's first ever Super Bowl. For the record, the play called in the huddle, "Sprint Right Option," was intended to go to Freddie Solomon. Good thing he was covered. Clark's leaping catch over Everson Walls is forever etched into the minds of 49ers fans, and into the history of the NFL.

Building a Bay Area Frankenstein

If I were to take the best attributes of Bay Area athletes and stitch them together to make a monster athlete, this is where I'd get the parts.

Left Arm—Vida Blue

Right Arm—Juan Marichal

Hands—Jerry Rice

Fingers—Jason Kidd

Finger Tips—Dwight Clark

Wrists—Barry Bonds

Forearms—Mark McGwire

Elbows—Larry Smith

Biceps—Jose Canseco

Shoulders—Wilt Chamberlin

Back—Vernon Davis

Hairy Back—Jeff Fassaro

Abs—Terrell Owens

Chest—Summer Sanders

Belly—Rod Beck

Feet—Rickey Henderson

Ankles—Tim Hardaway

Right Leg—George Blanda

Left Leg—Sebastian Janikowski

Thighs—Roger Craig

Calves—Larry Allen

Rear End—Art Shell

Hair—Mike Ricci

Eyes—Barry Bonds

Head—Bruce Bochy

Chin—Ken Norton, Jr.

Mouth—Rickey Henderson

Teeth—Mike Ricci

Brains—Joe Montana

Heart—Will Clark

Pituitary Gland—Manute Bol

Guts—Dave Dravecky

Balls—Jeff Kent

Asshole—Barry Bonds

A Dozen Unwritten Rules of Major League Baseball

The game has mystique, and a big part of it lies in the game's unwritten rules. There's a certain code of conduct players have to follow, and the path is passed down from Veteran to Rookie. Should you not follow, the chances of your team being involved in a bench-clearing brawl multiply tenfold. So, for the first time, let's put some of these "unwritten rules" down in ink.

12. The game is not yours to keep. Pass it on. It is often said that Bonds was a bad teammate—but never by his teammates, who will tell you he's one of the best hitting coaches they've ever had. Veterans have a responsibility to teach young players the right way to behave as a big leaguer.

11. Cross dress your rookies. An elaborate Little Bo-Peep costume or uniforms from the local Hooters should do just fine. Hazing is part of the game, and it keeps clubs loose and rookies humble. Doesn't matter what your signing bonus was when walking to the bullpen wearing a "My Little Pony" backpack.

10. Play your best lineup when the game matters. Doesn't matter if you're 24 games out of first place. If the other team is in contention, give 'em your best punch. Field your strongest lineup for the integrity of the pennant race.

9. Pitchers don't talk to hitters. Thanks to free agency and a mobile upper class, these guys pretty much get to know lots of players on other teams, but on game day, the fraternizing should be kept to a minimum. Back in the day, conversation would never take place between a team's pitcher and the other team's hitters. There is nothing to gain from being friendly to a guy you want to beat.

8. Don't get caught stealing signs. What's the best way to get a pitcher to serve one in your ear hole? Have his catcher catch you peeking. Again, it's not against the unwritten rules to steal signs, just never get caught doing it.

7. Don't get caught relaying signs to teammates. Happens all the time in every game—again, just don't get caught doing it, or the next pickoff move will be meant for you, not the fielder.

6. Know your umpires. Learning the tendencies of other players isn't enough. At the Major League level, it's mandatory to know the tendencies of your umpiring crew as well. Some teams even go so far as to post pictures of umpires with bios and talking points so players can "chat up blue" in between pitching chances.

5. No deeking players into late slides. If an infielder is going to pretend he's about to field a ball to induce the runner into a slide, it better happen early. No base runner wants to grab dirt late in his run unless he has to. Bottom line, if you're going to risk injury, there'd better be a reason.

4. Don't swing 3-0 with a big lead. A common theme from many old-school managers is "don't abuse a big lead late." If you're up big, feasting on struggling pitchers before they throw a strike is a big no-no. It could cause a serious case of bean ball to break out the next day.

3. No stolen bases with an eight-run lead. Again, this comes from the school of not abusing big leads late in a game. The unwritten rule used to be, "don't steal if you're up by five runs after six innings. Some of the newer, more hitter-friendly parks, however, have re-defined what a big, late lead really is. Consider this rule ignored in the hitting-friendly parks in Cincinnati, Arizona, Boston—and Colorado, before the Rockies starting using a humidor to deaden balls.

2. No bunting to break up a no-hitter after the sixth inning. It's one of the cardinal, unwritten rules never to be messed. Should you play with fire, expect repercussions and being treated like an outcast. Nothing pisses off a manager more than watching his pitcher lose a no-no on a drag bunt late in the game.

1. No staring, no posing: Develop a timely home run trot. The simple way to put it, and a common theme you'll hear coming from every dugout, "Don't pimp your own homerun." Even the superstar sluggers catch heat when they stand at home plate too long, admiring their own work. When you circle those bases, never look at the pitcher or into the opposing dugout, and that jog had better be brisk.

All ten names have something in common: Another man who's grown to fame, with the exact same name.

10. Willie Brown. The Raiders' Brown filled up the screen with his interception return in Super Bowl XI. The other was San Francisco's dapper mayor, who helped fill up Chin Basin by greasing the political skids to build the Giants a new park.

9. Jimmy Johnson. The former 49ers DB is in the Pro Football Hall of Fame. The ex-Cowboys coach is a member of the hair-care products HOF.

8. Eddie Plank. The former Athletics star won 326 games from 1901-17. The ex-Giant made it into nine games in 1978-79.

7. Ken Norton. Heavyweight boxer and his heavy-hitting 49ers linebacker son.

6. Eric Wright. Former Niner cornerback was one of three rookies to start in defensive backfield for team in Super Bowl XVI. Late NWA rapper Eric "Eazy E" Wright had the right attitude to play in the NFL.

5. John Taylor. The bassist provided the thump on numerous Duran Duran hits in the 1980s, and made the ladies scream. The WR of the same name never got hungry like a wolf waiting too long for Joe Montana to throw him the ball, but made plenty of 49ers fans scream.

4. Kevin Mitchell. By the end of his playing career, the husky former Giants MVP was as large as his namesake on the 49ers special teams' squad.

3. Brian Wilson. Though fans often thought (much like the Beach Boys) "Wouldn't It Be Nice" for the Giants closer to throw a clean ninth inning, he made the All-Star team in 2008.

2. Eric Davis. Crafty 49ers DB, and near-the-end-of-the-line Giants OF.

1. Michael Jackson. The Giants reliever led the NL with 81 appearances in 1993, the same year the King of Pop purchased 81 giraffes.

Numbers That Should Be Retired

The Bay Area teams do a great job honoring their past, but there are always over-looked details, such as these ten numbers that need to be retired with no further delay.

10. S.F. Giants No. 22—Will Clark. The most popular Giant of the Humm-Baby era, "The Thrill" was the face of the Giants remarkable late Eighties resurgence.

9. 49ers No. 8—Steve Young. He's already in the Hall of Fame, won an MVP and set Super Bowl records. So why the wait?

8. Warriors No. 17—Chris Mullin. The W's best pure shooter not named Rick Barry.

7. Oakland Raiders No. 12—Kenny Stabler. The Raiders have a policy against retiring uniform numbers, leaving this iconic slinger's digits available to any third string quarterback.

6. Oakland A's No. 34—Dave Stewart. The third most victorious pitcher in A's history, Stewart's number actually is retired, but in honor of another player, HOF reliever Rollie Fingers, who also wore No. 34. There's no law preventing a number from being retired twice.

5. Oakland Raiders No. 00—Jim Otto. As if anyone in Silver and Black would have the gumption to roll double snake eyes on their jersey ever again.

4. Oakland A's No. 35, 24—Rickey Henderson. Maybe the A's are waiting to retire Rickey's numbers because the "greatest of all times" hasn't actually officially retired himself.

3. Oakland A's No. 10—Tony LaRussa. He certainly is squirrelly—and would fight for squirrel rights—but there's no denying the impact that the animal-loving LaRussa has made on Bay Area baseball.

2. Oakland Raiders No. 16—George Blanda/Jim Plunkett. The dual kings of Bay Area reclamation projects.

1. S.F. Giants No. 25—Barry Bonds. The club has already retired his lounge chair and widescreen TV. The next logical move is his number.

If confidence is sexy, here's the beefcake. Bonds not included.

10. John Matuszak. The larger-than-life 6-foot-8, 285 pound 'Tooz was a Raiders cartoon character and always the life of party. The lineman was in his prime the week of Super Bowl XV, prowling New Orleans' French Quarter just a few wee hours prior to kickoff.

9. John Montefusco. San Francisco's ultimate cocky bastard didn't predict he would pitch a no-hitter against the Braves in late 1976—but if he had, no one would have batted an eye. "The Count" once predicted he would strikeout Johnny Bench four times in night and was still unrepentant after the All-Star knocked him out of the game with a first-inning homer.

8. Terrell Owens. A four-sport superstar in high school, T.O. excelled at just two things with the Niners: scoring TDs and showboating. Originally a quiet third-round pick in 1996, Owens quickly blossomed into a star and proved it to the nation in 2000 when he rushed to mid-field at Dallas after scoring a pair of touchdowns to bask in the glory on the Cowboys' famous star. He'd be #1 on the list, but didn't really develop his superior pain-in-the-ass act until he got to Philly.

7. Rick Barry. There's precious little highlight footage of Barry in his prime, but the few cuts that do exist prove he was one of the most exciting multi-faceted players ever, and a shoot-the-lights, in-your-face trash-talker.

6. Ronnie Lott. Like a heat-seeking missile, Lott laid the wood every single second of his football life. No one was shocked—grossed out maybe, but not shocked—when Lott had part of a mangled pinkie finger amputated in the mid-1980s so he could get back on the field sooner.

5. Ted Hendricks. At 6-foot-7, 220 pounds, Hendricks was built like a basketball player, but saved his slams for anyone dumb enough to tote a football anywhere near him. The Stork's long wingspan was custom built for batting down passes and corralling offensive players as if they were baby calves.

4. Jack Tatum. "The Assassin." He was called a cheap-shot artist by anyone not affiliated with the Raiders, but Tatum said he was only doing his job. Which he did, like a man possessed.

3. Jeffrey Leonard. Until the 1987 playoffs, "Ol' Penitentiary Face" was a local act. Then he famously put "one flap down" and did a slow cruise around the base paths. Opposing Cardinal fans responded by throwing everything from cowbells to loose change at Leonard.

2. Reggie Jackson. Before stirring the Yankees' cocktail, Reggie had his swaggering swizzle stick working overtime in Oakland. He was sports' perfect marriage of talent and uber-ego.

1. Kenny Stabler. For the Snake, "performance enhancing" came in a whiskey bottle. He once said: "The fatter I got, the drunker I got, the more women I got." And the more comebacks he orchestrated.

Seriously, they're not even football players . . . but how important is a sure-footed kicker? Ask any team that's lost by 3. But it's not just the points; it's the field position—the first weapon in any great defensive attack. Here's to the 10 best who applied foot to ball.

10. Mike Coffer, Kicker. Six seasons with San Francisco and back-to-back Super Bowl rings. Good leg that was at the right place at the right time.

9. Joe Nedney, Kicker. A proud graduate of San Jose State, Nedney spent a season in Oakland before joining the Niners in 2005, his eighth NFL team. He earned team Co-MVP honors in his first season in San Francisco, and was as much of a team leader as a place kicker can be. A great guy, his most controversial moment happened in 2007, when he got fined for giving a fan the "one-fingered-salute" in a loss to the Saints.

8. Chris Bahr, Kicker. After shunning a pro soccer career, Bahr became a Raider in 1980 after a few seasons with the Bengals, and quickly kicked his way into the team's record books. Bahr, a member of two championship teams, is second in most FG and FG attempted, and is second in franchise history with 817 points scored.

7. Sebastian Janikowski, Kicker. "Sea Bass, the Polish Cannon." The reputation he earned at Florida State as a rabble-rouser was tailor made for the Raiders—so perfect, in fact, that Al Davis had to have him, and made sure of it when he selected him with the 17th overall pick of the 2000 NFL draft. A touchback-inducing machine, Janikowski holds the franchise record for highest percentage of FG made (78%) and is one of the strongest and biggest kickers in NFL history.

6. Andy Lee, Punter. With punts of 71, 74, and 81 yards under his belt already, Lee is on his way to becoming one of the best punters, if not the greatest, in San Francisco history. Averaged an NFL-best 47.3 yards per punt in 2007, and was rewarded with his first trip to the Pro Bowl.

5. Shane Lechler, Punter. Holds the NFL record for punting yards averaged with at least 250 attempts at 45.69 yards. A three-time Pro Bowler with the Raiders, Lechler has been one of the premier special teams weapons in the NFL since 2000.

4. Tommy Davis, Kicker/Punter. In 1960, Davis' 19 FG were good enough and often enough to lead the NFL in field goals. But it wasn't an era of specialty, and Tommy earned his keep as the Niners punter, too. He went on to lead the NFL with a 45.6 punting average in 1962, and is still third all-time in yards per punt. For the better part of a decade, Davis was the only kicker on the team.

3. Ray Wersching, Kicker. If not for Jerry Rice, Wersching's 979 points would stand atop the 49ers record book for most points scored. He'll have to settle for second place and two Super Bowl rings. Ray also worked as a CPA, has an Insurance Agency in Redwood City, and was indicted by a Federal Grand Jury for embezzling more than $8 million in 2006.

2. Ray Guy, Punter. The first-ever punter selected in the first round of the NFL draft turned out to be one of the best bets in team history. Guy kicked the Raiders out of trouble for 14 seasons, and only three other players in franchise history appeared in more games. A seven-time Pro Bowler, three-time Super Bowl Champion and member of the NFL's 75th Anniversary Team, Guy's punts had so much hang time, opponents once checked the ball for helium.

1. George Blanda, Place Kicker, Quarterback. He holds the Raiders franchise records for Most Points (863), Most Extra Points (395), Most Consecutive Extra Points (201), Most Extra Points in a Single Season (56) and Most Career Field Goal Attempts (249). Beyond that, Blanda was no ordinary kicker. In addition to his record 26 seasons of professional football, he was also a gun-slinging quarterback who threw for nearly 27,000 yards with 236 TD. He made several key contributions under center for the Raiders, including getting the team into the 1970 AFC title game. He was the record holder for most career INTs until Brett Favre picked him off for the #1 spot.

Beyond the 24-foot high right field wall, outside the Giants' beautiful downtown ballpark, you can take yourself on a free walking tour of the greatest moments in the stadium's history. All of the bronze plaques are unique pieces of art themselves, signifying, in order, the moments, teams, players, and games fans will never forget.

1. April 11, 2000—Opening Day, Pacific Bell Park. Ah yes, forget what the Dodgers did to Giants pitching that beautiful afternoon, and please forget the original name of the stadium, forever etched right here.

2. 2000 NL West Division Champs Pennant. Shaped like a pennant you'd see hanging in a boy's bedroom, the Giants opened their magnificent new location by winning the division crown that season.

3. Bonds' 500th HR—April 17, 2001. Beat L.A. 3-2, splash hit. Bonds' handprints and autograph are pressed into the surrounding concrete. See, Barry did play here!

4. Bonds' All-Time Single Season HR Champ. Of the all the bronze plaques, I think this one's the coolest design. It resembles two baseball cards overlaying each other with Bonds on top and his stats underneath.

5. Bonds' 600th HR. Apparently Barry couldn't be bothered to get his hands dirty with concrete again.

6. 2002 NL League Champs. Along with Barry's prodigious climb up the HR chart, the Giants did more than a little winning along the way.

7. Wire-to-Wire 2003 Division Champ Pennant, 100-win season. The Giants opened and closed strong in yet another great regular season that fell short in October.

8. 660th HR, Barry Bonds ties Willie Mays—April 12, 2004. A special day for Giants fans as Bonds tied his godfather for third on the all-time homerun list. Both Bonds and Mays are pictured on the plaque. However, Barry's swinging a bat while Mays is just standing there.

9. 700th HR—Sept 17, 2004. No turning back now. It was only a matter of time before the record would fall, and this is when we all knew it. And it's the only plaque that remembers this place was once called SBC Park.

10. Rob Nen, 300th Save—Aug 6, 2000. Bonds can't have all the bronze glory on the walk outside the park, so here's a salute to the "The Nenth Inning" and the greatest closer in team history. Nen's impressive stats in San Francisco are there to be seen: 314 career saves, 2.89 career ERA.

11. Bonds' 715—May 8, 2006. The number says it all, and Bonds isn't on the plaque, but his victim's name that day is etched forever: Byung-Hyun Kim. It's the only plaque to borrow from another San Francisco icon; the towers of the Golden Gate Bridge are part of the design.

12. Jason Schmidt, Career High 16 Strikeouts—June 16, 2006. Ugh. First he gets a plaque, and then he becomes a Dodger? Oh well, that's baseball. Before crossing party lines however, Schmidt gave the Giants the best seasons of his career. In his last year with the club, he buzzed through the Marlins lineup in dominant fashion that night. Schmidt tied the franchise strikeout record established by Hall of Famer Christy Matthewson, October 3, 1904.

13. All Star Game—July 10th 2007. The entire baseball world came to the shores of McCovey Cove for one of the most beautiful mid-summer classics ever played. The third—and hopefully final—corporate name change to AT&T Park gets its first mention on this bronze beauty.

14. #756. The moment Giants fans had been waiting years for was delivered to them, at home, by Mr. Bonds himself. On the plaque, the answer to sports' newest trivia question: Who served up the historic pitch? Nationals pitcher Mike Bacik, August 7, 2007.

The designers of AT&T Park built a baseball cathedral. Around that cathedral, stand the Gods of San Francisco Giants baseball. There are five bronze pieces of artwork displayed proudly outside baseball's most scenic stadium, and each is unique and magnificent. Any first-time trip to a Giants game would be incomplete without having a look at all of them. Each statue has the players' stats, Hall of Fame plaque, and several quotes about the player. Here is what's said about each Giants great.

1. The Willie Mays Statue, corner of Third and King Street.

"He should play in handcuffs, to even things out a bit." Jim Murray, L.A. Times.

"All in all, I most enjoy watching him run bases. He strides, his spikes digging up great chunks of infield dirt; the cap flies off at second, he cuts the base like a racing car, looking back over his shoulder at the ball, and lopes grandly into third, and everyone who has watched him finds himself laughing with excitement and sheer delight." Roger Angell, *The Summer Game*

"If somebody came up and hit .450, stole 100 bases and performed a miracle in the field every day, I'd still look you in the eye and say Willie Mays was better. He could do the five things you have to do to be a superstar: hit, hit with power, run, throw and field. And he had that other magic ingredient that turns a superstar into a super superstar. He lit up the room when he came in. He was a joy to be around." Leo Durocher, former Giants manager.

"Willie has two weaknesses—a pitch thrown behind his back and a fly ball 20 rows into the stands." Leo Durocher.

"The only person who could have caught that ball, hit it." Bob Stevens, *San Francisco Chronicle*.

"Mere numbers...cannot show the flying cap, the basket catch, the quick feet, the whirl and throw that are etched not in the record books, but in the precious memory. It is debatable there has ever been a player with Mays' baseball instinct or, yes, intellect. The exquisite subtleties of his play only eventually become apparent to fans." Ron Fimrite, *Sports Illustrated*.

"Willie Mays and his glove: where triples go to die." Fresco Thompson L.A. Dodgers Executive.

"He was the most exuberant and exciting player of his generation, one of the most extraordinarily gifted ball players to ever step on a diamond. He could do everything and he could do it better than anyone else with a joyous grace." Arthur Daley, *N.Y. Times*.

2. Juan Marichal Statue, outside the Lefty O'Doul Gate.

"He can throw all day and hit a space no wider than two inches—in, out, up, down. I've never seen anyone as good as that." Pete Rose.

"If you don't get Marichal out of the game by the third inning, forget it. He is going to beat you." Curt Gowdy.

"I still think bunting against Marichal is a good idea. The only trouble is he won't give you a pitch you can bunt." Jim Wynn.

"If Marichal's first pitch doesn't get over, he's got 9 others to throw at you. Juan Marichal is the best pitcher in baseball." Ed Kranepool.

"When you really have to win a game, Marichal gives me confidence. Juan rises to the occasion. He thrives on competition. The tougher the situation, the better he is." Alvin Dark.

3. Orlando Cepeda Statue, corner of Third and King Street.

"He's annoying every pitcher in the league. He is strong, he hits to all fields, and he makes all the plays." Willie Mays.

"I've always regarded Orlando as the greatest right-handed true power hitter I ever saw in our day." Willie McCovey.

"This is the best right-handed pure power hitter for a young player I've ever seen." Bill Rigney, 1958.

Bill Rigney to Whitey Lockman, Spring Training, 1958.

Rigney: "What's your assessment of Orlando?"

Lockman: "He's a few years away."

Rigney: "No, he's ready now!"

Lockman: "A few years away...from the Hall of Fame."

4. Willie McCovey, on the shores of McCovey Cove. Walk across the historic Third Street Bridge into China Basin Park, and soak in one of the best views of AT&T Park on way to the McCovey statue. There, instead of a series of quotes, you'll find Stretch's story. Around his statue, you'll find the names of the "Willie Mac Award" winners. It's a wonderful place for true Giants fans to visit.

5. Seal Statue, behind the park at the Marina Gate. The least known of the statues, based on its location behind the park, sits a seal balancing a baseball on its nose. There used to be a plaque explaining that it was a tribute to San Francisco's baseball past, however, it was either removed, or stolen.

The Best of Ten through One

Since this is a book of (mostly) #10 through #1, these are the Bay Area athletes who did the most on behalf of their digit.

10 – Tim Hardaway.

9 – Reggie Jackson.

#8 – Steve Young.

#7 – Kevin Mitchell.

#6 – Bill Russell (USF).

#5 – Jason Kidd.

#4 – Miguel Tejada.

#3 – Daryle Lamonica.

#2 – Dick Dietz.

#1 – Billy Martin.

When they built the Giants' new ballpark, they thought of everything, including ways to keep kids interested and entertained. Funny, when I was a kid, the major league baseball game being played right before my eyes was enough for me. But times have indeed changed. Here are a couple of distractions perfectly designed to stop little Billy and Sally from squirming, and to give Mom and Dad a chance to take five or watch a little baseball.

5. Historic Third Street Bridge. Opened in 1933. At the time, it was the largest moving bridge in the world. Now dwarfed a hundred times over, the Third Street Bridge is partially closed for pre-game foot traffic. Take a walk over the bridge into China Basin Park to see the McCovey Statue, and one of the best views outside of AT&T Park. Disregard the several homeless people who sit in the same spot season after season pestering fans.

4. Barry Bonds Junior Giants Field. Ahh, it's a slice of baseball heaven for the 12-and-under crowd, offering a chance to actually play baseball. What a concept. It's a place to drop the kids off pre- or post-game while Mom and Dad enjoy a stroll to read in the plaques around China Basin Park. The plaques pay tribute to each Giants team from 1958-2000, when the team moved to its new downtown location.

3. Lights of Left O'Doul's Gate. When leaving the park at night, kids glow with the same neon glee that lights the O'Doul's Gate. A bright, colorful, electric animation of one of the park's unique features: "the splash hit." A little seal pops up to greet the ball . . . the kids love it.

2. The Coke Slide. If there is one thing that disturbs me, it's the growing corporate presence inside our stadiums. Having said that, the 80-foot-long, neon Coke bottle in left field is pretty cool. So are the slides that, yes, even I have taken for a spin. The entire Coke Fan Lot would have me wetting my pants if I were a kid again. Along with the slide, there's the big, old-fashioned glove statue, and a mini-AT&T Park for the little ones only. The best thing, it's all free—with the price of stadium admission, of course.

1. The Cable Car. Our nation's only moving landmark isn't going anywhere at AT&T Park. A real, retired—and now permanently stationary—cable car sits in the arcade in right-center field. Once a common mode of transportation for all San Franciscans, this one is now basically a jungle gym with a bell that kids ring nonstop from the first pitch to the final out. By the way, "No Dodgers Fans Allowed."

The Smiths

We all know Mr. Smith went to Washington. Apparently, he came to the Bay Area several times, too. Here they are, ranked by their "Smithiness."

10. Alex Smith, 49ers. The #1 overall flop happens to be the worst "Smith" in San Francisco history.

9. Chris Smith, Giants. Former USC standout never panned out in San Francisco.

8. Otis Smith, Warriors. Could throw it down back in the day, but now throws down deals as the Orlando Magic's GM.

7. Greg Smith, A's. Believe it or not, even though it's one of the most common names in the world, Greg is the only Smith to play for the A's in their 40 seasons in Oakland.

6. Reggie Smith, Giants. Former Dodgers tough guy finished up strong in Orange and Black in his last major league season.

5. Larry Smith, Warriors. He was Mr. Mean to opponents and beloved by the home crowd for his physical style. Closest thing the Warriors had to an enforcer.

4. Bubba Smith, Raiders. Before Police Academy, Bubba didn't tackle roles in bad movies; he caught quarterbacks for Al Davis.

3. Joe Smith, Warriors. The first time a Smith was selected #1 overall by a Bay Area team. Joe played two and a half seasons with Golden State before being traded to Philadelphia, and turning into a journeyman.

2. Derek Smith, 49ers. Recorded more than 100 tackles in five of his seasons for the Niners.

1. Phil Smith, USF/Warriors. One of just five University of San Francisco players to have his number retired, Smith would play six seasons with the Warriors, and was a member of the only Championship team in franchise history.

Now that Baron Davis is off to L.A., he'll take Jessica Alba (courtside during the Warriors playoff run) with him. Ouch, that hurts. We'll just have to carry on with these ten celebrities who very well could be at the next game.

10. Brad Gilbert. The nut who stabbed Monica Seles with a penknife fits the profile of a Raiders fan, but it's not often the world of professional tennis mixes with the Silver and Black. However, one of the Raiders' biggest fans is Brad Gilbert, former pro and coach of Andre Agassi.

9. CC Sabathia. If the Raiders ever need an emergency tackle or the Warriors find themselves lacking at power forward, all they'd have to do is look in the stands, where they're likely to find CC. The pride and joy of Vallejo is a frequent visitor to both the Black Hole and the Warriors' courtside. Kids flock to him, and he's great with them, a total charmer.

8. Rob Schneider. *SNL* alum, *Deuce Bigalow* franchise icon and master Jeff Gillooly impersonator, S.F. native Schneider partied hearty with the likes of Ellis Burks and Jason Schmidt after the Giants won the 2000 NL west and '02 NL Championship. But we've got to hold Rob accountable. Like a true Hollywood resident, he's rarely seen during the lean years. Maybe he's off "makin' copies."

7. Tom Brady. The spring after winning his first Super Bowl, the Peninsula native found time in his busy schedule of dating actresses and supermodels to visit the Giants spring training site to hang with the Orange and Black. Though he occasionally appears incognito wearing a Red Sox or Yankees cap, Brady has professed his love for the G-men. Seen as often in the tabloids as in football previews, Brady is the closest thing to a full-fledged crossover celebrity the NFL has.

6. Ronnie Lott. He may not be a celebrity in the truest definition of the word, but if there were a line for autographs next to Brad Pitt, Ronnie's would be longer here in San Francisco. Sitting courtside at a Golden State game means seeing a lot of long legs (of players and Warriors Girls) and probably bumping into the 49ers legend. Lott has been a Warriors season ticket holder since the early 1980s.

5. Willie Brown. The Giants would not have their current downtown home without the help of hizzoner greasing the skids. But Brown is more of a football guy, taking full advantage of the free luxury boxes provided turn his eight years running City Hall. He's likely the most sharply dressed man in the stadium.

4. Carlos Santana. San Francisco-raised icon fell in love with both guitars and the Giants as a youth and can be spied darting around the ballpark, or courtside at Warriors games to this day. Gets extra points for not being a frontrunner.

3. Robin Williams. During the early glory days of the Giants' China Basin ballpark, the San Francisco funnyman was a frequent face near the Giants dugout railing. Williams was there as the Giants won the 2002 pennant and even got a hug from home run king Barry Bonds. By the way, *Patch Adams* was schlocky crap, but I may be the one guy who liked *Death to Smoochy*.

2. Danny Glover. The city-born-and-raised leading man didn't just show up when the cameras were on. The *Lethal Weapon* star was the Giants' secret weapon in the stands, clad in a Willie Mays jersey. Glover is a diehard Giants fan, so much so he even wrote the introduction to the Giants' official 50th Anniversary book.

1. Tom Hanks. As a teen, the Oakland-raised movie star was a peanut vendor at A's games, becoming bosom buddies with the couple thousand regulars at the Coliseum during the heart of the Charlie Finley regime. In interviews, the *League of Our Own* star cites his time hawking nuts with helping his acting method. Hands down, Hanks is the biggest Hollywood star to be openly pro-Oakland.

Ten Off-the-Field, Off-the-Wall Injuries

Death in the ring was considered glorious during the days of Gladiators. We're more civil (barely) than the Romans, and we often consider an on-field injury a badge of glory. These ten athletes and their boo-boos, however, qualified them for the inglorious badge of stupidity.

10. Lionell Simmons, Kings. OK, so I had to venture just outside the Bay Area for this one, but it has to make the list. The oft-injured small forward once said he developed carpal tunnel syndrome playing Game Boy.

9. Daric Barton, A's. First, the rookie's batting average hit rock bottom, then his head hit the bottom of a swimming pool. He missed playing time, but not a scalp full of stitches.

8. Jay Witasick, two trips to the Bay Area with stints for both the Giants and the A's. Witasick is also known for a very strange injury. As the story goes there was a watermelon in the garbage bag he was changing. He injured himself yanking on the unexpected weight.

7. Mike Ivie, Giants. After a horrible 1980 season, the Giants cut ties with their cult icon after he said he cut himself with a hunting knife. Cynics say he might have been looking for an easy way out, but got cold feet. Brutal.

6. Roger Metzger, Giants. He severed parts of two fingers with a band saw during a freak woodworking accident in the winter of 1979. He managed to return to the field the next season to play in 28 games. He managed two hits . . . one for each nub.

5. Carney Lansford, A's. American League pitchers never slowed down Carney, and neither did a foot of fresh powder on a snowy mountain trail. Before the 1991 season, Lansford fell off a snowmobile and never really recovered. He was out of baseball after 1992.

4. Randy Cross, 49ers. A world of NFL defenders couldn't trip the sure-footed blocker, but Marine World did. Cross mangled his knee when he fell off a playground attraction at the aquatic amusement park. It was meant for kiddies, not offensive linemen.

3. Ron Bryant, Giants. After winning 24 games in 1973, his slider didn't fall off; he fell off a swimming pool slide. Bryant suffered severe lacerations to his side and torso and was out of baseball within two seasons.

2. Monta Ellis, Warriors. Fresh off earning a six-year, $66 million contract, the young combo guard was forced to miss significant time in the beginning of the 2008-09 season when he severely sprained his ankle. It required surgery. After initially telling the Warriors he hurt himself playing a pick-up game, it was later learned that Monta actually fell off a Moped back home in Mississippi.

1. Jeff Kent, Giants. Suffered a broken wrist during Spring Training in 2002, and then lied about it, saying he did the damage when he was washing his truck. Turns out, Kent was popping wheelies on a motorcycle. When the truth came out, it got ugly. The injury greased the skids for his exit after that year.

When you ink a contract, you usually have to initial things "here, here and here" before you sign your name on the dotted line. For these ten guys, there was no difference between the two.

10. J.R. Phillips. Ex-Giant so bad he even struck out with his initials. Real name: Charles Gene.

9. J.B. Carroll. Initials of the enigmatic Warrior stood for Joseph Barry Carroll, not "Just Barely Cares."

8. J.T. O'Sullivan. John Thomas was a no-brainer over Alex Smith.

7. R.C. Owens. Raleigh C. caught the first alley-oop from Y.A. Tittle.

6. Y.A. Tittle. Yelberton Albert tossed the first alley-oop to R.C. Owens.

5. World B. Free. The original Ocho Cinco.

4. A.J. Pierzynski. Anthony John, first in the league in double plays, last in hearts of Giants fans.

3. K.C. Jones. Before participating in a zillion Boston Celtics championships, he helped lead USF to national titles in 1955-56. FYI, K.C. stands for K.C.

2. P.J. Carlesimo. Peter J. got all choked up over, and by, Latrell Sprewell.

1. J.T. Snow. Jack Thomas was the son of a Ram and grew up a Dodgers fan, but will forever be remembered as a Giant.

What's Your Name?

Check this out ... I wrote a poem: "One forgets the name . . . given by his Mother, when one becomes famous...using something other." Here are nine guys you already know, and one guy you will know, by their other names.

10. Tyrone Curtis "Muggsy" Bogues, Warriors.

9. William "Bubba" Paris, 49ers.

8. Leon Joseph "Bip" Roberts, A's, Comcast Sports Bay Area.

7. Mack Neal "Shooty" Babbitt, A's, Comcast Sports Bay Area.

6. Johnnie B. "Dusty" Baker, Giants.

5. Charles Theodore "Chili" Davis, Giants.

4. Eric Augustus "Sleepy" Floyd, Warriors.

3. Roland Glenn "Rollie" Fingers, A's.

2. Rigoberto "Tito" Fuentes, Giants.

1. Giants top prospect, and record bonus baby: Gerald "Buster" Demp Posey, III. Buster the Third? Are you kidding me? Is that a great name, or what? He's gotta be a lock with a name like that, right?

Ten Spiritual Names

Though I walk through the shadow of the valley of Bay Area athletes, I shall fear no one with a biblical sounding name.

10. Larry Shepard, Giants. Only spent one season in San Francisco. Guess he wasn't "The Good Shepherd."

9. Garry St. Jean, Warriors. GM, then coach after P.J. was fired. For every Jason Richardson drafted by Saint Jean, there was a Vonteego Cummings.

8. Joe Angel, Giants announcer. The fans never converted.

7. Jesus Alou, Giants. No need to explain.

6. Bob St. Clair, 49ers. Not just a Saint, but also a God to old-school 49ers fans.

5. Ricky Churchman, 49ers. Maybe his NFL career would have lasted longer than two seasons if he had played or prayed harder.

4. Moises Alou, Giants. Say it ten times fast . . . you'll get to "Moses Hallelujah."

3. Jason Christianson, Giants. Got into it with Bonds in 2005. Ended up with Barry throwing a cup of Coke—not holy water—at him. Would you believe . . . that was his last year with the team?

2. Matt Cain, Giants. If I read one more headline that says, "Cain was Able" I'm going to scream.

1. Randy Cross, 49ers. Won a trinity of Super Bowl rings, and played his entire career in San Francisco.

Despite glorious careers, these ten men have yet to be called home to their respective Hall of Fames, for whatever reason. Time to set the record straight.

10. Dwight Clark. If dominating your position during your era is a credential for induction to the Hall of Fame, then Clark should be in. With more than 500 catches, he excelled in the passing game, and became a prototype TE for the modern NFL. A little something called "The Catch" should only help his resume.

9. Mark McGwire. In 1999, The Sporting News ranked McGwire among the top 100 baseball players of all time, but the latest Hall of Fame vote says otherwise, and it's not because of his .263 lifetime batting average. Denying his entry into Cooperstown is a childish overreaction by sanctimonious voters who want to pretend steroids users were anything other than par for the course.

8. Chris Mullin. One of the greatest college players the Big East had ever seen turned into one of the sharpest shooting small forwards in NBA history. He averaged more than 25 ppg for five consecutive seasons, turned a dog franchise into a regular playoff participant, was a five time All Star, and won Olympic Gold in 1984 and again with the Dream Team in 1992. He is the only member of that team not in the Hall of Fame.

7. John Brodie. When he walked away from his 17-season career with the Niners, Brodie was the third leading passer in NFL history behind only Johnny Unitas and Fran Tarkenton. The third overall pick of the 1957 draft distinguished himself as an elite passer on a bad team, but he was good enough to be named the AP NFL MVP in 1970. Many believe that Brodie's close ties with the Church of Scientology hurt the consideration he most certainly deserves.

6. Ray Guy. I'll be first to tell you that every 53-man roster has 51 football players and two kickers, but Ray Guy was no ordinary punter. Voted to the NFL's 75th Anniversary Team, he is the standard by which all punters are measured. If football is about taking care of your assignment, no one did his job as well, or as often, as Ray. The College Football Hall of Fame has opened its doors, now it's time for Canton to follow suit.

5. George Seifert. Transition can cripple teams. But for the 49ers, passing the baton from Bill Walsh to Seifert was as seamless and smooth as anyone could have dreamed. On the staff since 1980, Seifert took over as the headcheese in 1989, capturing Super Bowl XXIV in his debut season. He'd stock the case again with the 1994 team, finishing 124-67 overall.

4. Tom Flores. With Super Bowl wins as a player, an assistant coach, and as the head coach the Oakland Raiders, how does this man get overlooked by the Hall of Fame of Professional Football? Despite the fact that he was only ten games over .500 in the regular season, he won more than 100 games with a postseason record of 8-3. On the trailblazing front, he was the first Hispanic-born QB to play professional football. With all the respect that Tony Dungy deserves for being the first African-American to win a Super Bowl, Flores was the first "minority" to call the Lombardi trophy his own, and he did it twice.

3. Roger Craig. In 1985, Roger went to no-man's land, becoming the first player in NFL history to rush for 1,000 yards with a 1,000 more receiving. With more than 13,000 yards from scrimmage, I would put my two Super Bowl rings on my middle fingers and raise them in the direction of Ohio. But Roger is too classy for that, which I believe, is just another reason why he should have a yellow blazer in his closet.

2. Jim Plunkett. Most people can't even believe than a Heisman-winning, two-time Super Bowl champion QB isn't in the Pro Football Hall of Fame, but he isn't. Forget his 198 career interceptions; the man threw for more than 25,000 yards with the UPI Rookie of the Year award in 1971, a Comeback Player of the Year award in 1980, and a little something Raiders fans like to call the Super Bowl XV MVP award. If nothing else, Plunkett should be enshrined under the credential of "Greatest Back-Up QB" of all time.

1. Don Nelson. Why would a man who owns half of Maui want to reside forever in Springfield, Mass.? Actually the better question is: What does the Basketball Hall of Fame have against Nellie? I don't know, but one of the game's great personalities and innovators should already be there. With five NBA titles in his playing days, all Nelson did with his coaching career was climb to #2 on the all-time wins list, and he's still going. Never one for the "old boys club," Nelson's devil-may-care attitude hasn't helped his standing with voters. But at this point, why should he care? Ask anyone who knows the game: Don Nelson doesn't need the Hall of Fame to be a hall of famer.

Founding Father, or clean-up hitter? Leader of the Free World, or trade bait? State of the Union, or state of your team's bullpen? Here are ten players who shared a surname with "the Big Cheese."

10. Herb Washington (A's) and George Washington. The first elected President of these United States, and the first non-glove-owning designated pinch runner in baseball history.

9. Glenn Adams (Giants) and John Adams. A reserve OF, and the nation's first back-up President.

8. Lester Hayes and Rutherford B. Hayes. A DB who loved stickum, and a leader who probably stuck gum under the Oval Office desk.

7. Mark Grant and Ulysses S. Grant. A Civil War hero turned 18th President, and the lure that helped snag Kevin Mitchell from the Padres in 1987.

6. Cole Ford (Raiders) and Gerald Ford. Nixon's pardoner lampooned for falling down stairs, and the deranged Raiders kicker who could have been the protagonist in the film "Falling Down."

5. Marc Wilson (Raiders) and Woodrow Wilson. Two of the stiffest leaders ever in both of their chosen fields.

4. Ray Buchanan (Raiders) and James Buchanan. Complete opposites.

3. Wendell Tyler (49ers) and John Tyler. One dropped the football a lot, the other became president when William Harrison dropped dead just weeks into his Presidency.

2. Reggie Jackson and Andrew Jackson. Reggie paid off in the clutch so often his picture should be on money, too. Just ask him.

1. Lincoln Kennedy and Abraham Lincoln and John F. Kennedy. Highly regarded Raider couldn't have picked two better Presidents to share a name with.

Here we are in 2008, the final season of Yankee Stadium. Wonder how long it will be 'til Wrigley Field and Fenway Park are memories as well. Fans have become used to changing times—if they have not, they'd better come around quickly. Here's a list of ten things that, in just my lifetime, have become extinct.

10. The Importance of Boxing. With the growing popularity of mixed martial arts, you can pretty much kiss the sweet science goodbye. Every now and then, there's a young middleweight with lightning-fast hands who grabs our attention, but never for an extended time. With the current state of the heavyweight division, it's safe to say that ever since Lenox Lewis knocked out Mike Tyson, the sport has been dropped to the canvas as well.

9. Umpire Chest Protectors. Remember the big blue pillow protector that used to be a staple in Norman Rockwell paintings? Yeah, bye bye. Trust me, never hit an umpire in his chest. They're now armored like tanks. They wear vests under their uniforms that could probably stop bullets.

8. Legitimate Nicknames. Crazy Legs. Night-Train. Magic. Doctor. Oil Can. Shoeless. Sweetness. Where have all the great nicknames gone? If not for the XFL's "He Hate Me" we wouldn't have had anything to talk about in years. In an age where marketing is key, how did this art form die?

7. Player/Managers. Talk about a sign of the times, you'll never see a player/manager, a la Pete Rose, again. Now if a player is old enough to manage, by definition he's too old to play. The pressure to win is enough to make a player shrink. Can you imagine if you had to set the lineup too, and deal with the media questions afterwards?

6. Marge Schott. Of course Margie isn't coming back. She's dead. But she represents something more. In a day of 'round-the-clock sports coverage, there will never again be room for bigoted hate-mongers to enjoy such power, even if she was "just acting her age." There is no more room in sports for intolerance—unless, of course, you're gay.

5. Astroturf. And good riddance! Although there's no substitute for a little terra firma, the advances in synthetic turf technology now make the old playing surface look like the Brady Bunch's backyard.

4. The Good Seats. For you and me to enjoy, that is. Only corporate clients and individual Masters of the Universe can afford two down low. Ever-expanding ticket prices have moved the average family of four to the upper deck or bleachers for good. Great tickets at the parks opening in N.Y. in 2008 cost roughly the same as a trip to Mexico.

3. Scheduled Double Headers. Major League Baseball sent a loud-and-clear message to its owners about 15 years ago: squeeze every nickel you can out of your fans. And so, we wave goodbye to the scheduled double header. What used to be a rite of passage for kids in every NL and AL city is now only offered in twi-night form, where you'll have to pay two admissions.

2. Senior Leadership. Maybe the most disturbing of all trends. There is now the perception that if you're in college your senior year, there's a major problem with your game. With millions of tempting dollars waiting in the pros, if you ever see a NCAA team starting five seniors, you're probably watching the NIT. So often kids are tempted to make the leap before they're ready, and suffer dire consequences.

1. Peace and Quiet. And it's never ever coming back. Pulsating music, deafening drum beats, electric scoreboards that are constantly spinning, selling or blinking, a shrieking PA announcer . . . and that's just batting practice. Oh, how I long for the days of simple organ music, or the chance to actually talk to the person sitting next to me. Got my hot dog and beer . . . now where are the earplugs?

Ten Bright Spots in Bay Area Sports

As the A's move all-star caliber players in their prime . . . as the Giants continue to turn in losing season after losing season . . . as the 49ers drift further away from NFL royalty . . . as the Raiders... well, we got the Raiders, too. These are lean days for Bay Area fans. Without a title to hang our collective hat on since the Niners' last Super Bowl win, here are ten reasons for fans to keep the faith.

10. Warriors crowds. While corporate crowds dull environments everywhere, the Warriors unquestionably draw the best crowds not just in the Bay, but the entire NBA. The energy at Oracle Arena for their first-round playoff upset over the Mavericks was unlike anything we'd seen before.

9. Matt Cain. Don't let his record fool you. A closer look at the numbers proves this kid can pitch. For two straight seasons Cain has led the National League in tough-luck-losses, and has received a miniscule amount of run support. What a waste. Cainer finished with the tenth lowest ERA in 2007, when the team scored two or fewer runs in 21 of his starts. He's a horse and a 20-game winner if the Giants get their lineup together.

8. JaMarcus Russell. The #1 overall pick of the 2007 Raiders draft will have to deal with coaching changes along with NFL defenses as long as he's in Silver and Black, but there's little doubting his ability. A physical freak for the position, the strong-armed quarterback out of LSU will need to develop patience in the pocket, and with Al Davis. At least he's got a little help...the next name on this list.

7. Darren McFadden. Loving speed, Al Davis ignored some glaring needs in the 2008 NFL draft, and took the lightning-fast Razorback with the fourth overall pick. In a very small sample size, it appears to be a good choice. McFadden burst into the NFL with breakaway ability and is one of just a few reasons for Raiders fans to dream of returning to their gloried past.

6. Brad Ziegler. Another Billy Beane draft-day success story, and this one comes with a sidearm delivery. Ziegler announced his presence with authority in 2008, setting a new Major League record with 39 consecutive scoreless innings pitched to begin his career. His jersey would likely be a big seller if fans weren't afraid of his impending trade—'cause after all, that's what the A's do.

5. Frank Gore. A steal as the 65th overall pick of the 2005 NFL Draft, Gore has established himself as one of football's premier running backs. A fantasy football hero, he's not bad in reality either, establishing the 49ers franchise rushing record with 1,570 yards in 2006, becoming the first player in San Francisco history to lead the NFC in rushing.

4. Monta Ellis. A dynamic combo guard, and the Warriors and their fans are heavily invested. With a new contract and new responsibilities as "the man," it's time for Monta to stop riding mopeds and drive the Warriors back to NBA respectability. The second-round draft pick averaged over 20 points in just his third NBA season.

3. Patrick Willis. The 11th overall pick of the 2007 NFL draft joined the 49ers and led the NFL in tackles on the way to being named the NFC/NFL Defensive Rookie of the Year He made the Pro Bowl and was named first team All Pro. The only other Niners player to do that was Ronnie Lott. Needless to say, we could be looking at an all-time great.

2. The San Jose Sharks. Boasting a wild crowd of their own, the Sharks are the #1 draw in San Jose, and are routinely ranked among the favorites to win the Stanly Cup. And since they're the only realistic Bay Area contender for a crown anytime soon, now would be a great time to deliver. Everyone knows it, most of all the franchise, which has pulled out all the stops to do so. San Jose enters 2008-09 with renewed hope, and new coach Todd McLellan.

1. Tim Lincecum. After making his debut with the Giants in 2007, Lincecum's first full season in the Majors was an announcement (punctuated with an All-Star selection) that S.F. could have its next big thing. An 18-5 record, with an NL-best 265 strikeouts, for a team that only won 72 games. He'll be the ace going forward, and has already been dubbed "The Franchise."

OK, the hardest part of this book is to rank, explain or justify. How do I define a Bay Area athlete? If your career touched the Bay at the college level but you went on to pro success elsewhere, is that good enough? What if the player was born here, but immediately moved? How many "bonus points" do I give to a player who was beloved? How many points do I take away if a great player never won a title? How do I compare a great player from the '20s or '60s to a modern NFL player? I worked on this for months, and honestly, I can't explain it . . . so let the debate begin.

101. Tiger Woods. We'll start with Tiger, because if we didn't we'd likely have to finish with him, considering he's on pace to become the greatest, and wealthiest individual athlete the world has ever known. Although he's not exactly "Bay Area," Tiger spent two years at Stanford where he won the NCAA Individual Golf Championship in 1996. When not crushing Majors, you can catch-a-Tiger sitting courtside every now and then at Maples Pavilion. He's on the list—yet officially, off the list because he would distort it too much.

100. Baron Davis. Labeled a "coach killer" before being traded to the Warriors, Davis breathed life back into his career, a near-dead Golden State franchise, and a fan base that had endured 12 straight non-playoff seasons. Although he'll be lustily booed when he returns as a Clipper, Davis' leadership and drive brought the Bay Area one of the greatest playoff upsets in NBA history and electrified Oakland more than any one single player since the Run TMC era.

99. Curt Flood. Raised in Oakland, Flood never played for a Bay Area team, but paved the way for free agency by fighting baseball's reserve clause. Flood's efforts pioneered the way every single sports league in the world conducts business with its players.

98. Rob Nen. With 206 saves in five seasons, Nen turned the ninth inning into "The Nenth Inning" along with the ever-present song "Smoke on the Water" by Deep Purple. He's the Giants' career saves leader, led the league in saves in 2001, and was selected to three All-Star Games.

97. O.J. Simpson. Got his start running the football at Galileo High School, right on the corner Van Ness Ave and Bay Street. "Johnnie Law" finally caught up with him in Vegas in 2008. He would be ranked considerably higher if not for all the knife and gun waving.

96. J.T. Snow. A Giants fan favorite who turned in Gold Glove season after season, Snow is widely recognized, even by Dodgers fans, as one of the game's greatest defensive first basemen. So beloved is Snow, the Giants had him sign a one-day contract and ceremonially put him in the starting lineup for one game so he could retire in Orange and Black.

95. Alice Marbel. In the early 1930s she became the best U.S.-born female tennis player after growing up in San Francisco. She would win four U.S. singles titles and Wimbledon in 1939.

94. Jason Schmidt. Dominated the Giants rotation and the rest of the National League when he came to San Francisco via a trade with Pittsburgh. Never had a double-digit loss total attached to his name in 5 and a half seasons with the Giants. He started games one and four of the 2002 World Series, and tossed a 2-0 shutout in the NLDS the next season.

93. Kevin Johnson. Before he ran for mayor of his hometown of Sacramento, K-J practiced distribution of funds as one of the best point guards to ever play four years at Cal, where he dropped the first triple-double in Pac 10 history.

92. Ray Guy. If there's ever going to be a punter selected to the Football Hall of Fame, it will be Guy, who spent his entire career getting the Raiders out of trouble. Three Super Bowl rings and he never had a punt returned for a TD. When it comes to doing your on-field job, no one was better.

91. Felipe Alou. The first Dominican player to routinely play Major League Baseball, he would have a distinguished career that began with him playing for the Giants, stopping in Oakland, and finished with him managing San Francisco from the dugout at AT&T Park.

90. Y.A. Tittle. Ten seasons in San Francisco for an iconic quarterback who battled for playing time with Frankie Albert and John Brodie. But with a decade of battling at Kezar Stadium, he's earned a place here, and in the Hall of Fame.

89. Bobby Bonds. A blend of power and speed that led him to become baseball's first 30/30 man, and father of the man who would surpass his own and nearly all other baseball careers.

88. Brick Mueller. A two-time All-American tailback at the University of California and the featured player on one of college football's most historic teams. He also became an Olympian, winning the silver medal for high jump at the 1920 Antwerp Games.

87. Lynn Swann. Out of Serra High School in San Mateo where he became a standout track star on his way to getting a full ride to USC, and a Hall of Fame career with the Steelers. As graceful an athlete the brutal game of football has ever seen.

86. Tony Gonzalez. After becoming a premier pass-catching TE in Berkeley, all Tony would become is one of the greatest players at his position in the history of the NFL. A sure-fire Hall of Famer when he hangs it up with the Chiefs, he also tasted the Sweet Sixteen as a member of the Golden Bears' basketball team.

85. Deion Sanders. In one season in San Francisco, he brought swagger to the 49ers secondary and hit .285 in 52 games for the Giants. Too bad "Prime Time" was just passing through.

84. K.C. Jones. Ran the point, with Bill Russell in the middle, for the University of San Francisco's back-to-back NCAA title teams. The SF native would also win Olympic gold and nine NBA Championships, all with Big Bill right there in the middle.

83. Daryle Lamonica. "The Mad Bomber" won two AFL MVP awards but was on the wrong end of Super Bowl II. Nevertheless, his big arm defined Oakland's deep, downfield attack in the late Sixties and early Seventies.

82. Candice Wiggins. The all-time leading women's scorer in the history of the Pac 10 conference, and Stanford women's hoops as well.

81. Joe Morgan. A stellar baseball player at Castlemont High School in Oakland before going on to become a Hall of Fame second baseman. Although the iconic elbow flap enjoyed its finest days with Cincinnati's Big Red Machine, Morgan's career also included stops with both the Giants and A's.

80. Matt Biondi. The Palo-Alto-born swimmer chose the pool at Cal, not Stanford, and went on to become one of the country's most decorated swimmers, and an Olympic Hall of Famer.

79. Ricky Watters. With amazing hands and high-stepping running style, he helped the 49ers reach three consecutive NFC title games, and scored a post-season record five TDs against the Giants in the Divisional Round in 1994. In Super Bowl XXIX he scored three more times, tying a mark held with just three other men, two of whom were also 49ers—Jerry Rice and Roger Craig.

78. Rich Gannon. The NFL journeyman found a home in John Gruden's Raiders offense, and found the end zone time and time again. He also found two straight Pro Bowl MVP awards, which has never been done before. In 2002, Gannon "the Cannon" threw for nearly 4,700 yards and 28 TDs, winning the regular season MVP award, but losing Super Bowl XXXVII.

77. Gino Marchetti. Hall of Fame linemen who led the fabled undefeated 1952 USF Football team as a student, he'd go on to become one of the NFL's early defensive masters.

76. Sal Bando. A leader on the field and leader in RBIs for three A's teams that dominated the early Seventies. Four-time All Star who finished second, third and fourth in three different MVP votes.

75. John Elway. Football turned out the be the right choice for Stanford's two-sport standout athlete who played two years in the Yankees' minor league system. Had his pro career been based in the Bay Area, there's no telling where he'd have been on this list, or how much different NFL history would be.

74. Patrick Marleau. A career Sharkie and consummate leader down in San Jose. The Sharks are the only NHL team Captain Pat has ever known.

73. John Brodie. Born in San Francisco, he played his entire NFL career in Niners Red and Gold, and was named the league's MVP in 1970. He brought the air attack to the West Coast and by the time he retired, Brodie had climbed all the way to third on the NFL's career passing list. The Niners have retired his number #12. The Hall of Fame should follow suit and open the doors to Canton.

72. Harris Barton. Drafted in the first round, he started 134 of his 138 career games for the 49ers. "Zeus" won three Super Bowls and is just as proud of his third place finish at the 2007 Pebble Beach National Pro-Am.

71. Dave Casper. The Tight End earned four straight trips to the Pro Bowl in Oakland and helped the Raiders win a pair of Super Bowls. Involved in two of the NFL's iconic plays, Casper was the "Ghost the Post," and fell on the football for the TD that would become known as "The Holy Roller."

70. John McEnroe. His demeanor may not have been suited for Palo Alto, but he tailored his game at Stanford, where he won an NCAA title before embarking on a pro career that would claim seven Grand Slam singles titles.

69. Dave Wilcox. "The Intimidator" defined defense on the West Coast before the West Coast offense defined the 49ers. He was fast enough to run with receivers of the day, and could bury you in the backfield for a four-yard loss.

68. Randy Cross. You'll find a pattern among great 49ers offensive linemen; they never played for another team. Cross was selected All Pro six times—or to look at it another way, twice the number of Super Bowl rings he owns.

67. Frank Robinson. This teammate of Bill Russell during his high school days would clearly rank much higher had his professional playing days been anywhere near the Bay. Although he managed the Giants he gets points deducted for his one season playing in Dodger blue.

66. Charles Haley. The only player in football history to win five championships. His first two came with the 49ers. A fourth-round draft-day score, Haley wore out his welcome with head coach George Seifert and Steve Young after the two had to be separated. He was traded to the rival Cowboys after the `91 season, and won three more rings.

65. Jim Corbett. San-Francisco-born Heavyweight Champion of the World, "The Gentleman" was the first West Coast athlete to gain national respect in the now dying sport of boxing.

64. Joe Capp. The player who lead Cal to the 1959 Rose Bowl would return as coach, and cement his place in Memorial Stadium history. His lesser known escapades on the basketball court resulted in two consecutive Pacific Coast Conference titles for the Golden Bears.

63. Willie Brown. Took a Fran Tarkenton pass to the house for a then-Super-Bowl-record 75-yard INT return for TD in Super Bowl XI. Served the Raiders as defensive captain for ten of his 12 years in Oakland.

62. Terrell Owens. Eight seasons with the 49ers seem a distant memory for one of the most overexposed athletes of all time. As dominant on the field as he was distraction at all other times. An amazing athlete who was actually at his "most stable" in S.F. had a monster 2002: 100 catches, 1,300 yards, 13 TD.

61. Jose Canseco. Brash, brazen and bulked up by chemicals, there's no denying Jose's right to be on this list. He bashed his way into our collective conscience with the A's, and now won't leave us alone.

60. Jason Giambi. Another A's MVP who got his cash somewhere else, Giambi was Oakland baseball during his time in the East Bay. He also seems to have spent some time hanging around BALCO headquarters as well.

59. Kevin Mitchell. Powered the Giants to the 1989 Pennant and stocked his trophy case with the NL MVP in the same season. Slugged his way into the hearts of fans, and can still be caught around the park on a regular basis.

58. Bob St. Clair. Born, raised and played his whole life with distinction in the city of San Francisco. A 49ers legend and gentleman who provides a link to the game's gloried past.

57. Ted Hendricks. The Stork was simply one of the nastiest linebackers to ever put on pads. He was legend from the time he stepped on the field, and personified the Silver and Black D.

56. Leo Nomellini. "The Lion" was the first pick in Niners history, and it's safe to say they nailed it after ten Pro Bowl selections, a retired number and a bust in the Football Hall of Fame.

55. Cliff Branch. Fourteen seasons in the vertical passing game, and one of the premier deep threats in Raiders history, Branch burned corners by the quarter. Won three Super Bowls for Mr. Davis and wore just two jerseys in his NFL career, one for the Oakland Raiders and one for the Los Angeles Raiders.

54. Miguel Tejada. A top A's prospect who turned in a stunning MVP performance down the stretch in 2002, and also turned into one of baseball's most dependable shortstops, and of course, now plays somewhere else. Hero of "the streak".

53. John Henry Johnson. A workhorse Hall of Famer who could open or run though holes on the football field. Part of the famed 49ers' "Million Dollar Backfield."

52. Evgeni Nabokov. Between the pipes he's a San Jose staple, and a leader in nearly every franchise net-minding stat. Won the Calder and the loyalty of life-long Sharks fans.

51. "Lefty" O'Doul. Beloved by the entire city of San Francisco, where he was born, raised and died. O'Doul was baseball before the Major Leagues came West. A PCL player and manager of historical consideration, he was one of the pioneering players credited with bringing the game of baseball to Japan.

50. Dwight Clark. Nine years for the Niners. Two Pro Bowls, two All-Pro seasons, two Super Bowls and one amazing catch that change football forever in San Francisco.

49. Jesse Sapolu. The "Quiet Hawaiian" spent his entire career in San Francisco and was rewarded with four Super Bowl rings, just one of six players in team history to do so.

48. John Taylor. A superhero in Super Bowl XXIII, Taylor was a career Niner and turned himself from a special-teams standout into one of the NFL's most dependable targets. He'd make two trips to Honolulu, and two more trips to the Lombardi Trophy.

47. Tom Brady. A grad of Junipero Serra High School, the kid from San Mateo grew up watching the Niners play. He's creeping up on his idol, Joe Montana, on the NFL's all-time great QB list. But he's not there yet. Who knew the kid who went to Ann Arbor would end up with Super Bowls and supermodels?

46. Joe Thornton. In short time Thornton has proved to be one of the best players to ever wear a Sharks jersey. He'll rocket up the next version of this list should Lord Stanley find the way to San Jose.

45. Tim Hardaway. UTEP two-stepper put his foot in his mouth with some insensitive remarks about the gay community, which, in all places is bad, but in the Bay Area, is way uncouth. He's making amends; he used to make crazy buckets for the Warriors.

44. Hank Luisetti. A game changer of the first degree, Luisetti was a scoring machine for Stanford with his patented, running one-handed shot. He did for guards what George Mikan did for big men.

43. Jimmy Johnson. Before there was "Prime Time" the 49ers shutdown cornerback had a Jimmything. Good enough to play both ways, the path he chose lead him to the Hall of Fame.

42. Tom Meschery. Hooped it up in San Francisco as the son of a Russian immigrant, and was hardscrabble because of it. Once led the NBA in fouls, and can be found among the Warriors retired jersey numbers.

41. Hugh McElhenny. "The King" claimed his 49ers throne early, winning the NFL's Rookie of the Year in 1952. Thirteen seasons in San Francisco; one bust in Canton, Ohio.

40. Art Shell. Who are the greatest tacklers in NFL history? Art Shell and Anthony Munoz. That's the list. Shell is a dignified man, but his loyalty to Al Davis came back to bite him a second time around as coach.

39. Owen Nolan. *O Captain! My Captain!* six times over. Owen Nolan defined a franchise and would easily be on the Mount Rushmore of Sharks Hockey.

38. Chris Mullin. Warriors fans hope Mully can sink his free agent and draft picks as smoothly has he sank his buckets. Now the General Manger, once the sharpest shooting forward in franchise history not named Barry.

37. Mark McGwire. Had a trip to Capitol Hill and had a great fall from grace because of it. However, his power in Green and Gold was prolific, as were so many home runs. Some day the sun will shine on Mark McGwire again. Cooperstown, however, is a different story.

36. Matt Williams. Gruff and hard to the core, Williams could hit you 30 dingers and pick it all day long at third. He's earned his respect with dirty unis and cold-as-ice stares.

35. Fred Biletnikoff. Known for big plays when down and distance mattered most. It's amazing that no cigarettes from his two-pack-per-day habit got stuck to the stickum on his hands.

34. Jeff Kent. "Booooooooo!" I know, I know, I know. But Giants fans, you're nuts. He's one of the game's greatest second basemen, and he was an MVP in Orange and Black.

33. Dave Stewart. MVP in the quake series of 1989, "Smoke" could blow your doors off with one cold glance. Four straight 20-win seasons don't come around that often anymore.

32. Bert Campaneris. A stout speedster who helped the A's grab three World Series in the Seventies. He put on the jersey more times than any other Oakland A's player.

31. Kenny Stabler. A wild child MVP who lead the Raiders to the first Super Bowl the Bay Area had ever seen in January 1977. "The Ghost," could not have gone "to the post" without the slithering Snake.

30. Jackie Jensen. A son of San Francisco and one of the most complete athletes in Bay Area history, Jensen was the first person to appear in both the Rose Bowl and the World Series.

29. Gene Upshaw. Obliterated anyone on the wrong side of the Raiders line, because that's who it belonged to: Upshaw owned the line of scrimmage and would go on to represent every player on both sides of it after his playing days.

28. Rollie Fingers. Did A's fans know the man they were watching was changing the way baseball would be played? Fingers' fastballs changed the game in the late innings.

27. Nate Thurmond. The legends feared "Big Nate," and the respect he's earned in NBA circles is all the street cred he needed. But some tasty BBQ didn't hurt either.

26. Roger Craig. Over a grand on the ground, and with grabs before anyone else in a single season, Craig was a perfect fit for the West Coast system. He would have been a fantasy football god had we gotten down like that back then.

25. Jim Plunkett. A Heisman in Palo Alto and a legend in Silver and Black. When Raiders fans close their eyes, it's their #16 they see dropping back.

24. Tim Brown. A class act and consummate pro, the similarities between Timmy and Jerry Rice are stunning. The difference in their ranking however is the difference in Super Bowls.

23. Wilt Chamberlain. One of the greatest players in NBA history would surely rank higher had he been in the bay longer than two seasons.

22. Will Clark. The sweet-swinging Thriller always brought his lunch box to work. Blue collar and clutch, Giants fans can't imagine the late Eighties or early Nineties without him.

21. Jim Otto. Fired off the line with snap precession, destroying defenders while wearing the double bullets on his jersey. Should be next to the word "Raider" in the dictionary.

20. Dennis Eckersley. With Hall-of-Fame hair and the sweet 'stache to boot, Eck made closing cool . . . and Cooperstown doing it.

19. Jim "Catfish" Hunter. Iconic in every way; perfect once.

18. Jason Kidd. One of the greatest point guards to ever touch a basketball, he was born in San Francisco and killed it on court for Cal.

17. Gaylord Perry. You couldn't tell what was on the ball because it was too busy being thrown past you. The Hall of Famer would be the first pitcher to be named Cy Young in both leagues.

16. Orlando Cepeda. As true a Giant as there has ever been, "the Baby Bull" was a hit in the city and on the field, and paved the way for a wave of Latino talent.

15. Reggie Jackson. Three World Titles with the A's allowed him to do all the yapping he wanted ... and he wanted to!

14. Vida Blue. Electrified the Oakland Coliseum like no one before and none since.

13. Juan Marichal. One of the most proven and artful pitchers in Major League history. Would be a #1 starter for countless franchises, but belongs to Giants fans.

12. Steve Young. Bonus points to the MVP Hall of Famer for proving all the doubters wrong. He let 49ers fans know that football may have begun, but didn't end, with Joe. His Super Bowl record six TD passes is still the finest postseason performance in franchise history.

11. Mark Spitz. Michael Phelps cashed in, but Spitz paved the way. If the record were still his alone, he'd have made the top ten.

10. Ronnie Lott. The number one name in defense in a town that always has to keep its guard up.

9. Rick Barry. If Barry were in his prime today, he'd be "Great White Hyped" more than anyone in history and he'd deliver. He's one of the greatest scorers, free-throwers and passers in hoops history.

8. Willie McCovey. A true San Francisco Giants legend and hometown favorite, "Stretch" is often found ranked #1 in the hearts of old-school Candlestick die-hards.

7. Joe DiMaggio. Born in Martinez but raised downtown, "The Yankee Clipper" always left his heart in his true hometown of San Francisco. His funeral was held in North Beach's Saints Peter and Paul Roman Catholic Church on March 11, 1999. I was one of thousands who passed the church that day to pay respects.

6. Rickey Henderson. The best lead-off man in baseball history, Ricky defined the A's and redefined how the game was played. One of the smartest players the game has ever seen.

5. Bill Russell. Back-to-back NCAA titles before becoming the greatest teammate the world of sports has even known. Russell is Bay Area bred, before his Celtic glory days.

4. Jerry Rice. Pound for pound, one of the greatest sportsmen in the history of competition. His countless records and reputation for out working the entire football world are legend.

3. Willie Mays. Quite possibly the most complete player in baseball history, and one of the most beloved. If the "Say Hey Kid" finishes only third, it just shows you how amazing San Francisco sports have been.

2. Barry Bonds. A paralyzing player for pitchers and history to deal with, Bonds' bat and presence loomed larger over this city than even his Godfather. Quite simply, Bonds was the most feared hitter in baseball history.

1. Joe Montana. He wasn't big, fast or strong, but he's unquestionably the single most beloved and important athlete in the history of San Francisco. Win four World Championships and they'll remember you as #1 forever, too.

Index

Murphy, Dwayne, 41
Murphy, Troy, 173
Murray, Rich, 85

N

Nabokov, Evgeni, 59, 61, 231
Nabor, John, 168
Nedney, Joe, 202
Nelson, Darrin, 130
Nelson, Don, 97, 220
Nen, Rob, 68, 205, 226
Neumann, Paul, 158
Nevers, Ernie, 130
Nolan, Owen, 59, 60, 232
Nomellini, Leo, 12, 175, 230
Norris, Mike, 46
North, Billy, 47, 77
Norton, Ken, Jr., 87, 195, 198

O

Oakland A's, 30, 33–35, 39–48, 67, 78, 110, 155, 157
Oakland Invaders, 124
Oakland Oaks (ABA), 125
Oakland Oaks (PCL), 124
Oakland Raiders, 29, 51–54, 111
Ocean Beach, 99
O'Connor, Fred, 149
O'Dell, Billy, 24
Odem, Blue Moon, 42, 45
O'Doul, "Lefty," 231
Ogden, Bud, 183
Ogden, Ralph, 183
Oski the Bear, 93
O'Sullivan, J. T., 216
Otto, Jim, 54, 199, 233
Owens, Billy, 157
Owens, R. C., 216
Owens, Terrell, 73, 137, 140, 172, 194, 200, 230
Ozolinsh, Sandis, 60

P

Papal Mass, 70
Paramount, 80
Paris, William "Bubba," 121, 217
Park, Gary, 178
Parrish, Tony, 176
Pastorini, Dan, 139, 152
Payton, Gary, 186
Perry, Gaylord, 15, 26, 68, 156, 233
Perry, Joe, 13
Peterson, Julian, 176
Phillips, J. R., 84, 216
Phillips, Mel, 176
Piazza, Mike, 19, 86, 141
Piersall, Jimmy, 181
Pierzynski, A. J., 140, 216
Pinson, Vada, 128
Plank, Eddie, 198
Plummer, Gary, 190
Plunk, Eric, 157
Plunkett, Jim, 52, 54, 56, 131, 137, 151, 167, 183, 199, 220, 233
Polonia, Luis, 107
Portugal, Mark, 89
Posey, Gerald "Buster" Demp, III, 217
Prieto, Ariel, 85
Primeau, Wayne, 153
Pronger, Chris, 60

Q

Quicksilver Messenger Service, 82
Quinn, Greg, 65

R

Radborn, Charles "Old Hoss," 148
Rader, Dave, 22
Radnich, Gary, 178, 183

Raiders, 158, 166–67
Rambis, Kurt, 184
Raney, Hal, 181
Rathman, Tom, 166
Rauch, John, 57
Reese, Archie, 175
Remenda, Drew, 60
Restaurants, 63–66
Reuschel, Rick, 153
Ricci, Mike, 58, 105, 195
Rice, Jerry, 13, 106, 136, 167, 170, 176, 194, 234
Richmond, Mitch, 49, 157, 172
Ridlehuber, Preston, 52
Righetti, Dave, 89, 183
Rigney, Bill, 69
Rijo, Jose, 157
Riley, Preston, 72
Ring, Bill, 91
Rios, Armando, 154, 172
Ripken, Cal, Jr., 147
Roa, Joe, 154
Roberts, Leon Joseph "Bip," 217
Robinson, Frank, 129, 186, 229
Robinson, Jackie, 27
Robinson, Jeff, 153
Robinson, Ted, 126, 181
Rodgers, Andre, 84
Rogers, Will, 112
Rohde, Len, 175
Rohn, Dan, 155
Rolling Stones, 70
Rose, Pete, 147
Roseboro, Johnny, 19, 79
Rosen, Al, 76
Rowand, Aaron, 86
Rudi, Joe, 40
Rueter, Kirk, 25
Russell, Bill, 171, 187, 209, 234
Russell, JaMarcus, 145, 224

S

Saatsaz, Cyrus, 98
Sabathia, CC, 212
Saber Kittens, 93
Sadecki, Ray, 24, 158
St. Clair, Bob, 12, 175, 189, 218, 230
St. Jean, Garry, 218
San Francisco Demons, 124
San Francisco downtown, 99
San Francisco Golden Gaters, 125
San Francisco Seals, 125
San Francisco Spiders, 124
San Francisco Warriors, 135, 153
San Francisco 49ers, 110, 111, 146, 155–56, 166–67
San Franscisco Shamrocks, 124
San Jose Sharks, 58–61, 145, 225
Sanders, Deion, 87, 228
Sanders, Summer, 168, 194
Sanford, Jack, 25
Santa Cruz, 100
Santana, 83
Santana, Carlos, 213
Santangelo, F. P., 172
Santiago, Benito, 69
Sapolu, Jesse, 231
Sapp, Warren, 89, 139
Saroyan, William, 112
Schafer, Lee, 158
Schmidt, Jason, 25, 143, 154, 205, 227
Schneider, Rob, 212
Schollander, Don, 168
Schott, Marge, 222
Seifert, George, 219
Seikaly, Rony, 139
Sheehan, Tom, 149
Shell, Art, 53, 57, 149, 171, 195, 232
Shepard, Larry, 218